ATLAS OF MAGICAL BRITAIN

BY THE SAME AUTHORS

Mysterious Britain
Mazes and Labyrinths of the World
The Secret Country
A Guide to Ancient Sites in Britain
Alien Animals
Bigfoot Casebook
Earth Rites
The Evidence for Bigfoot and Other Man-Beasts
Sacred Waters
Ancient Mysteries of Britain
Modern Mysteries of Britain
Modern Mysteries of the World

ATLAS OF MAGICAL BRITAIN

JANET
AND
COLIN BORD

CHARTWELL
BOOKS, INC.

This edition produced for Book Sales Inc.

First published in Great Britain in 1990 by
Sidgwick & Jackson Limited

ISBN 155521 945 4

Printed in Singapore

CONTENTS

GLOSSARY

BARROW A prehistoric earthen burial mound. NEOLITHIC ones were long and covered burial chambers built of stone; in the later BRONZE AGE, round and without stone chambers. Round barrows are also called tumuli (one = tumulus); burial mounds built of stones are called cairns.
BRONZE AGE In the West, approximately 2100 BC to 700 BC, when bronze was used to make tools and weapons.
CAIRN See BARROW.
CAPSTONE A very large stone forming the roof of a BARROW). Today the covering earth mound has often gone, leaving the burial chamber exposed.
CAUSEWAYED CAMP An area of land bounded by banks and ditches, constructed in the early NEOLITHIC period possibly as meeting places or for performing rituals.
CIST A prehistoric tomb made of stone slabs set on edge, covered by a CAPSTONE and often sunk into the ground.
CUP-AND-RING MARKS Prehistoric rock carvings in the form of a cup-like hollow surrounded by concentric rings. They are thought to be Bronze Age, but their meaning is unknown.
CURSUS A linear Neolithic monument resembling an avenue bounded by banks and ditches; the Dorset cursus is over 6 miles long. Their purpose is unknown.
DOWSER A person who is sensitive to emanations from underground water or natural energy currents etc. Some use hazel twigs which jerk when the desired substance is located; others use only their hands.
EARTH ENERGY Researchers into LEYS and prehistoric sites have theorized that running through the earth are natural energy currents, which can be located by sensitive people, and that prehistoric man may have constructed his stone circles etc. to mark or utilize these energies.
FIRST-FOOTING At midnight on 31 December, in Scotland and northern England, male first-footers visit houses to bring good luck in the New Year; they carry a gift of coal, a loaf, a bottle of whisky or other customary item.
GREEN LANE Many ancient thoroughfares in Britain have been abandoned and now survive as grassy 'green lanes'.
INCORRUPTIBILITY When the coffins of saintly people are opened years after their deaths, the bodies are often incorrupt, or undecayed, e.g. St Bernadette of Lourdes.
IRON AGE The latest prehistoric period, when iron was used for tools (800 BC to the Roman invasion of AD 43).
LEYS Early this century, Alfred Watkins identified alignments of prehistoric and later sites which he felt marked prehistoric trackways, though later researchers feel that leys may mark lines of EARTH ENERGY.
MAZE England's ancient mazes were cut into the turf and there is only one path from outside to centre. There are links with the Cretan labyrinth and the Minotaur legend, but the history of the turf maze is not clear-cut.
MOTTE AND BAILEY A medieval fortification comprising an earth mound (the motte) on which a stone or wood tower was built, linked by drawbridge to the bailey, a separate enclosure with timber buildings.
NEOLITHIC The New Stone Age (4000 BC to 2000 BC), the time of the earliest stone structures to survive in Britain.
OLD CALENDAR In 1752 Britain 'lost' 11 days when we adopted the European calendar. This meant that festivals were on different days, e.g. Old Christmas Day is 6 January.
PELE-TOWER (also **PEEL-TOWER**) Fortified houses built around the Scottish border as a protection against raiders.
PSYCHIC MANIFESTATIONS Inexplicable events such as ghosts and poltergeists.
REIVER A raider, especially on the Scottish border.
SABBAT A gathering of witches, at which the participants worship their gods and goddesses with feasting, dancing, singing and sometimes sex magic.
TUMULUS See BARROW.
UFOs AND UFO ENTITIES Short for 'unidentified flying object', UFO is sometimes taken to mean 'alien spacecraft', but there is no real evidence that they or their occupants come from outer space.
WARLOCK A sorcerer or black magician.
WELL-DRESSING The annual custom of decorating well-heads with pictures made from flower petals and other natural substances, particularly popular in Derbyshire.

A NOTE ON THE MAPS

Place-names rather than site-names are marked on the maps, and each place-name represents one or several sites of interest. The nature of the most important site (or sites) at each place is indicated by a symbol, as follows:

- ● prehistoric or Roman site (e.g. stone circle)
- ■ building (e.g. church, castle) or town
- ▲ other man-made structure (e.g. well, maze, road)
- ♦ natural landscape feature (e.g. hill)

The special features of each site are indicated by a colour in the appropriate shape, as follows:

- ● ■ ▲ ♦ ghosts, hauntings and fairies
- ● ■ ▲ ♦ legends (e.g. giants, the Devil, underground passages, witchcraft legends, hidden treasure, Arthurian legends, dragons) and traditional customs (e.g. morris dancing)
- ● ■ ▲ ♦ Christian centres and church siting legends
- ● ■ ▲ ♦ other significant features (e.g. leys, mazes, zodiacs, earth energies, monsters, black magic)

★ Places which are particularly worth visiting.

INTRODUCTION

As THE PACE OF LIFE in Britain today grows ever faster, with new pressures being unceasingly placed upon the countryside, it sometimes seems as if the whole of Britain will soon be overwhelmed, leaving no traces of the events of the previous six thousand years. But luckily many fascinating relics of our past do survive. The earliest structures still to be seen are the causewayed camps, henge monuments and long barrows of the Neolithic people who arrived here around 4000 BC. Admittedly the very best structures of the Neolithic period and all later times are now protected by such organizations as English Heritage and the National Trust and so are theoretically safe from harm, but many lesser monuments which lack official guardians have also survived against all odds, and provide us with tangible links between our present age and earlier times. So many of these monuments, the lesser as well as the greater, have the power to rekindle the dying flame of magic and mystery which is so often lacking in today's mechanistic age.

The people of past centuries wove imaginative stories around the notable features of their landscape: the strange-shaped hill, the stone circle whose purpose was unknown, the church in an unexpected location; and giants, dragons, the Devil, fairies and witches, as well as folk heroes such as King Arthur and Robin Hood, became part of the local tradition handed down from generation to generation. Although we can now smile at their apparent gullibility, their landscape was alive for them in a way it no longer is for us today. And behind the superstitions and now-derided beliefs there may have been echoes of the thought patterns of our ancestors – those long-gone people who built the burial chambers and erected the standing stones whose real purpose we no longer understand. Research into leys (alignments of ancient sites) and earth mysteries suggests a far deeper significance for the stone structures than is yet generally realized: early man may have found a way to tap into the earth's life-giving energy currents and use them for his own purposes, which included fertility for himself, his crops and his livestock. Traces of rituals apparently designed for this purpose still survive in some of the traditional customs like the Abbots Bromley Horn Dance (Staffordshire), the Padstow 'Obby 'Oss festivities (Cornwall) and the Queensferry Burryman (Lothian).

Just as seemingly outlandish traditions and customs may be based on long-forgotten rites, so are ghost stories often based on factual happenings. Undoubtedly some of them are tales embellished in the telling, but many of the ghosts we describe have been seen, for ghosts and poltergeists are a real mystery even today, albeit one largely ignored in our scientific world. In addition there are tales here of hidden treasure, underground passages, and holy wells with healing powers. There is no part of Britain where such tales have not survived, and many of the places are still in existence, not yet having been built over or ploughed away.

There are, of course, far too many sites for them all to have been included in this atlas, so we have tried to select ones which can be visited now, and where there is something still to see. We have given brief directions where we felt it was necessary, plus Ordnance Survey map references for the most difficult sites to locate. Our choice has been a personal one, maybe sometimes idiosyncratic, but giving, we hope, a taste of what survives of magical Britain as the year 2000 approaches.

We have divided the mainland of Britain (plus close offshore islands) into 16 areas covering two or more counties each, beginning in the south-west with Devon and Cornwall, and ending with the northern half of Scotland. Certain themes are found throughout the country – for example church-siting legends where a church was being built on one site but its stones were overnight mysteriously removed elsewhere, until the builders gave in and adopted the new site. But other themes are more localized – for instance tales about Robin Hood, whose territory covers much of the north of England but who is rarely heard of elsewhere. King Arthur, however, was a national rather than a local hero, and his name appears widely throughout western and northern areas. Being more hilly and rocky than the east, the west and north are also the main regions where prehistoric stone structures have survived; they are naturally much rarer in other parts, where outcrops of rock are infrequent and building materials therefore unavailable. Consequently, legends describing standing stones as people turned to stone for some transgression are confined to the areas where standing stones are a landscape feature. But strange-shaped hills, large and small, occur in all parts except the flattest, and so stories of giants dropping spadesful of soil are not confined to any particular region.

Taking the country region by region, we can see more clearly how the local legends and the geography of an area are quite closely linked. Devon and Cornwall are both relatively unspoilt counties, with wild upland areas littered with prehistoric sites and subsequently rich in folklore: King Arthur, petrifaction legends, ghosts and ley-lines are all well represented. Further east, Somerset, Dorset and Hampshire are nearer to large urban centres, yet still retain their quiet rural corners, and Dorset is especially well endowed with antiquities. Somerset is dominated, mysteriously speaking, by Glastonbury with all its Arthurian connections, while Hampshire is rich in ghosts and hidden treasure. The south-east of England is host to a mixture of traditions: prehistoric sites litter the South Downs, along with folklore involving fairies, giants and the Devil. But military and religious invaders have left their mark in Kent: in the haunted site of the Battle of Hastings, and in the early Christian sites, especially at Canterbury.

West of London, despite modern developments and an urban population spilling over into rural areas, Avon, Wiltshire, Oxfordshire and Berkshire still have plenty for the seeker of mysterious places. Wiltshire is famous for its prehistoric sites, structures of stone and earth whose purpose archaeologists still puzzle over, while Oxfordshire's most famous group of antiquities, the Rollright Stones, are probably the richest in folklore and legends of any group of prehistoric sites in Britain. Berkshire's main mysterious area centres on Windsor, with its haunted castle and Great Park.

Even London has much to offer in the way of magic and mystery. Although there are few prehistoric sites in the capital and the counties to the north (Buckinghamshire, Bedfordshire, Hertfordshire and Essex), other subjects take their place, and we find an area full of ghosts, Devil stories, underground passages, witchcraft, church-siting legends - even some dragons. Eastern England too (Cambridgeshire, Norfolk and Suffolk) has plenty of hidden treasure, underground passages, giants, ghosts, Devils and, most numerous of all, the fearsome phantom black dog, calf-sized and with glowing eyes, which still patrols certain favourite haunts.

To the west, Gloucestershire and the county of Hereford and Worcester both have a wealth of folklore, particularly holy wells. Northamptonshire and Warwickshire are rich in ghosts. Further west again, in Wales, both north and south are relatively unspoilt, with mountain and lowland overflowing with intriguing remains around which have grown a host of legends about fairies, ghosts, heroes, saints and holy wells, treasure, King Arthur, dragons, lost settlements, moving stones, mermaids and evil spirits.

The middle England counties of Leicestershire, Shropshire, Staffordshire, West Midlands, Derbyshire, Lincolnshire and Nottinghamshire, though less well endowed with visible remnants of prehistory, make up for this lack in other ways. The northern counties, from Cheshire in the south-west, through the industrial conurbations of Merseyside and Greater Manchester, to Lancashire, Yorkshire, and further north to Cumbria, Northumberland, Durham, and not forgetting the 'new' counties of Humberside, Cleveland, and Tyne and Wear, show a strong contrast between the industrialized areas in the west and east, and the open moorland along England's spine. Although the cities have had almost all their mysterious places eradicated, out on the moors it is a different story. This is especially true in Northumberland, Cumbria, and across the sea on the Isle of Man.

Many different kinds of scenery are covered in the two sections devoted to Scotland, from lonely mountains without roads and people, to busy cities; from the islands off the west coast where in some respects time has stood still, to the industrial Lowlands where the 20th century is ever-present. In the remoter areas, every hill, every mountain, every loch had its ghost or monster or giant or Devil tale, and the human inhabitants knew their environment in a way that has been lost by people today, who travel from place to place by car and thus see nothing of the tiny details that go to make up their environment. If we were all as closely in touch with our surroundings as was usual in rural areas only a few decades ago, there is no knowing what strange happenings would be reported, which are now unnoticed through lack of witnesses. But if you find yourself out in the mountains in some of the dramatic weather that the Highlands regularly experience, you will not find it hard to understand how to our ancestors the landscape seemed alive with superhuman entities, monsters and evil spirits. In our modern world, largely insulated from nature, we are in danger of losing the sense of awe that wild places can inspire, so a visit to the wilder parts of Scotland is recommended for those wishing to rediscover the spirit of the earth.

In each section our favourite sites are starred, so that travellers short of time can be sure to visit those places most worth seeing. But a more leisurely exploration of some of the remote and forgotten places we describe will bring its rewards, for in escaping even briefly from the roar and bustle of the late 20th century you may recapture faint echoes of times long past. We hope that our suggested journey of exploration down the country lanes to the unspoilt churches, and across the high moorland to the lonely standing stones, will reveal to you many places where a magical aura still survives undiminished after hundreds and thousands of years.

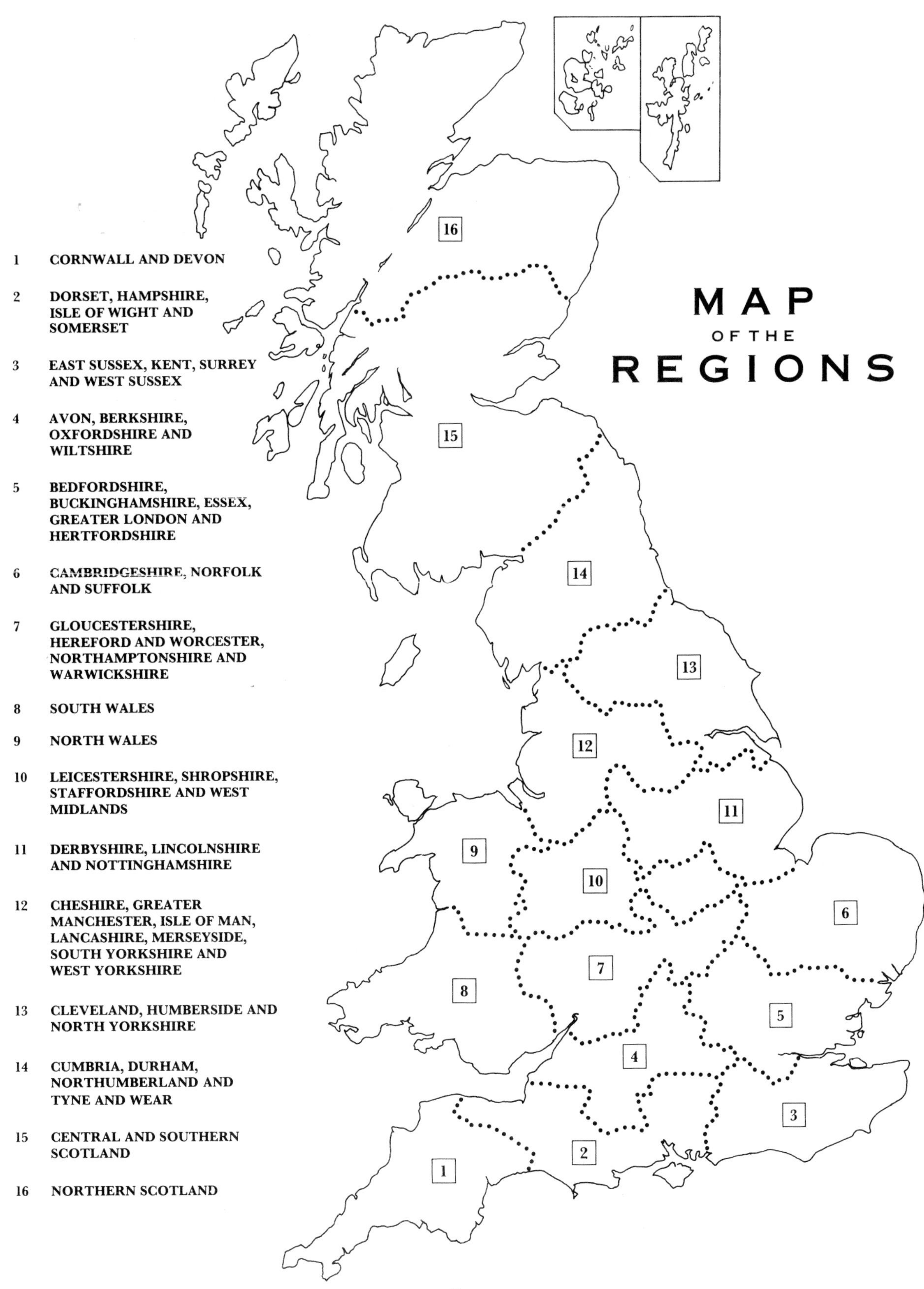

MAP
OF THE
REGIONS
16
15
14
13
12
11
10
9
8
7
6
5
4
3
2
1
1 CORNWALL AND DEVON
2 DORSET, HAMPSHIRE, ISLE OF WIGHT AND SOMERSET
3 EAST SUSSEX, KENT, SURREY AND WEST SUSSEX
4 AVON, BERKSHIRE, OXFORDSHIRE AND WILTSHIRE
5 BEDFORDSHIRE, BUCKINGHAMSHIRE, ESSEX, GREATER LONDON AND HERTFORDSHIRE
6 CAMBRIDGESHIRE, NORFOLK AND SUFFOLK
7 GLOUCESTERSHIRE, HEREFORD AND WORCESTER, NORTHAMPTONSHIRE AND WARWICKSHIRE
8 SOUTH WALES
9 NORTH WALES
10 LEICESTERSHIRE, SHROPSHIRE, STAFFORDSHIRE AND WEST MIDLANDS
11 DERBYSHIRE, LINCOLNSHIRE AND NOTTINGHAMSHIRE
12 CHESHIRE, GREATER MANCHESTER, ISLE OF MAN, LANCASHIRE, MERSEYSIDE, SOUTH YORKSHIRE AND WEST YORKSHIRE
13 CLEVELAND, HUMBERSIDE AND NORTH YORKSHIRE
14 CUMBRIA, DURHAM, NORTHUMBERLAND AND TYNE AND WEAR
15 CENTRAL AND SOUTHERN SCOTLAND
16 NORTHERN SCOTLAND

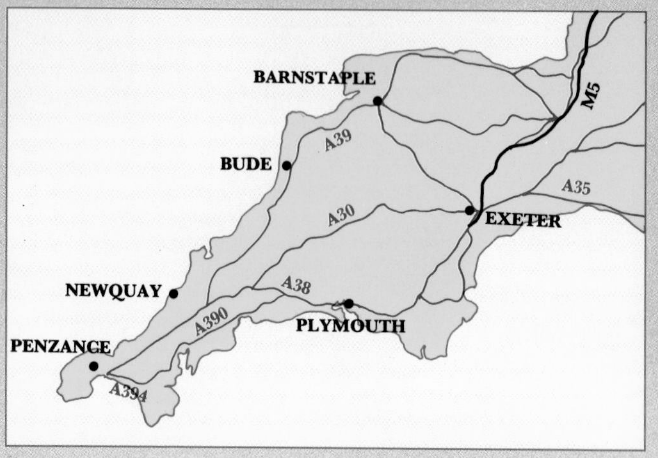

CORNWALL AND DEVON

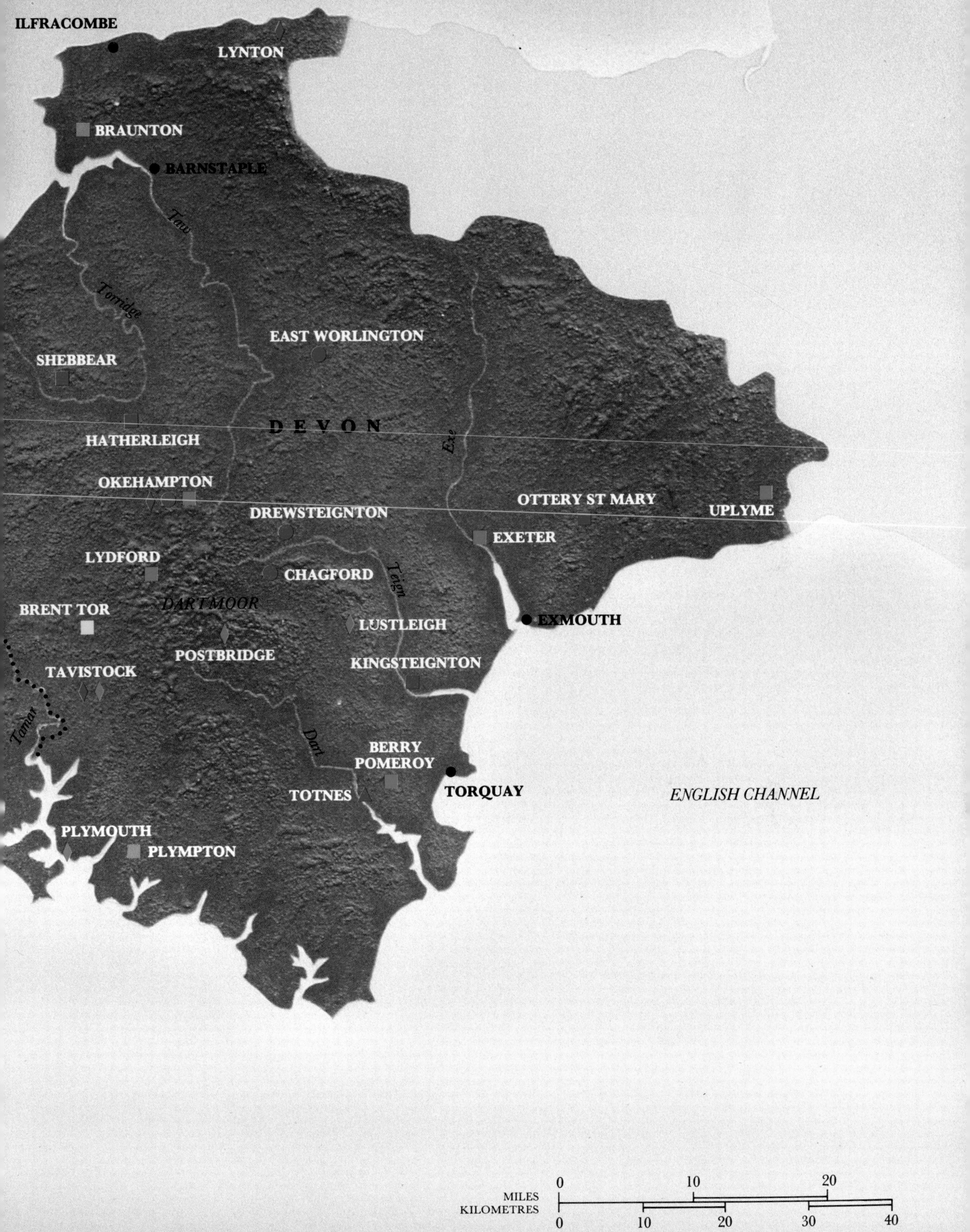

ILFRACOMBE
LYNTON
BRAUNTON
BARNSTAPLE
Taw
Torridge
EAST WORLINGTON
SHEBBEAR
DEVON
HATHERLEIGH
Exe
OKEHAMPTON
OTTERY ST MARY
UPLYME
DREWSTEIGNTON
EXETER
LYDFORD
CHAGFORD
Teign
DARTMOOR
BRENT TOR
EXMOUTH
LUSTLEIGH
POSTBRIDGE
KINGSTEIGNTON
TAVISTOCK
Tamar
Dart
BERRY POMEROY
TOTNES
TORQUAY
ENGLISH CHANNEL
PLYMOUTH
PLYMPTON
MILES
KILOMETRES
0
10
20
0
10
20
30
40

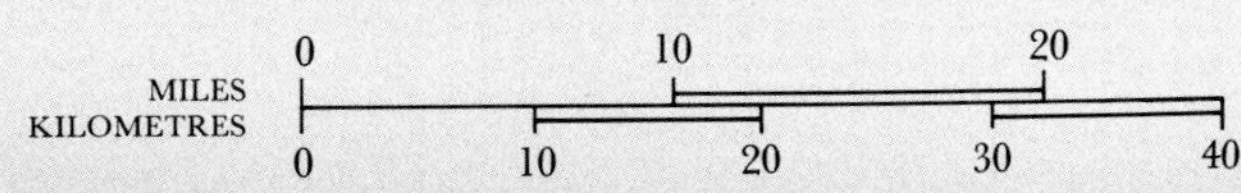

CORNWALL

BODMIN MOOR

Dozmary Pool. GHOST; ARTHURIAN LEGEND. Jan Tregeagle was reputed to be an evil lawyer who sold his soul to the Devil, as a result of which his ghost was given endless tasks by clergymen in an attempt to save it. One of these tasks was to empty Dozmary Pool (said to be bottomless) with a leaky limpet shell.

This atmospheric lake is also the place where Sir Bedivere threw away the sword Excalibur at King Arthur's command as he lay dying; a hand emerged from the water to grasp the weapon. *8 miles NW of Liskeard, close to road between St Neot and Bolventor (Jamaica Inn) (SX 195745).*

The Hurlers Stone Circles. PETRIFACTION LEGEND; UNCOUNTABLE STONES. These three Bronze Age stone circles standing side by side were named from the belief that they were men turned to stone for playing the game of hurling on the Sabbath. It was also once believed that the stones could not be accurately counted. *Immediately NW of Minions, itself 4 miles N of Liskeard (SX 258713).*

FALMOUTH

Falmouth Bay. SEA MONSTER. A creature known as Morgawr, the Cornish for 'sea giant', is said to dwell in the sea around here. There were many sightings in 1976, for example from Pendennis Point, Rosemullion Head and Parson's Beach. Two fishermen off Lizard Point saw 'a great head like an enormous seal [with a] long neck .... The body was black and the head was grey and we saw a total length of about 22 feet ... a big rounded back [with] humps on the top.' Although there have been more sightings since, the mystery remains unsolved.

FOWEY

Castle Dore and Tristan Stone. ARTHURIAN LEGEND. Castle Dore was an Iron Age fort, the possible home of Cunomorus, a local king who had a son called Drustanus. He may have been the Tristan who was the lover of Isolde. The Tristan Stone nearby (not now in its original position) has a worn 6th-century inscription: DRUSTANUS HIC IACIT CUNOMORI FILIUS (Drustanus, son of Cunomorus, lies here). *Tristan Stone beside A3082 just outside Fowey; Castle Dore 2 miles NW beside B3269.*

GUNWALLOE

Church. SITING LEGENDS. According to one legend, this church was intended to be built elsewhere in the parish, but the building materials were mysteriously removed every night to the present coastal location. Another tradition tells the story of a shipwrecked traveller who vowed to build a chapel at the place where he had escaped from the waves. So close is it to the sea that the churchyard walls have more than once been washed away. *3 miles S of Helston (SW 660206).*

HUDDER DOWN

Deadman's Cove. GHOST. In 1978, a man dressed in black standing by the sea was approached by a couple who were amazed to see him fade away. *Off B3301 3 miles NW of Camborne.*

LAND'S END

Lyonesse. DROWNED LAND. The cliffs at Land's End were once the entrance to a fertile land which, according to legend, was drowned by the sea in the 11th century. Lyonesse reached as far as the Scilly Isles 28 miles south-west, and the islands contain clear evidence of a drowned landscape - so perhaps Lyonesse is more than a legend. Some people have claimed to have had visions of a lost city from the cliffs at Land's End: Edith Oliver twice saw a jumble of domes, spires, towers and battlements far out to sea.

MADRON

Holy Well. HOLY WELL. This ancient holy well, still in use, is a good one to visit to capture the atmosphere of how holy wells used to be in earlier centuries when they were still widely used. Here you are likely to find rags tied to the surrounding bushes. People have done this for hundreds of years; either it represents an offering to the spirit of the well, or alternatively it was believed that as the rag rotted away, so would the owner's ailment disappear. Close to the well are the ruins of a stone baptistery, through which the water runs. One famous cure happened in 1640, when a boy crippled playing football followed the ritual of bathing in the well on three successive Thursdays in May, then sleeping on a nearby grassy mound known as St Madern's Bed. Other ailments successfully cured included colic and rickets. Baptisms took place here; and contemporaneously with Christian rites, pagan rituals continued, like that performed by unmarried girls who in May would float a cross on the water, the number of bubbles arising indicating the number of years before they would marry. *From Morvah road ½ mile W of Madron follow track signposted to well, opposite entrance to Trengwainton Estate (SW 446328).*

Lanyon Quoit. GIANT. This fine prehistoric burial chamber, with an 18-foot capstone supported on three upright stones, was for obvious reasons known as the Giant's Quoit and the Giant's Table. *1½ miles NW of Madron, beside road to Morvah (SW 430337).*

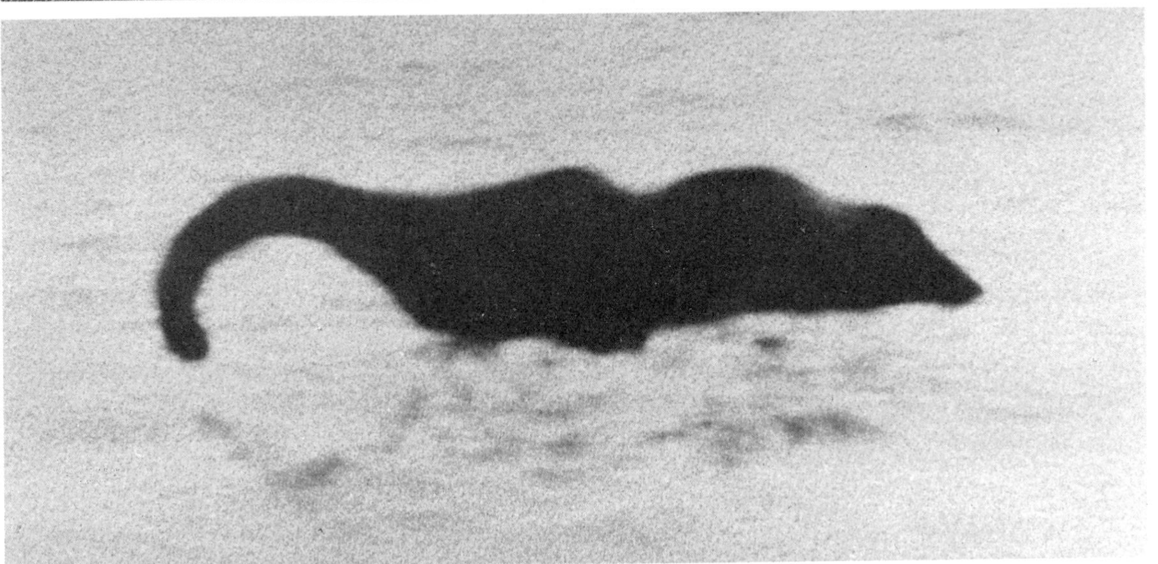

ABOVE The prehistoric burial chamber known as Lanyon Quoit
BELOW Morgawr, the Cornish sea monster, photographed off Falmouth in 1976

St Michael's Mount, seen from Marazion

Men-an-Tol and Men Scryfa. HEALING STONE; TREASURE. Three stones, one circular with a large hole through it, stand in a line on the open moor in the West Penwith area, where there are enough prehistoric sites to keep enthusiasts happy for weeks. The Men-an-Tol (holed stone) and its companions are probably all that remains of a prehistoric burial chamber, which sometimes incorporated holed stones, perhaps to allow access to the interior chamber. The holed stone here, known last century as the Devil's Eye, became famed for its healing ability. Adults climbed through the hole to cure rheumatism, and children were passed through it to cure rickets and scrofula.

Men Scryfa (written stone) carries a worn early Christian inscription. As with many other old stones in Cornwall, there was a belief that gold lay buried beneath it. Some time ago, a man who had a recurring dream of a crock of gold dug a pit around the base of the stone; he found nothing, but the stone collapsed and has only been re-erected in recent years. *Both sites reached by walking along track from minor road between Madron and Morvah, 4 miles NW of Penzance (Men-an-Tol: SW 426349. Men Scryfa: SW 427353).*

MARAZION

★ St Michael's Mount. GIANTS; SAINTS; LEY. This offshore island, linked to Marazion by a causeway, was said to have been built by the giant Cormoran and his wife. They were using white rock, which had to be carried some distance, so Cormoran's wife tried to cheat by bringing local greenstone in her apron instead. Cormoran kicked her when he found out, her apron string broke, and she dropped the stone. In later years a small chapel was built on the stone, and it became known as Chapel Rock.

In AD 495, some fishermen had a vision of St Michael over the summit of the Mount. Thereafter it became a Christian settlement, and there are still some remains of the various monastic buildings. St Keyne came on a pilgrimage here and left her influence on a rough stone seat known as St Keyne's Chair (see *St Keyne*). Whichever one of a newly married couple first sits on the chair, he or she will dominate the marriage.

St Michael's Mount also marks one end of a long-distance alignment or 'geomantic corridor' called by its discoverer John Michell the 'St Michael Line', for in its course across country it links numerous St Michael sites including Brentor church (see *Brent Tor*, Devon) with prehistoric sites like the Hurlers stone circles (see *Bodmin Moor*), and many other significant ancient sites (see Hamish Miller and Paul Broadhurst's book *The Sun and the Serpent* for an investigation of the Line).

PADSTOW

May Day Festivities. ANCIENT CUSTOM.
The atmosphere in Padstow is electric on 1 May, when the coming of spring is celebrated with enthusiasm. Throughout the day, two 'Obby 'Osses, with their attendant teasers and mayers, move round the town. The following crowds sing the traditional songs about the arrival of spring and summer. Some of the accompanying rituals relate to the bringing of fertility: any young girl whom the 'Oss manages to envelop in his skirts will gain a husband or a baby within the year; the 'Oss used to visit Treator Pool where it splashed the spectators with water, to bring good luck; and there used to be a man-woman among his followers, a symbol of fertility. The town is decorated with flags, bunting and greenery, and in the centre stands a maypole, around which dancing takes place.

PENHALE

Penhale Sands. BURIED TOWN. According to legend, Langarroc, a fine town with seven churches, once stood on the land now covered by sand dunes. A storm arose as a punishment for the people's bad ways, and the town was completely buried. There may be some truth in this legend, because ancient human skeletons have been found and a tiny 7th-century church has been recovered. This can be visited, but unfortunately looks more like an air-raid shelter than a church, following its 'restoration' with concrete. *5 miles SW of Newquay.*

REDRUTH

Carn Brea. GIANTS. This prehistoric hillfort was traditionally the home of the giant John of Gaunt. On the hill are stones called the Giant's Cradle, the Giant's Coffin, the Giant's Wheel and other giants' possessions. *1 mile SW of Redruth.*

ST AGNES HEAD

Chapel Porth. GIANT. The legend tells that the giant Bolster could stand with one foot on Carn Brea and the other on St Agnes Beacon, 6 miles apart. He fell in love with St Agnes, but she soon grew tired of him, and asked him to prove his love by filling a hole in the cliffs at Chapel Porth with his blood. What he didn't know, but she did, was that the hole was bottomless. The unsuspecting love-sick giant opened a vein in his arm with a knife, and the blood flowed until he died. There is said to be a red stain at Chapel Porth showing where Bolster's blood fell. *On coast 1 mile N of Porthtowan.*

St Keyne's well, named after a 5th-century virgin

ST BURYAN

The Merry Maidens, the Pipers and the Blind Fiddler. PETRIFACTION LEGEND. The Merry Maidens are now a stone circle, but were originally (according to legend) a group of young girls turned to stone for dancing on the Sabbath. The Pipers, two tall standing stones not far away, were turned to stone while trying to escape. The Blind Fiddler almost managed to get away, but he too was turned to stone. It is also believed that the stones cannot be moved, and cattle used to pull them away are said to have collapsed and died. *Merry Maidens and Pipers beside B3315 about 3 miles SW of Penzance; Blind Fiddler beside A30 just W of Catchall (Merry Maidens: SW 433245. Pipers: SW 435248. Blind Fiddler: SW 425282).*

Boleigh Fogou. DEVIL; WITCHES. Not far from the Pipers is an underground chamber of the kind called, in Cornwall, a fogou. (There is another good one at Carn Euny prehistoric village near Sancreed.) Being constructed close to Iron Age settlements, they may have originally been used for storage purposes, though other suggestions have included hiding places and ritual structures (perhaps symbolizing the Earth Mother's womb). At Boleigh the stone-roofed passage is 4½ feet wide and 36 feet long. In folklore it was said that witches held sabbats here, and the Devil played his pipes for them; the witches would change into hares and run into the fogou. *In garden of Rosemerrin House off B3315; ask permission to visit (SW 437252).*

ST DENNIS

Church. SAINT'S DEATH. Set in a weird landscape of china clay workings and granite stone walls, this church may have acquired its dedication from the Cornish word *dinas*, meaning fort, for it stands inside an Iron Age hillfort. The circular churchyard wall is a clue to the site's antiquity. In legend, the death of St Dennis in Paris by decapitation was marked by a fall of blood on to the stones in St Dennis churchyard, an occurrence occasionally repeated since, to warn of an impending disaster. St Dennis may also be 'Dimilioc' where a siege and the death of Duke Gorlois took place in the Arthurian stories as told by Geoffrey of Monmouth. *5 miles NW of St Austell.*

ST JUST

Carn Gluze Barrow. FAIRIES. Although this is a burial site, it looks rather different from the usual prehistoric tombs, taking the form of a massive stone wall enclosing a pit and burial cists, originally covered by a domed roof. Cremated human bones and early pottery were found during excavations, and there is some evidence that this site was in use from the Neolithic through the Bronze Age, covering perhaps a thousand years – so this may once

The ruins of Tintagel Castle

have been an important ritual site, revered and visited in the way that our ancient cathedrals are today. But despite its antiquity the only surviving folklore relating to Carn Gluze is that tin miners returning home at night from their work used to see lights burning, and rings of fairies dancing on and around the barrow. *½ mile W of St Just, reached along lane leading to Cape Cornwall, forking left off this lane on edge of town (SW 355312).*

ST KEYNE

St Keyne's Well. HOLY WELL. A 5th-century virgin, St Keyne, performed many miracles and eventually retired to Cornwall to live near the well bearing her name, on the waters of which she laid a spell. In the words of Southey's poem:

If the husband of this gifted well
Shall drink before his wife,
A happy man henceforth is he,
For he shall be master for life.
But if the wife should drink of it first,
God help the husband then!

One unfortunate Cornishman told a sad tale as he sheepishly shook his head:

I hasten'd as soon as the wedding was done,
And left my wife in the porch;
But i' faith she had been wiser than me,
For she took a bottle to church.

Beside lane ½ mile S of St Keyne, itself 2 miles S of Liskeard.

ST LEVAN

St Levan's Stone. SAINT'S LEGEND; ARTHURIAN LEGEND; HOLY WELL. In the churchyard sits a huge split boulder where the saint was said to rest after going fishing. He struck the rock with his fist and split it open as a memorial to himself. The wizard Merlin is said to have spoken this prophecy:

When with panniers astride,
A pack-horse one can ride
Through St Levan's Stone,
The world will be done.

Being so close to the church, this stone was probably of some significance in pagan times long before the church was built. The remains of the saint's well can also be visited on the cliffs a short walk to the south. *3 miles SE of Land's End.*

TINTAGEL

★ Tintagel Castle and Merlin's Cave. ARTHURIAN LEGEND. Although widely known as King Arthur's birthplace, Tintagel's claims to Arthurian connections are somewhat tenuous. There may have been a monastic settlement here in the 5th or 6th century, or even a chieftain's stronghold, but the only 'evidence' is Geoffrey of Monmouth's placing of the king's birth here, rather than in Wales as would have been expected of a Welsh writer. So perhaps he *was* following a genuine tradition when he wrote in the 12th century of events six hundred years earlier. Whatever the truth may be, Tintagel Castle (but not the over-commercialized village) is well worth a visit: its clifftop location is stupendous.

From a cove down on the shore, Merlin's Cave can be entered. The wizard Merlin assisted in Arthur's conception by using his magic powers to help King Uther Pendragon to disguise himself as Gorlois, the husband of Igerna. In this disguise, the King seduced Igerna, who later gave birth to Arthur. Merlin's ghost is said to wander in the cave.

VERYAN

Carne Beacon. TREASURE. Gerennius, Cornish saint and king, is said to be buried in this prehistoric round barrow in a golden boat with silver oars, but excavations have found nothing. *1 mile S of Veryan, itself 7 miles SE of Truro.*

WARBSTOW

Warbstow Bury. GIANT; ARTHURIAN LEGEND. One of Cornwall's finest Iron Age hillforts was also said to be the home of a giant, killed when the giant of Launceston Castle threw a tool at him.

A long mound inside the fort was known as Arthur's Grave, but there is no evidence to link the king with this site, and there are many 'Arthur's Graves' in Britain (see especially *Glastonbury*, Somerset). *Beside lane W of Warbstow, itself 10 miles E of Tintagel; footpath goes through fort.*

ZENNOR

Zennor Quoit and Church. GIANT; ARTHURIAN LEGEND; MERMAID. The 'quoit' is a prehistoric burial chamber on the moor above the village, said to have been erected by a giant (hence its local name of the Giant's Quoit) and to be immovable; if it *is* taken away, the stones will come back by themselves.

Zennor also has an Arthurian tradition: when this stretch of coast was invaded by the Danes, the King and his men defeated the invaders at Vellan, west of Pendeen.

In Zennor church, a 15th-century carved bench-end commemorates a reputed visit from a mermaid. In human disguise, she fell in love with Matthew Trewhella, the churchwarden's son and a fine singer, and they left the village together. It was believed locally that she had enticed him into the sea, and according to legend, his voice can still be heard singing from beneath the waves. *On coast 5 miles SW of St Ives (Quoit: SW 469380).*

Brentor church, sited on top of lonely Brent Tor

DEVON

BERRY POMEROY

★ **Berry Pomeroy Castle.** GHOSTS; TREASURE. Ghosts seen here include a woman in a long hooded cape, and the sound of a crying baby has been heard.

The legend of hidden treasure concerns a young man from Totnes who dreamed of finding an iron pot filled with gold. Just after midnight he set out in stormy weather towards the castle, and on the road met a doctor to whom he told his tale. The doctor persuaded him to return home, saying he could look for the treasure in the morning. Next day the young man went to the castle and found that the hiding place of his dream had been recently disturbed, and there was no pot of gold. Shortly afterwards, the formerly impoverished doctor seems to have come into some money. *Berry Pomeroy 1 mile E of Totnes; castle in woods to N and open to public.*

BRAUNTON

Church. SITING LEGEND. St Brannoc, founder of this church, may have come to Devon from Wales in the 6th century. He had a vision that he should build a church at the place where he would see a sow suckling her piglets. The saint is said to be buried somewhere in the church, and visitors today can see a roof boss with a carving of the pigs, as well as a bench-end depicting St Brannoc himself. *5 miles NW of Barnstaple.*

BRENT TOR

★ **Brentor Church.** SITING LEGEND; LEY. The inaccessible location of this small church, on top of a rocky tor, is attributed to the Devil, who nightly moved the building materials uphill from the original site until the people gave in and built it on the tor. St Michael then appeared, disapproved of the church's location and kicked the Devil downhill, throwing a large rock after him. This legend can be seen as symbolizing the conflict between the old pagan religions (led by the Devil) and the new Christianity (led by the saint). Christian churches were often built on sites which were important to pre-Christian peoples, and indeed evidence of an earthwork has been found around the rock on which Brentor church was built. Whether the Christians were attempting to subdue the pagans by taking over their sites, or were themselves involved in some pagan practices, is unclear; similar legends occur throughout Britain.

This church is also on the St Michael Line (see *Marazion*, Cornwall). *Brentor church 4 miles N of Tavistock.*

CHAGFORD

Longstone, Shovel Down. MOVING STONE. This standing stone was said to move round slowly at sunrise so that each face was warmed in turn by the sun. The Grey Wethers stone circles on Sittaford Tor (2 miles south-west) were also said to do the same. Nearby there are prehistoric stone rows on Shovel Down; these led to burial cairns, and so were presumably built for ritual purposes, but nothing is really known about them. *Shovel Down 2 miles SW of Chagford; stones reached from lane to N (SX 660856).*

DREWSTEIGNTON

Spinsters' Rock. SITING LEGEND. Four large stones form this monument, which may be all that remains of a Neolithic burial chamber. Originally it was part of a much larger complex of standing stones with avenues of stones forming a cross, one arm of which led towards Spinsters' Rock; however an insensitive farmer removed all the standing stones, and now only Spinsters' Rock survives. According to legend it was built by three spinsters (i.e. spinning ladies) to amuse themselves early one morning after delivering the wool they had spun. *2 miles W of Drewsteignton, in field beside minor road (SX 700908).*

EAST WORLINGTON

Long Stone. DEVIL. This prehistoric standing stone has five crosses carved on it, one on the top and one on each side. This was often done, presumably to Christianize stones and dispel any lingering paganism that might still attach to them. According to folklore, it was thrown here by the Devil and now cannot be moved: it has proved impossible to shift it, even when using horses. *East Worlington 8 miles SE of South Molton; Long Stone close to road to Meshaw, $1\frac{1}{2}$ miles N of village (SS 775159).*

EXETER

Exeter Cathedral. GHOST. A phantom nun is said to haunt the cloisters, appearing usually about 7 p.m. near the south wall of the nave. She walks for a few yards before vanishing.

LUSTLEIGH

Hunter's Tor, Lustleigh Cleave. GHOSTS. Two women riding over the Tor in 1956 came across about 12 men on horseback, accompanied by others on foot and some greyhounds. The men were all in medieval costume, and the women thought they were on location for a film. Curious, they followed the horsemen until they were hidden by a stone wall. Seconds later, when the women rode past the wall, the medieval party had disappeared, nor could the women find any hoofprints in the soft ground other than their own. *Hunter's Tor 2 miles NW of Lustleigh, itself 3 miles NW of Bovey Tracey; footpath runs over Tor.*

LYDFORD

Lydford Castle. GHOST. Judge Jeffreys is the unexpected ghost here, sometimes appearing as a black pig. *8 miles SW of Okehampton.*

LYNTON

The Valley of Rocks. PETRIFACTION LEGEND. Legend has it that when the Devil came across a man called Ragged Dick and his friends dancing here on a Sunday, he turned them into slate. The rock formation is still known as Ragged Dick. *Just W of Lynton.*

OKEHAMPTON

Branscombe's Loaf and Cheese, Sourton Common. DEVIL. Walter Branscombe was a 13th-century bishop of Exeter who rode to outlying parts of the county to visit his flock. The legend has it that, while returning across Dartmoor with his servant one day, he was offered refreshment by a stranger on condition that the bishop addressed him as 'Master'. They were just about to accept the bread and cheese when the servant spotted cloven hoofs beneath the stranger's long cloak, and, realizing that he was the Devil, knocked the food from the bishop's hand. The bishop made the sign of the cross, and the Devil vanished. Today the loaf and cheese can still be seen on Corn Ridge - two round granite boulders much bigger than the others. Not far away are the Slipper Stones, where the bishop lost his slippers. *Sourton Common about 4 miles SW of Okehampton (SX 553891).*

Nine Stones, Belstone. PETRIFACTION LEGEND. This circle of 17 stones, which once surrounded a cairn that has now disappeared, are said to be maidens turned to stone for dancing on the Sabbath. They still dance at noon, so it is rumoured. *On moor ½ mile SW of Belstone, itself 2 miles SE of Okehampton (SX 612928).*

Okehampton Castle. PHANTOM DOG. In the guise of a black dog, Lady Howard haunts the castle grounds. She has to pluck one blade of grass nightly and carry it to her old home in Tavistock, continuing until there is no grass left around the castle. A path near the castle has been named 'Lady Howard's Walk'.

PLYMOUTH

Shaugh Bridge. PHANTOM HOUNDS; DEVIL. The Wild Hunt, Yeth (i.e. Heath) or Wish Hounds have been heard in several areas of Devon. These are packs of ghostly hounds, portents of death and disaster and also known in other areas of Britain. They are not seen, but only heard as they pass overhead on stormy nights. Shaugh Bridge was said to be often visited by the Wild Hunt and the Devil, who would try to lead travellers to the edge of Dewerstone Rock, from where they would fall off the cliffs into the river below. The Devil's cloven hoofprints were, so it is said, once seen in the snow on the cliff. *Shaugh Bridge crosses River Plym NW of Shaugh Prior, 6 miles NE of Plymouth centre.*

PLYMPTON

Church. SITING LEGEND. Crownhill Castle was said to have been the original intended site for this church, until the Devil intervened by continually moving the building stones down to the new site, where the church was finally built. *E of Plymouth.*

POSTBRIDGE

Bellever and Huccaby. FAIRIES. Devon folklore is rich in tales of fairies, here often called pixies. They were believed to dance in the stone circles on Dartmoor, including the one near Huccaby Tor. A young Postbridge man, who frequently walked the 5 miles across the moor to Huccaby when he was courting a girl there, one night is said to have got caught up by a group of pixies dancing near Bellever Tor. They danced around him all through the night, making him spin around, until by dawn he was exhausted and resolved to give up courting. He never did marry. *S of Postbridge (Bellever Tor: SX 645765).*

Postbridge. PHANTOM DOG; PHANTOM HANDS. South-east of Postbridge, in the Cator Common area, there have been sightings in the last 50 years of a large white ghost dog - a slender animal like an Afghan or Saluki. When a woman spoke to it, it vanished. This may be the ghost of an old type of deer- or wolf-hound, a kind of dog rarely seen today.

In the 1920s, several road accidents were believed to have been caused by ghostly presences on the main road south-west of Postbridge at Nine Mile Hill. The drivers said the steering wheel was pulled by invisible hands; a motorcyclist felt 'large, muscular, hairy hands' close over his and drive the machine off the road.

STOKE

Church. SAINT; GHOST; HOLY WELL. The church is said to have been built at the place where St Nectan had his head cut off, picked it up, put it back in place, and walked away as if nothing had happened. This may be a memory of the ancient Celtic head cult, in which the head was venerated as the most important part of the body. The Celts collected and preserved their enemies' heads, and they also carved stone heads, some of which survive today.

In 1973 the vicar saw a figure in a monk's habit in the churchyard. He stood on the grass to wait for him, thinking it was unusual to see a monk there, but then the figure disappeared. Other people, too, have seen the phantom monk.

There is also a holy well at Stoke, St Nectan's Well, off the main street and down a steep path. *1½ miles W of Hartland.*

TAVISTOCK

Vixen Tor, Merrivale. WITCH. Many travellers on the moor lost their lives in the bogs when thick fog was caused, it is said, by a witch's spells. She used to perch high on Vixen Tor, but was outwitted by a man who was given a magic ring by the pixies. This made him invisible, and he was able to creep up behind her and push her off the Tor into the bog. *S of Merrivale, itself 4 miles E of Tavistock.*

Wistman's Wood. PHANTOM HOUNDS; GHOSTS. The Yeth Hounds were said to haunt this ancient wood, and a phantom funeral procession of monks in white robes has been seen. The twisted oaks are many hundreds of years old, and it has been suggested that this was a sacred wood where the druids worshipped. Its name may derive from the local word 'whisht', meaning 'eerie'. *Wood can only be reached by footpaths, e.g. from Two Bridges (NE of Princetown); from there, good mile's walk to N.*

TOTNES

Brutus Stone. HERO LEGEND. Brutus, the Trojan hero, is said to have planned to found a new Troy in Britain. He

CALENDAR OF EVENTS

February/March: Shrove Tuesday
ST COLUMB MAJOR, Cornwall. *Shrovetide Hurling:* Hundreds play an ancient game using a small silver-coloured ball.

1 May (May Day)
PADSTOW, Cornwall. *'Obby 'Oss Festival:* Processions of two hobboy horses and dancing followers throughout the day, to celebrate the arrival of summer (see entry for *Padstow*).

8 May
HELSTON, Cornwall. *Furry Dance:* Children and adults dance through the decorated town, taking good luck into the houses.

May: Spring Bank Holiday
KINGSTEIGNTON, Devon. *Ram Roasting Fair:* In the past, a lamb was killed and eaten, perhaps a relic of ancient sacrifices to the gods.

23 June
Cornwall. *Midsummer bonfires* on St John's Eve, on various hilltops, originally lit to strengthen the declining sun and bring fertility.

5 November
OTTERY ST MARY, Devon. *Tar Barrel Rolling:* A traditional variation on Bonfire Night celebrations, where men run carrying burning barrels. There is also a fire carnival at HATHERLEIGH (Devon) on the following Wednesday.

5 November
SHEBBEAR, Devon. *Turning the Devil's Boulder:* At night, bellringers turn a large stone outside the churchyard using crowbars, in order to protect the village from harm.

Tar Barrel Rolling, Ottery St Mary

landed in England on the banks of the River Dart, at the place where Totnes now stands. As he stepped from his ship on to a granite boulder he proclaimed:

Here I am, and here I rest,
And this town shall be called Totnes.

The stone where he is said to have stood, known as the Brutus Stone, is set into the pavement in Fore Street near the East Gate. Although the story was current in the late 16th century, it is unlikely to be based on fact. Possibly 'Brutus Stone' is derived from 'Bruiter's Stone' (from which the town crier 'bruited' his news), or from 'Brodestone' (big stone).

UPLYME

Black Dog Inn. PHANTOM DOG. This inn is so named because a ghostly black dog haunts Haye Lane close by. The dog crosses the Devon-Dorset boundary, a significant fact since phantom dogs are for some reason attracted to boundaries, as well as other old landscape features like ancient trackways, ponds, churchyards and prehistoric sites. There are hundreds of phantom dog legends throughout Britain. The animals are usually black in colour, calf-sized, and with glowing red eyes. Despite their frightening appearance, they rarely harm the people who see them (and people do still see them today). *NW of Lyme Regis.*

BRISTOL CHANNEL
CHEDDAR
MENDIP HILLS
BRENT
KNOLL
MINEHEAD
LUCCOMBE
DUNSTER
WATCHET
WILLITON
EXMOOR
WESTONZOYLAND
GLASTONBURY
QUANTOCK
HILLS
Parrett
LOW HAM
NORTON
FITZWARREN
BABCARY
SOUTH
CADBURY
SOMERSET
Tone
TAUNTON
SHAFTESBUR
YEOVIL
SANDFORD
ORCAS
BLACKDOWN
HILLS
BROADWAY
MONTACUTE
TRENT
CHURCHINGFORD
FOLKE
DORSET
THORNCOMBE
MELCOMBE
HORSEY
0
10
20
MILES
KILOMETRES
0
10
20
30
40
CERNE ABBAS
CHIDEOCK
EGGARDON
HILL
DORCHESTER
Frome
LYME
REGIS
ABBOTSBURY
PORTESHAM
WEYMOUTH
ISLE OF
PORTLAND
BRISTOL
A38
A36
A303
M3
TAUNTON
M5
WINCHESTER
A30
A33
M27
YEOVIL
SOUTHAMPTON
A27
A35
A31
PORTSMOUTH
BOURNEMOUTH
WEYMOUTH

ENGLISH

CHANNEL

DORSET HAMPSHIRE ISLE OF WIGHT AND SOMERSET

DORSET

BERE REGIS

Woodbury Hill. TREASURE; HOLY WELL. The Anchoret's Well inside this Iron Age hillfort was said to contain a golden table or tablet. On 21 September each year the local people used to come to the well and drink its water, which was believed to have healing powers. *Reached from minor road E of Bere Regis.*

BOTTLEBUSH DOWN

Roman Road. GHOSTS; FAIRIES. Tumuli, barrows, earthworks and other evidence of activity in prehistoric times are everywhere on the Downs, and at the point where the course of a Roman road crosses the B3081 many witnesses have seen a ghost on horseback. He was seen in 1924 by an archaeologist, R.C. Clay, who was driving home one evening. Mr Clay saw a horseman galloping ahead of him, then alongside him 50 yards away, and he was able to observe the figure in detail. The man wore a long flowing cloak, had bare legs, and seemed to be waving a weapon above his head; the horse had no bridle or stirrups. Mr Clay felt that the figure dated from the late Bronze Age (*c.* 2500 years ago), and also noted that horse and rider disappeared by a prehistoric burial mound.

Another man who rested on a barrow while crossing the Down was surrounded by 'little people in leather jerkins', who danced around him. *Bottlebush Down lies between Sixpenny Handley and Cranborne, about 10 miles N of Wimborne Minster.*

CERNE ABBAS

★ **Cerne Abbas Giant and Abbey.** GIANT; FERTILITY CUSTOMS; UNDERGROUND PASSAGE; HOLY WELL; LEY. Cut out of the chalk on a hill slope close to the village, the giant still stands 180 feet tall. No one knows when he was made, or by whom, though theories abound. The pagan god Hercules is one popular identification - but for the local people it was his unmistakeable male attributes which were the most important feature of the giant. He was considered to be a potent source of fertility, and women would sit on the figure to be cured of barrenness. Unmarried girls would pray at his feet that they would not die old maids; and married couples would hope to ensure a child by having intercourse on the figure. Another fertility custom was the May Day maypole dancing, and at one time a maypole (a phallic symbol) was erected annually in a small earthwork called the Trendle or the Frying Pan above the giant's head.

Not far away in the village are the ruins of an abbey, and an underground passage is said to run from the abbey to the site of St Catherine's Chapel on Cat-and-Chapel Hill. There are literally hundreds of rumoured underground passages throughout Britain, but only a few of them existed in reality.

Not far from the abbey St Augustine's holy well can still be seen. At one time it was the abbey's only water supply, and traditionally it began to flow where St Augustine struck the ground with his staff.

According to *The Ley Guide* (Devereux and Thomson) the Cerne Abbas sites of St Mary's church, the holy well, the abbey ruins and the Trendle lie in a straight line which continues through other antiquities to form a ley 7 miles long. *Footpaths from village uphill to Giant; abbey ruins also on N side of village; well can be reached through churchyard and down to right, along ancient cobbled path between tall lime trees.*

CHIDEOCK

Graveyard. PHANTOM DOG. There are many black dog legends in the West Country, such as the one at Uplyme on the Devon border. The Chideock dog was seen before the Second World War by a man walking home from Morcombelake to Chideock with a friend late one winter's night. It followed them along the road as far as the old graveyard at the crossroads in Chideock, and then as they watched in the bright moonlight it walked towards a gravestone and disappeared. *3 miles W of Bridport.*

CORFE CASTLE

Corfe Castle. GHOSTS. These spectacular ruins date back to the 11th century, though the site was already in use in Saxon times, and over the centuries many dramatic events have occurred here, some possibly having echoes in the present day. In AD 978 King Edward the Martyr was murdered here; 22 French noblemen were starved to death in the dungeons by King John; and there was a long siege during the Civil War before the castle fell to the Roundheads. In recent times local people have seen ghosts among the ruins, and over the last 20 years there have been sightings of a headless woman on the pathway to the castle. *5 miles NW of Swanage.*

DORCHESTER

★ **Maiden Castle.** GIANTS; UNDERGROUND PASSAGE. The surviving ramparts of this Iron Age hillfort are among the most impressive to be seen anywhere in Britain. Being on such a vast scale, it is not difficult to see why people thought the fort was built by giants.

A new item of folklore developed during the Second World War: that an underground passage 2 miles long ran from Maiden Castle into the centre of Dorchester and was used by the Home Guard. *2 miles SW of Dorchester; reached along lane from A354.*

The Cerne Abbas Giant, a fertility symbol carved into a chalk hillside

EGGARDON HILL

Hillfort. DEVIL; PHANTOM HOUNDS. A man was supposed to have been chased by the Devil across this fine Iron Age hillfort. It is also said to be haunted by Diana and her hounds, collecting the souls of the dead (similar to the Wild Hunt in Devon). *1 mile SE of Powerstock, reached from track off lane to E.*

FOLKE

Church. SITING LEGEND. Folke is a tiny settlement with a fine Gothic church next to the manor house. The church was being built in Broke Wood a mile to the south, but the materials were nightly removed to the present site by mysterious forces. *2 miles SE of Sherborne.*

ISLE OF PORTLAND

Isle of Portland PHANTOM DOG. Portland's ghost dog, shaggy-coated, as tall as a man and with fiery red eyes as big as saucers, is known as the Tow (rhyming with 'cow') Dog. He has been seen all over the island, from Chesil to the Bill, but he does not attack people - he only bars their way. *S of Weymouth.*

MELCOMBE HORSEY

Giant's Grave. GIANTS. A giant who lost a stone-throwing contest was believed to have died of disappointment and been buried in this mound; nearby are the two stones which were being thrown by the giants from Nordon Hill to Henning Hill. The stones were said to move when they heard the cocks crowing at Cheselbourne (the trick being that stones, being stone, can't hear!). *8 miles S of Sturminster Newton beside lane linking Cheselbourne with Melcombe Bingham to N (ST 757017).*

MILTON ABBAS

Milton Abbey and St Catherine's Chapel. UNDERGROUND PASSAGES; KING'S VISION. From the fine abbey church, legend has it that three tunnels ran: to Winterbourne Houghton church 1½ miles to the north-east, to Quarleston Farm at Winterbourne Stickland 2 miles to the north-east, and to Delcombe Manor 1½ miles to the north. The labour and construction problems presented by such tunnels make their existence unlikely.

Just east of the abbey on a hill is St Catherine's Chapel. This simple building was erected at the place where King Athelstan had a vision of victory in battle in the 10th century; on his return from a successful expedition he built the chapel before founding the monastery here. People would visit the chapel on pilgrimage, and it can still be visited. *6 miles SW of Blandford Forum.*

PORTESHAM

Hell Stone. DEVIL. The Devil was said have been playing quoits on the Isle of Portland 8 miles away when he threw over to Blackdown Hill the stones that form this tomb. The monument is a Neolithic chambered long barrow, with nine upright stones supporting a large capstone. It lay in ruins until 1866, when it was inaccurately reconstructed. *½ mile N of Portesham and reached by footpath (SY 606867).*

SANDFORD ORCAS

Manor House. GHOST. The fine Tudor manor house is supposed to be haunted by a farmer who hanged himself in it. Wearing a white smock, he has been seen several times walking past the kitchen window. A ghostly old lady has been observed climbing a staircase, and other figures

Maiden Castle, the remains of an Iron Age hillfort

have also been seen. Strange harpsichord music has been heard, as well as heavy footsteps, and some people have smelled tobacco smoke and incense. *1 mile NE of Yeovil; open to public.*

SHAFTESBURY

Shaftesbury Abbey. GHOST; TREASURE. The Saxon abbey was once an impressive building, but now only ruins remain. The abbey's treasures were said to have been buried on the site by a monk, who died taking to his grave the secret of their location. Now his ghost walks in the ruins, disappearing by a wall where there was once a doorway. He appears to be walking on his knees, presumably because the ground level has been raised in more recent times. *W of Market Place.*

SHAPWICK

Badbury Rings. ARTHURIAN LEGEND; TREASURE. This Iron Age hillfort still has prominent defensive earthworks and is one of several places identified as Mount Badon, where King Arthur fought the Saxons in AD 518 and defeated them. There is also said to be a golden coffin buried here. *Reached by footpath from Blandford Forum–Wimborne Minster road which passes nearby (SU 963030).*

STUDLAND

The Agglestone. DEVIL. The Devil was sitting on the Needles, legend has it, when he threw this 20-foot rock at Corfe Castle (or Bindon Abbey or the spire of Salisbury Cathedral, according to whichever version you hear). But it fell short and landed on the heath west of Studland. Alternative names for it are the Devil's Anvil and the Devil's Nightcap. *1 mile W of Studland and 2 miles N of Swanage (SZ 023828).*

THORNCOMBE

Forde Abbey. GHOST. Originally a Cistercian abbey dating back to the 12th century, the enlarged building is now an unusual and impressive private house. Occasionally a ghostly black monk is seen in the Monk's Walk in the cloisters, and in the Great Hall. He may be Thomas Chard, the abbot who built the Great Hall and tower in 1500. *Forde Abbey 3 miles SE of Chard and 1 mile NW of Thorncombe; sometimes open to public.*

TRENT

Trent Barrow. ARTHURIAN LEGEND; GHOSTS. The pool in this earthwork is one of the places where King Arthur's sword Excalibur is said to have been thrown. Interestingly, it is only a few miles from *South Cadbury* Castle (see Somerset), which may have been Camelot. Ghostly galloping hooves and wailing voices are rumoured at Trent Barrow, following an incident when a coach and horses with all the passengers aboard drove into the pool. *1 mile E of Trent, itself 1 mile NE of Yeovil.*

WOOL

Hethfelton House. PHANTOM COACH. It is said locally that at midnight a ghostly coach-and-four drives down the lane in a southerly direction alongside the Holy Stream, towards the River Frome. *Coach's route ½ mile NE of Wool, itself 5 miles W of Wareham.*

HAMPSHIRE

BASING

Basing House. TREASURE; GHOST. The house was blown up by the Roundheads in 1645; but beforehand, so it was said, the owner, the Marquis of Winchester, melted down all his gold, and in the shape of a golden calf this treasure was buried beneath the house. It still lies hidden under the ruins.

The ghost of Oliver Cromwell is also said to walk near the ruins. *1 mile E of Basingstoke.*

BEAULIEU

Beaulieu Abbey. GHOSTS. There have been numerous reports of ghostly monks at the abbey, which was founded in 1204 and continued as an active monastery until its dissolution in 1538. Sometimes the monks are seen: in 1965 a woman saw a brown-robed monk sitting reading a parchment scroll; and in 1977 another woman saw two monks walking along a path. As she watched, they vanished. Sometimes the monks are heard but not seen: in 1960 the then curator of the Montagu Motor Museum heard slow footsteps as of men carrying a burden, then sounds like grave-digging. His cottage overlooks what was probably the monks' burial ground. He has also heard the sound of monks chanting, as have others, and some people have smelt incense. *7 miles S of Southampton.*

BREAMORE

Breamore House. GHOST; MAZE. This is a fine 16th-century red-brick manor house haunted by a lady in a poke bonnet, reputedly the wife of an early owner, murdered by her son. She appears when the current owner is soon to die. Nearby is a fine Saxon church, and in a clearing in the woods is a turf maze known as the Mizmaze. *1 mile NW of Breamore, itself 7 miles S of Salisbury; open to public.*

CALENDAR OF EVENTS

Early January
NEWCHURCH, Isle of Wight. *Blessing of the Plough:* On Plough Monday, farm work used to resume after the Twelve Days of Christmas. On Plough Sunday the plough is blessed at a church service.

February/March: Shrove Tuesday
CORFE CASTLE, Dorset. *Shrovetide Football:* Street football played to maintain an ancient quarrymen's right of way.

Easter: fifth week following (Rogation Sunday)
MUDEFORD, Dorset. *Blessing the Sea:* In some coastal parishes, the nets, boats and the sea are all blessed; the priest sometimes sails out into the harbour, as at Mudeford.

1 May (May Day)
MINEHEAD, Somerset. *Hobby Horse Festival:* A hobby horse tours the town and also visits DUNSTER; on the evenings of 2 and 3 May he visits neighbouring hamlets.

13 May (Old May Day)
ABBOTSBURY, Dorset. *Garland Day:* Flower garlands on wooden frames were taken on to boats and thrown into the sea, possibly as an offering to the sea-god. Now the garlands are simply carried through the village.

24 December (Christmas Eve)
ANDOVER, Hampshire. *Mummers' Play:* The participants wear coloured paper streamers while performing 800-year-old play.

24 December (Christmas Eve)
DUNSTER, Somerset. *Burning the Ashen Faggot:* An old Christmas ritual still performed at the Luttrell Arms Hotel.

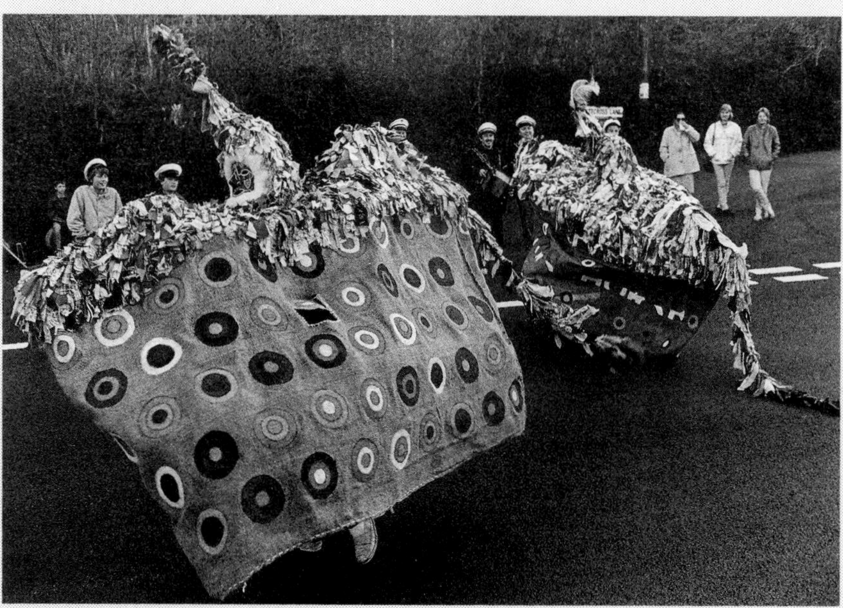

Minehead Hobby Horses

COPYTHORNE

Money Hills. TREASURE. These round barrows were said to contain hidden treasure. *Beside lane at NE end of Copythorne, itself 3 miles NW of Totton (SU 318151).*

HAYLING ISLAND

South Hayling. DROWNED CHURCHES. According to legend, Hayling Island was once connected to Normandy by land. There were also said to have been churches in

South Hayling which were overwhelmed by the sea in the 14th century, though their bells are sometimes still heard ringing out beneath the waves. Over the centuries there has been considerable erosion of Britain's coastline, so it is not impossible that Hayling Island once extended further south. Until the 18th century, the Isle of Wight could be reached across the sands from the mainland at low tide. *E of Portsmouth.*

HIGHCLERE

Church. MONSTER. A yew tree by the church was once, apparently, home to a grampus - a kind of dolphin - which chased the villagers and made loud breathing noises which caused great annoyance. (No wonder it puffed and panted, being somewhat out of its element in a tree!) A priest banished it to the Red Sea, where it must stay a thousand years; but the date of its likely return is unknown, for the date of its banishment is also unknown. *4 miles S of Newbury.*

MEONSTOKE

Old Winchester Hill. SITING LEGEND. An Iron Age hillfort crowns this prominent hill, with fine views as far as the Isle of Wight. In the 2nd century BC it may have been a tribal centre, and a tradition grew up that it was intended to be the original site of Winchester, but the building materials brought here were mysteriously transported 10 miles to the north-west, where Winchester was finally built. *2 miles NE of Meonstoke, reached by path from lane leading SE from Warnford.*

NETLEY

Netley Abbey. PROPHETIC DREAM. These 13th-century ruins have been preserved because of a dream that an 18th-century owner, Walter Taylor, had. Taylor bought the abbey, which had been used as a private dwelling since the Dissolution of the Monasteries, and planned to use the stone as building materials elsewhere. He dreamed that the keystone of an arch fell on him, but disregarded this warning and started demolition; when he was indeed killed by a stone falling from a window arch, all demolition was halted. *On E side of Southampton Water; open to public.*

NEW FOREST

Rufus Stone. GHOST. King William II, known as Rufus because of his red hair and ruddy complexion, died in a hunting accident (or was murdered) in the New Forest on 2 August 1100. It has been suggested that William Rufus was a divine victim, sacrificed in a pagan ritual in order to promote the vigour and fertility of the kingdom. His body was taken in a cart to Winchester, and it is said that on the anniversary of his death the king's ghost follows the route from the forest to Winchester. The Rufus Stone now marks the place of William's death. *2 miles SW of Cadnam, close to lane leading to Upper Canterton from A31.*

SILCHESTER

Roman Town. GIANT; DEVIL. In Roman times Silchester was a thriving town called Calleva Atrebatum, and some fine Roman remains can still be seen there, including a large stretch of Roman wall 15 feet high. The town was at some time also said to be the home of a giant named Onion, and coins found in the ruins were known as Onion's pennies. The story goes that he threw a stone, now known as the Imp Stone, a mile away to its resting place beside a road crossing the Hampshire-Berkshire border, and the marks of his huge fingers are supposed to be still visible on the stone.

The Roman road which led east from Silchester - its course is still traceable today - is known as the Devil's Highway. *6 miles N of Basingstoke.*

WINCHESTER

★ Winchester Cathedral, Castle Hall and St Catherine's Hill. SAINT; ARTHURIAN LEGEND; GHOST; LEY; MAZE. Winchester has long been an important town, and was the capital of England when William the Conqueror was king. In the 9th century St Swithun was bishop here, and the site of his tomb can still be seen in the cathedral. Pilgrims visited it, and many miracles were reported.

In Castle Hall near Westgate, the 13th-century great hall houses 'King Arthur's Round Table', divided into segments for the king and 24 knights. Although very old, it is unlikely to have been genuinely Arthur's, though the medieval author Sir Thomas Malory believed so, and he located Camelot at Winchester in his *Morte d'Arthur.*

Castle Hall is now an assize court, and in 1973 a prisoner cleaning the cell block below the great hall saw a ghost disappear through a wall. He wore a frock coat and three-cornered hat.

According to Paul Devereux and Ian Thomson's *Ley Guide*, Winchester lies on an 11-mile ley (alignment of ancient sites) from Tidbury Ring to a tumulus beyond St Catherine's Hill. The Winchester sites on the ley are St Bartholomew's church, Hyde Gate and the Lady Chapel at the Cathedral. The next point is St Catherine's Hill, a mile south-east of the town centre. There was an Iron Age hillfort on the hill, and in the 12th century a small chapel dedicated to St Catherine was built, of which slight traces remain.

East of the tree clump holding the chapel ruins is a turf maze known as the Mizmaze. It may be 18th-century, or it may be much older - no one knows. But it lies exactly on the line of the ley.

ISLE OF WIGHT

GODSHILL

Church. SITING LEGEND. The fine Norman church on a hilltop was originally planned to be built in the valley below, according to legend; but every morning the builders would find the previous day's work demolished and the stones carried uphill by unknown hands, so they gave in and the location was changed. *4 miles NW of Ventnor.*

MOTTISTONE

Long Stone. GIANT; DEVIL; DRUIDS. The 13-foot stone is a probable remnant of a Neolithic long barrow. Legend has it that the stone was thrown here by a giant, the smaller stone being thrown by the Devil; alternatively the Devil dropped some stones from his overloaded cart.

There was also a belief that the druids used to meet at this stone. *Reached along footpath through woods, starting opposite church (SZ 408843).*

QUARR HILL

Quarr Abbey. GHOST; TREASURE. These monastic ruins, half a mile from the new Benedictine abbey, are said to be haunted by the ghost of Henry II's queen, Eleanor of Aquitaine, who was believed to have been buried here in a gold coffin. In fact she lived and died on the mainland, not at Quarr, so the ghost must be that of some unknown woman. *1 mile W of Ryde; track leads past old and new Quarr Abbeys.*

SOMERSET

BABCARY

Wimble Toot. ZODIAC. This tree-covered tumulus marks the breast of the Virgo figure in the Glastonbury Zodiac (see *Glastonbury*). Virgo is the fertile Earth Mother, and Wheathill lies at her feet. Her profile and front are outlined by the River Cary, and she is lying on her back, her head pointing west. Tumuli are often breast-shaped, and 'toot' is a variant of 'teat'; Wimble Toot certainly resembles a breast lying on the fertile farmland, and so is appropriately placed in the zodiac outline. *Can be seen from lane ½ mile S of Babcary, itself 7 miles N of Yeovil (ST 560280).*

BRENT KNOLL

Brent Knoll. DEVIL; ARTHURIAN LEGEND. Brent Knoll is an isolated hill surrounded by the Somerset Levels and crowned by the single ditch and rampart of an Iron Age hillfort. According to tradition, it was formed from a shovelful of earth thrown down by the Devil when he was digging out Cheddar Gorge.

In Arthurian legend it was the Mount of Frogs, and three giants lived there. The knight Ider, who had the task of challenging them, galloped off and killed all three without waiting for Arthur and the knights who were going to help him.

The occult writer Dion Fortune saw Brent Knoll as a sacred mount where dwelt colonists from Atlantis. *Brent Knoll 6 miles S of Weston-super-Mare; from East Brent, footpath by church leads S to hill, ½ mile away.*

BROADWAY

Church. SITING LEGEND. There are two legends to explain why the church is located where it is, a mile from the village centre. According to the first it was being built in the village, but the day's work was each night undone and the materials carried away to the new site. Alternatively, the Devil threw three stones at the existing church, but missed. However, the local people decided to move the building further away just in case he should keep trying and demolish it.

There is an interesting old cross in the churchyard. *Broadway 2 miles W of Ilminster; church along road towards Ilton.*

CHEDDAR

Cheddar Gorge. DEVIL. When the Devil first saw the Mendip Hills they were smooth in outline, and legend has it that he decided to spoil them by digging out a deep channel which became the Gorge. His first spadeful of rock and soil he threw out to sea, and it became the islands of Steep Holme and Flat Holme. The next load became Brent Knoll (see *East Brent*), and he also meant to destroy Minehead and Watchet, but when he jumped over the River Parrett the basketload of soil he was carrying flew off in all directions.

CHURCHINGFORD

Robin Hood's Butts. ROBIN HOOD; WARRIORS' GRAVES; GIANTS; TREASURE. Robin Hood was said to have used these three tumuli for target practice, but it was also believed that the bodies of warriors killed in battles between the Danes and Saxons (or in the Civil War) were buried there.

Another tradition was that they were formed by giants throwing clods of earth at one another. The largest mound was supposed to concealed a hoard of gold, but no one could reach it because however much they dug, the holes would fill up again overnight. *1 mile E of Churchingford, around where Churchingford–Bishopswood road crosses B3170 to Taunton (ST 234126).*

Glastonbury Tor, famous for its Arthurian associations, is topped by a 13th-century tower

EXMOOR

Caractacus Stone, Winsford Hill. GHOSTS; TREASURE; PHANTOM DOG; DEVIL. Ghostly horses, a waggon and their driver are said to haunt this place: when the driver tried to drag the stone away in order to find the treasure hidden beneath it, the stone fell and killed him.

Winsford Hill is also haunted by a black dog with glowing eyes; on seeing it, the traveller must wait until it vanishes before continuing.

Not far away in the valley, Tarr Steps form a very old 'bridge', supposedly built by the Devil for his own use, across the River Barle. *B3223 crosses Winsford Hill NW of Dulverton; Caractacus Stone not far from road, under shelter close to crossroads called Spire Cross, easterly arm of which goes to Winsford village 1 mile away. Westerly road leads to Tarr Steps. (Caractacus Stone: SS 890336.)*

GLASTONBURY

★ Glastonbury Abbey, Glastonbury Tor and Chalice Well. ARTHURIAN LEGEND; HOLY WELL; FAIRIES; MAZE; ZODIAC; LEY. Identified as the Isle of Avalon where King Arthur was buried, Glastonbury is famous for its

Arthurian connections and a haven for those seeking a mystical atmosphere. The abbey, whose substantial ruins still survive in the town centre, was founded around AD 700, though what can be seen now is much later: St Mary's Chapel or the Lady Chapel is 12th-century, the

Ruined Glastonbury Abbey

Abbot's Kitchen is 14th-century, and the abbey church building covers at least these three centuries. Close to the Lady Chapel, in the monastery burial ground, the monks claimed to have discovered the remains of King Arthur and Queen Guinevere; they were reburied by the monks in their church at a site now marked by a notice-board. Historians doubt that the monks really did find Arthur's grave, but no one can be certain, and it is not impossible.

Joseph of Arimathea is said to have come to Glastonbury and built a church on the site where the Lady Chapel now stands. He brought with him a staff, which he planted on Wearyall Hill and from which the Holy Thorn grew. Descendants of this non-native tree, which blooms around Christmas, can be seen in the abbey grounds and by St John's church in the town. Joseph also brought to England the Holy Grail, which according to one legend is now concealed in Chalice Well. Another name for this was Blood Spring, from the redness of the water – caused, in fact, by its iron content. The well is in a garden at the foot of the Tor, the hill which is Glastonbury's other major feature.

On top of the Tor is a tower, all that remains of a 13th-century church dedicated to St Michael. An entrance to Annwn, a fairy realm, was believed to exist on the Tor and the 6th-century St Collen once met Gwyn ap Nudd, king of the fairies, on top of the hill. Collen entered the king's palace, but when Gwyn offered him fairy food he sprinkled holy water around and immediately found himself alone once more on the empty hilltop.

Visitors may notice ridges or terraces around the hill. It has been suggested that these mark the course of an ancient labyrinth, and that pilgrims followed its spiral course to the top. In an even more speculative theory, the Glastonbury area is claimed to be a huge zodiac, its signs marked out by natural and man-made landscape features. This Glastonbury Zodiac, or Temple of the Stars, is a circle 10 miles across. Glastonbury town and the Tor lie within the figure of Aquarius, here represented by the mystical bird the phoenix.

The Tor also lies on a 21-mile ley extending from Butleigh church to Brockley church (for details see *The Ley-Hunter's Companion* by Paul Devereux and Ian Thomson).

LOW HAM

Church. DRAGON. According to legend, the Dragon of Aller lived in Athelney Fens and caused considerable problems for the people round about: it made raids on them and their livestock, burning crops and trees with its fiery breath, until it was killed by a local man. A spear said to be the weapon he used can still be seen in Low Ham church. *3 miles W of Somerton.*

LUCCOMBE

Dunkery Hill. DEVIL. The 1700-foot hill, high up on Exmoor, was supposedly formed when the Devil was digging out the Punchbowl on Winsford Hill: he dumped the rock and soil here, to form Dunkery Hill. On the north-east promontory are three large stone cairns dating back to the Bronze Age; two of them are called Joaney How and Robin How, but there is no surviving folklore to explain these names. It is possible that they derived from Robin Hood and Little John. *S of Luccombe, itself 5 miles SW of Minehead; cairns E of road from Luccombe (SS 908426).*

MONTACUTE

Montacute House and St Michael's Hill.

UNDERGROUND PASSAGE; STRANGE DREAM. An underground passage at least a mile long was said to run from Montacute House to Ham Hill, south of Stoke-sub-Hamdon. Ham Hill is the site of a 210-acre hillfort, one of the largest in Britain. Though it is now much damaged by quarrying, there are still some impressive ramparts to be seen.

Between the two locations is St Michael's Hill. A local sexton once dreamed that he should dig on top of the hill; he ignored the dream, but it came to him again, and after the third time he organized the digging. A huge stone was found which split in two revealing a crucifix of black flint, another of wood, an old bell and a book. An ox-cart was harnessed to transport the items, and they ended up at Waltham in Essex. There an abbey was built where the oxen halted, the big flint crucifix being placed over the altar. *Montacute 3 miles W of Yeovil, and Ham Hill 1 mile further W; hillfort can be explored by footpaths; Montacute House open to public (National Trust).*

NORTON FITZWARREN

Norton Camp. DRAGON. Following a battle in the hillfort known as Norton Camp, a dragon was said to have been formed by 'spontaneous generation' from the pile of dead bodies. It terrorized the neighbourhood until it was killed by a local hero,Fulk Fitzwarine.The events are commemorated on a carved and painted rood-screen (*c.* 1500) in the church (or did the rood-screen inspire the dragon tale?). *Norton Fitzwarren 2 miles W of Taunton, and camp on hill N of church, crossed by footpaths.*

SOUTH CADBURY

South Cadbury Castle. ARTHURIAN LEGEND. Following archaeological excavations at this Iron Age hillfort, it has been tentatively identified as the site of King Arthur's Camelot. There are also local traditions connecting the place with Arthur. At midsummer, he and his knights are said to ride over the hill and down to a spring beside Sutton Montis church. The sound of ghostly riders is also heard on winter nights along an old track called Arthur's Lane, and there was a belief that Arthur lies sleeping inside the hillfort. *South Cadbury 4 miles SW of Wincanton; footpath leads to fort from main street S of church.*

WATCHET

St Decuman's Well. HOLY WELL. The well is a hillside spring covered by a small stone shelter, and the water flows into three basins. According to legend, St Decuman was decapitated by local pagans, but he picked up his head, washed it in the well and popped it back in place. After this the water became endowed with healing powers. *Well 200 yards W of St Decuman's church, overlooking town.*

WESTONZOYLAND

Sedgemoor Battlefield. GHOSTS. Since the battle in 1685 there have been numerous sightings of ghostly soldiers all around this area. In one instance a couple driving across Sedgemoor nearly ran into some men carrying staves and pikes. *3 miles E of Bridgwater.*

Chalice Well at Glastonbury, reputedly the resting place of the Holy Grail

WILLITON

Battlegore. DEVIL; GIANT. The stones among the earthworks may be the remains of a prehistoric tomb, or they may be connected with a 10th-century battle, but according to legend they were thrown here in a contest between the Devil and a giant. On the leaning stone the Devil's handprint can be seen. *Beside road to Watchet, ¼ mile NW of Williton.*

EAST SUSSEX
KENT
SURREY
AND
WEST SUSSEX

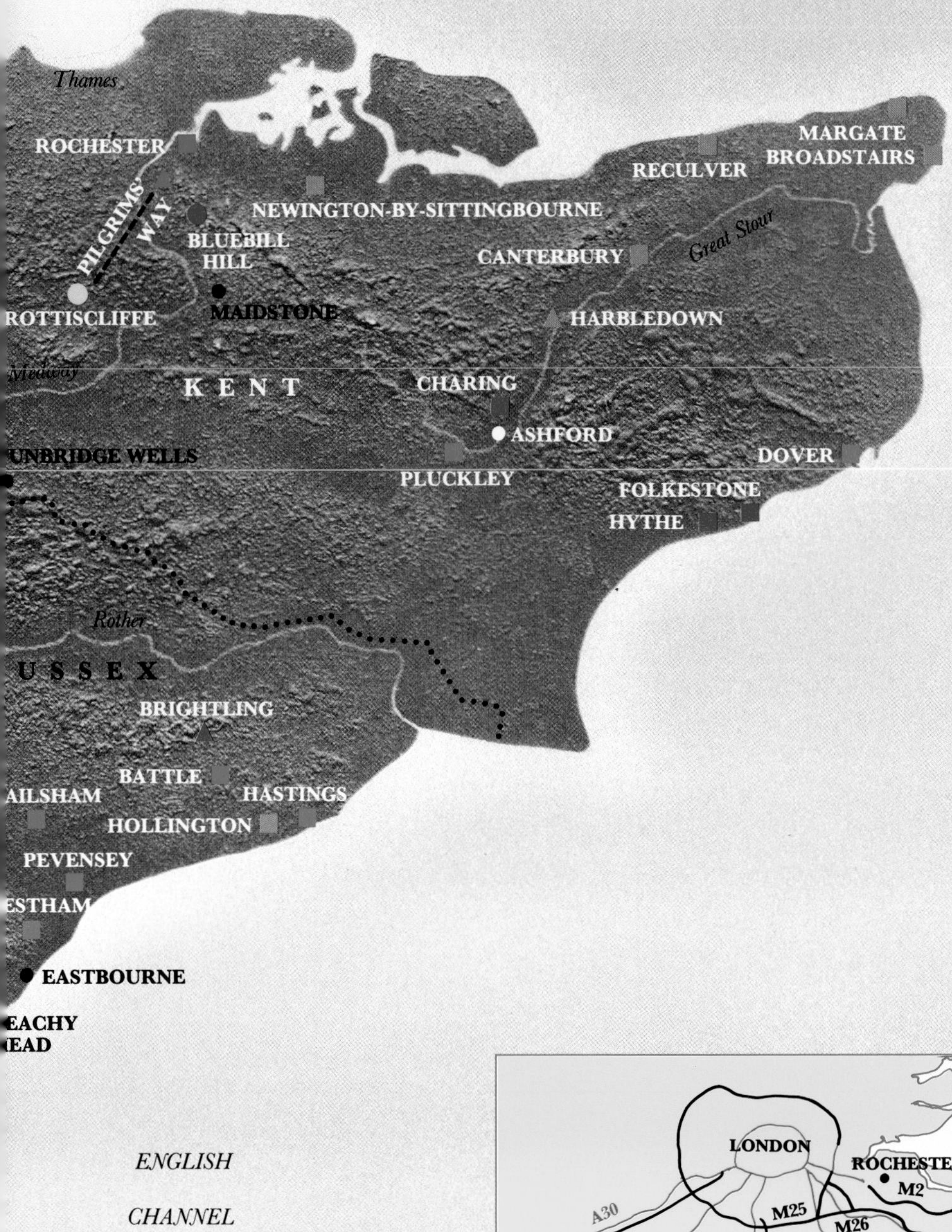

Thames
ROCHESTER
PILGRIMS' WAY
BLUEBILL HILL
NEWINGTON-BY-SITTINGBOURNE
RECULVER
MARGATE
BROADSTAIRS
CANTERBURY
Great Stour
ROTTISCLIFFE
MAIDSTONE
HARBLEDOWN
Medway
KENT
CHARING
ASHFORD
UNBRIDGE WELLS
PLUCKLEY
DOVER
FOLKESTONE
HYTHE
Rother
USSEX
BRIGHTLING
BATTLE
AILSHAM
HASTINGS
HOLLINGTON
PEVENSEY
ESTHAM
EASTBOURNE
EACHY
EAD
ENGLISH
CHANNEL

LONDON
ROCHESTER
MARGATE
M2
CANTERBURY
A30
M25
M26
A2
A258
A20
M3
GUILDFORD
M23
A21
M20
DOVER
FOLKESTONE
A3
A23
TUNBRIDGE WELLS
A259
CHICHESTER
A27
HASTINGS
BRIGHTON
EASTBOURNE

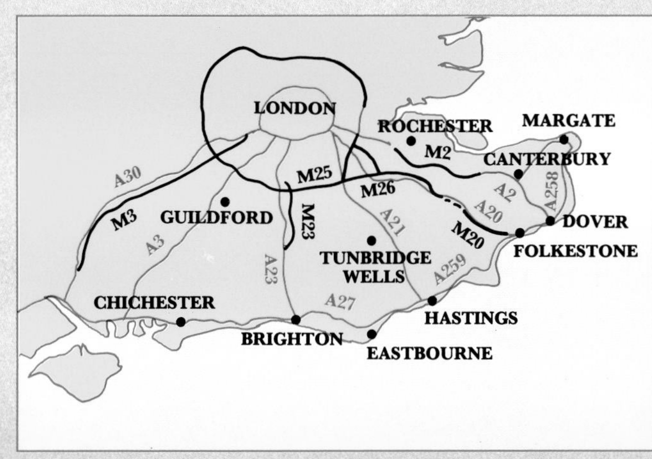

EAST SUSSEX

ALFRISTON

Church. SITING LEGEND. The church stands on an ancient mound, although originally, according to legend, it was intended to be built elsewhere. Each morning the builders found their work destroyed and the stones thrown over on to the mound. They didn't know whether to persist in the original location or move the site, but when a 'wise man' saw four oxen lying on the mound in the shape of a cross this was taken as a sign that the church should be built there. *6 miles NW of Eastbourne.*

BATTLE

Battle Abbey. GHOSTS. William the Conqueror founded the abbey at the site of the Battle of Hastings (1066), and the High Altar of William's church was sited on the spot where King Harold II fell. The church no longer survives, but the spot is now marked by Harold's Stone. The main battlefield lies on the hillside to the south, and the ground is said to run red with blood when it rains. Numerous ghosts have been seen in the area in recent years, including a Norman knight in Abbot's House, a lady in red on the stairs in Abbot's House and in the ruins, a lady in grey near the Great Hall, and a monk in the abbey gateway. On the anniversary of the battle, the ghost of the first man killed rides across the battlefield, or so it was believed. *6 miles NW of Hastings; Battle Abbey open to public.*

BEACHY HEAD

Beachy Head. GHOSTS. This high cliff has a fascination for those contemplating suicide, but whether this is solely because it is a perfect place to jump off, or whether there is an evil atmosphere here that impels the unsuspecting over the edge, is not known. Nor is it always clear whether the ghosts seen here are of suicide victims, or are a manifestation of the evil atmosphere said to have been sensed here. One of the ghosts seems to be a suicide victim, as she has been seen stepping over the edge. Another ghost is a lady in grey, seen on the cliff-edge path; and a black monk is said to beckon people to their deaths. *SW of Eastbourne.*

BRIGHTLING

Churchyard. FOLLY; DEVIL. The pyramid which dominates the churchyard was built to the instructions of 'Mad Jack' Fuller, a local squire who died in 1834. Two other local follies of his are Brightling Needle and the Sugar Loaf. 'Mad Jack' is said to be sitting, mummified, inside his tomb on an iron chair, with a bottle of claret on a table, and surrounded by broken glass to stop the Devil coming to take him away. To call up the Devil, or 'Mad Jack' himself, run backwards seven times round the tomb. *5 miles NW of Battle.*

BRIGHTON

Royal Pavilion. GHOSTS. The Prince Regent's Indian-style residence, built in the late 18th century, has an underground passage said to be haunted by the Prince, but he does not appear in the state rooms. Between the two world wars, a caterer checking his preparations on the night before a banquet saw a woman in a long dress, bonnet and shawl, who walked through the room where the laid tables stood, but the attendant said no one left the building.

St Peter's Church, Preston Park. GHOST. A couple walking in the churchyard in the 1970s saw and spoke to a lady in medieval costume, who they thought was wearing fancy dress for a pageant. They were puzzled when she ignored them, and they could not hear her footsteps, and so they turned round - to see her fade away by a large tomb. *In N Brighton, on Preston Drive close to Preston Manor.*

DITCHLING

Ditchling Beacon. PHANTOM HOUNDS; PHANTOM DOG. Wish or Witch Hounds were believed to race overhead here, chasing the souls of the damned, while the road between Ditchling and Westmeston, on Black Dog Hill, was supposed to be haunted by a phantom headless black dog. *Ditchling 6 miles N of Brighton; Ditchling Beacon on Downs S of Westmeston and Ditchling.*

GLYNDE

Mount Caburn. DEVIL; GIANT; TREASURE. An Iron Age hillfort crowns this hill, traditionally formed from a clod of earth thrown here by the Devil while feverishly digging out the Devil's Dyke (see *Poynings*, West Sussex). A giant called Gill who reputedly lived on the Downs would throw his hammer from the summit of the Caburn. Somewhere in the hill were said to be buried a silver coffin and a knight in golden armour. *¾ mile W of Glynde, itself 2 miles SE of Lewes (TQ 444089).*

HAILSHAM

Michelham Priory. GHOST. The 13th-century priory buildings are haunted by a Grey Lady, who has been seen near the gatehouse. She is also said to visit sleeping occupants of a certain bedroom, looking down on them for a moment before leaving the room through the closed door. *2 miles W of Hailsham and 7 miles N of Eastbourne; open to public.*

'Mad Jack' Fuller's pyramid in the churchyard at Brightling

HASTINGS

Hastings Castle. GHOSTS. On autumn evenings the ghost of Thomas à Becket is said to appear in the ruins. More reliably reported recent ghosts include a woman, possibly a nun, dressed in brown, seen digging near the entrance to a dungeon. *On Castle Hill, overlooking town and beaches.*

HOLLINGTON

Church. SITING LEGEND; DEVIL. Away from the village and surrounded by woods, this church stands on an isolated site said to have been chosen by the Devil, who nightly transferred the building materials to this spot until one day someone passing by found a church newly erected. *On N outskirts of Hastings; church W of village.*

PEVENSEY

Pevensey Castle. GHOSTS. Very impressive remains survive of this Roman coastal fort: in Roman times the sea came right up to the south wall, but now the ruins lie a mile inland. The Normans built a castle inside the Roman wall, now ruined, though the dungeons and part of the keep can still be seen. The ghost of Lady Pelham walks the walls at dusk, and ghostly sounds of battle have been heard. A phantom army led by William Rufus is said to wend its way across the marshes to the castle from the sea, re-enacting an attack on the castle. *4 miles NE of Eastbourne.*

WEST FIRLE

Firle Beacon. GIANT; TREASURE. The long barrow on the hill was said to be the burial place of a giant who lived up here. He regularly quarrelled with another giant on Windover Hill and they would throw boulders at one another; one of them struck and killed the Windover giant, who can still be seen on the hillside (see *Wilmington*).

There is also said to be a silver coffin buried somewhere on Firle Beacon. *3 miles NW of Alfriston; footpaths cross Downs (long barrow: TQ 486058).*

WESTHAM

Church. GHOST. Not far from *Pevensey* Castle (see entry) is this church, where in 1978 a visitor saw a ghost. A man in a modern suit was walking along the path from the church door; when the witness smiled and spoke, the man vanished. He has also been seen by other visitors. *4 miles NE of Eastbourne.*

WILMINGTON

★ The Long Man of Wilmington and Wilmington Church. GIANT; TREASURE; LEY. The Long Man is truly a giant - a chalk-cut figure over 200 feet tall outlined on the steep hill slope of Windover Hill. The date of his original cutting (he now has a more permanent outline) is unknown; nor is it clear who he was meant to represent, though many suggestions have been made, including a warrior, a god, and a giant who was killed by another giant living on Firle Beacon (see *West Firle*). Another legend has it that he fell and broke his neck, his body being outlined in chalk where he lay before it was buried in a long barrow on the hilltop. A Roman in a golden coffin is said to lie buried beneath the Long Man.

The fact that the Long Man holds two long staves led the discoverer of leys, Alfred Watkins, to identify him as a Dodman, a prehistoric surveyor. Ley researcher Paul

The Royal Pavilion at Brighton, said to be haunted by the Prince Regent

Devereux found that a 2-mile ley links the Long Man with a tumulus in Friston Forest and a round barrow on Windover Hill, both to the south, and with the medieval priory and nearby church at Wilmington to the north. A tradition linked church and priory by a short tunnel, which would have run along the course of the ley and may be confirmation of it. Wilmington church is also interesting for the huge, ancient yew tree standing in the churchyard, perhaps dating back a thousand years to the earliest use of this site for religious (Christian or pagan?) purposes. The proximity of the Long Man to this ancient sacred site suggests some definite connection between them. *1½ miles NE of Alfriston: Long Man on Windover Hill S of village; footpaths cross hill from lane to Litlington.*

The chalk-cut giant known as the Long Man of Wilmington

KENT

BLUEBILL HILL

Kit's Coty House and Little Kit's Coty House. BURIAL SITES; RITUAL; UNCOUNTABLE STONES. Kit's Coty House is the more impressive of these two tombs, with a large capstone balanced on three upright stones. It is said to mark the burial place of Kit or Catigern, killed in a 5th-century battle which is sometimes refought by ghostly soldiers. It is said that an object placed on the capstone at the full moon will disappear if you walk around the stones three times.

Little Kit's Coty House, not far away, is now a confused pile of stones, said to be uncountable and therefore sometimes called the Countless Stones. *Off A229 3 miles N of Maidstone and just S of Bluebell Hill (Kit's Coty House: TQ 745608; Little Kit's Coty House: TQ 744604).*

CANTERBURY

★ **Canterbury Cathedral.** GHOSTS; HOLY WELL. Canterbury is an important landmark in the history of Christianity in Britain, and there has been a cathedral here since the end of the 6th century. The present building dates from at least 1100 - the date when the crypt, the oldest part, was completed. No visitor should miss walking through the crypt, preferably choosing a time when there are few other visitors and the powerful atmosphere can be absorbed in calm and quiet.

Perhaps the most dramatic event in the cathedral's history was the bombing in the Second World War. Bombs fell in the precincts all around, but the cathedral itself was miraculously spared. A much earlier drama was the murder of Archbishop Thomas à Becket in 1170. The site of his murder inside the cathedral is marked, but there are no reports of his ghost walking there. One ghost of the many that undoubtedly do haunt the cathedral and its precincts is the monk seen walking contemplatively in the cloisters, who vanished after passing one witness; he has also been seen by others.

A well in the infirmary cloisters, known as St Thomas's Well, was said to flow with blood ever since the water was used to clean the floor after Becket's murder. Miraculous powers were ascribed to objects which had been touched by St Thomas, and the well water (judiciously coloured pink to promote the link with the saint's blood) was claimed to have healing powers. So many pilgrims visited the shrine of St Thomas of Canterbury that at the height of the cult it was as popular as Lourdes is today.

St Martin's Church, St Pancras Church and St Augustine's Abbey. EARLY CHURCH SITES; DEVIL. In Canterbury can be seen many remains of very early Saxon churches, dating from the time of St Augustine's arrival late in the 6th century to convert the pagans to Christianity. St Martin's church is still complete - the chancel and some blocked Saxon doorways are particularly old. King Ethelbert was probably baptized here, in AD 597.

The other churches are now ruined, but St Pancras is interesting as the probable site of a heathen temple used by King Ethelbert before he converted to Christianity. The Devil is said to have been so annoyed at the King's conversion that he attacked the church, and left the marks of his talons in the wall of the south porch.

Bonfire procession at Lewes

CALENDAR OF EVENTS

6 January (Twelfth Night)
GILL ORCHARD, HENFIELD, West Sussex. *Apple Howling:* Verse chanted at apple trees, plus horn-blowing and howling, to wake them up and make them bear a good crop.

January
MARGATE, Kent. *Blessing of the Sea:* To celebrate Epiphany, a Greek Orthodox service is held and a crucifix decorated with flowers thrown into the sea.

May
NEWINGTON-BY-SITTINGBOURNE, Kent. *Blessing of the Cherry Orchards:* Crop-blessing processing.

25 July
EBERNOE near Petworth, West Sussex. *Horn Fair:* On St James's Day, a horned sheep is roasted and its head and horns presented to the winning cricket team.

5 November (Guy Fawkes Night)
LEWES, East Sussex. *Bonfire Night:* Seven bonfire societies in fancy dress form torchlight processions, and effigies are burnt.

24 December (Christmas Eve)
HYTHE, Kent. *Hoodening:* Hooden horse goes round pubs with handbell ringers, carol singers and morris dancers in several East Kent locations in addition to Hythe: FOLKESTONE (Christmas Eve), CHARING (Whitsun), CANTERBURY (first Saturday in September), BROADSTAIRS (August Folk Week).

DOVER

Dover Castle and Roman Lighthouse. GHOSTS. A headless drummer boy, murdered during the Napoleonic Wars, is said to haunt the castle, an impressive building begun shortly after the Norman Conquest. Even older, however, are two buildings in the castle grounds - the church of St Mary-in-Castro, which is a much restored late Saxon building, *c.* 1000, and the Roman pharos (lighthouse) which stands at its west end. This was built in AD 43, though the top half is a medieval restoration. The ghosts of a Roman soldier and a monk in a black cowl have been seen here.

HARBLEDOWN

Black Prince's Well. HEALING WELL. The water of this well was believed to cure leprosy, hence its other name of Leper's Well. The well is close to St Nicholas Hospital, founded for the relief of lepers in 1084. *Harbledown just W of Canterbury; well behind St Nicholas Hospital (near church) at foot of hill.*

KEMSING

St Edith's Well and Kemsing Church. HOLY WELL; GHOST. St Edith was a Saxon princess born in Kemsing, and the water from her well was believed to cure eye troubles. A procession to the saint's well still takes place annually on or near her day, 16 September.

At the end of December every year a ghostly knight is said to visit the church, where he kneels in prayer. Legend identifies him as one of the men who killed Thomas à Becket in Canterbury Cathedral. *3 miles NE of Sevenoaks.*

PILGRIMS' WAY

Pilgrims' Way. GHOSTS; PHANTOM DOG. This ancient trackway, dating back to prehistoric times along part of its downland route, was followed in medieval times by pilgrims travelling between the cathedral cities of Winchester and Canterbury. Ghosts have reportedly been seen at various places along the Way. A rider with broad-brimmed hat and silver spurs, mounted on a fine horse, has been seen on a lane linking the Pilgrims' Way with Bearsted; he has spoken to people and been mistaken for a living person - until he vanished! Sometimes a horse's hooves have been heard but no ghost seen. At Eastwell Park near Ashford a ghostly horseman is said to ride every Midsummer's Eve from the Pilgrims' Way via the house and into the lake. Near Trottiscliffe, the ghost haunting the Way takes the form of a big dog. *Good stretch near Trottiscliffe, 7 miles NW of Maidstone.*

PLUCKLEY

Church, Churchyard and Village. GHOSTS; PHANTOM DOG. Pluckley has been named 'The Most Haunted Village in England' because of the number of ghosts witnessed there. In 1975, for example, 'a woman in a long white gown, gliding among the tombstones' was observed to vanish by a puzzled witness; and a ghostly white dog has been seen in the church. *5 miles NW of Ashford.*

RECULVER

Saxon Church. EARLY CHRISTIAN SITE; GHOSTS. In the 7th century AD, a priest named Bassa built a church on the site of a Roman fort. Only the outline now survives, but two towers of a later church still stand tall on what would be a fine coastal site, were it not for the modern developments which have spoilt it. A legend that crying babies can be heard on stormy nights was recalled when archaeologists dug up babies' skeletons in an excavation of the Roman fort. *3 miles E of Herne Bay.*

Interior of Canterbury Cathedral

The haunted Pilgrims' Way, route of Chaucer's pilgrims to Canterbury, near Trottiscliffe

ROCHESTER

Rochester Castle and St Nicholas Churchyard. GHOSTS. The castle battlements are said to be haunted by Lady Blanche de Warenne, accidentally killed by an arrow shot by her husband-to-be; an alternative account says that she committed suicide by throwing herself off the round tower. Strange footsteps have also been heard in the castle. A white-bearded figure is said to haunt at night St Nicholas churchyard, the place where Dickens wished to be buried. Rochester has many Dickens associations, and the author himself is reputed to haunt the area of the Corn Exchange.

TROTTISCLIFFE

Coldrum Chambered Tomb. LEY; UNDERGROUND PASSAGE; TREASURE. Ley hunter Paul Devereux has discovered a 4½-mile-long alignment (or ley) passing through this prehistoric tomb and linking it with several churches, including nearby Trottiscliffe church. Interestingly, there is a legend of an underground passage linking Trottiscliffe church and Coldrum tomb, which may be a folk memory of the ley.

The legend also tells of treasure hidden in the tunnel, which may be a distorted reference to the earth energy flowing along the ley. Archaeological excavations at the tomb revealed the remains of over 20 people who had been buried there, and today the large stones forming the burial chamber can still be seen. *7 miles NW of Maidstone; tomb ¾ mile E of church (TQ 654607).*

SURREY

ALBURY

Silent Pool. SACRED SITE. The upper of two pools in woodland was traditionally believed to be bottomless, and may have been a sacred pool where pagan rituals were performed. In more recent centuries the water from springs at Silent Pool was thought to have special qualities, and people at the local Sherbourne fair held on Palm Sunday would buy mugs of it. The story of a ghostly girl at the pool is a 19th-century invention of local author Martin Tupper. *In woods W of Sherbourne Farm, off A25 to Dorking, 4 miles E of Guildford.*

BLETCHINGLEY

Church. GHOST. Several people have seen, close to the memorial to Sir Robert Clayton, the ghost of a woman of several centuries ago. *3 miles E of Reigate.*

DUNSFOLD

St Mary the Virgin's Well. HOLY WELL. It was believed that the Virgin Mary appeared to pilgrims seeking cures at this well, whose water was said to be good for eye troubles. *5 miles SE of Godalming; well along lane from Dunsfold church.*

FARNHAM

Church. GHOSTS. A number of ghostly events have been recorded from this church: a visitor kneeling in a pew witnessed a pre-Reformation High Mass taking place at the altar; a curate and parson saw a ghostly old lady; while a wartime fire-watcher heard Latin being chanted and saw candles being carried in procession around the dark church.

FRENSHAM

Church. FAIRIES. A cauldron kept in the church was said to have been brought there by the fairies from Borough Hill somewhere nearby - possibly the hills on Churt Common known as the Devil's Jumps. Wherever it may have been, it was a fairy dwelling, and anyone knocking on a large stone on the hill could borrow whatever they desired. That, traditionally, is how the cauldron came to be in the church: but it was not returned on time, and no borrowing has since been allowed. *3 miles S of Farnham.*

GUILDFORD

Loseley House. GHOSTS. The 16th-century mansion is said to be haunted. A recent visitor saw a woman dressed in dark brown and with 'staring black eyes' standing at the foot of the stairs; others have seen her at the same spot, or gliding up the stairs. *2 miles SW of Guildford; open to public.*

St Catherine's Chapel and St Martha's Church. PILGRIMS; SACRED SITES. Both old buildings are on hilltop sites, linked by the Pilgrims' Way: pilgrims would visit them on their journey to Canterbury. St Catherine's Chapel, now ruined, was built in the 14th century on what was probably already a sacred site; St Martha's church was also erected on a pagan sacred site - there were once a stone circle and other old stones close by. A traditional fair formerly took place on St Catherine's Hill every 2 October until it was abolished because the celebrations got out of hand; and the hill of St Martha was a beacon where fires were lit. *Chapel of St Catherine less than ½ mile S of Guildford centre, off A3100 to Godalming; Pilgrims' Way crosses River Wey and after 2 miles in easterly direction St Martha's church is reached.*

REIGATE

St Mary's Church. GHOSTS. Within a few days in 1975, the same person heard a ghostly choir singing in the locked, dark church and saw a woman walking down the path to the church, fading away when only a few feet from the witness. She was observed again some months later, wearing the same long white dress seen by the first witness. *In Chart Lane.*

WEST SUSSEX

ARUNDEL

Arundel Castle. GHOSTS. At least four ghosts are said to haunt this Norman-style (Victorian rebuilt) castle, seat of the Dukes of Norfolk: a girl in white who jumped from Hiorne's Tower after an unhappy love affair; a kitchen boy who haunts the great kitchen, and now is heard cleaning pots and pans; a 'blue man' poring over books in the library; and late one night in 1958 a trainee footman saw in the corridor ahead of him a man in a light grey tunic, whose image faded as the footman watched.
A white bird of ill omen is also said to flutter against the castle windows when a member of the family is about to die. *9 miles NW of Worthing; open to public.*

BOSHAM

Church. DROWNED BELL. The church dates back to Saxon times when Bosham was a busy port from where King Harold set sail to Normandy: both the church and the manor house are represented in the Bayeux Tapestry. During a Viking raid in the 10th century, the church's tenor bell was stolen and taken away in a boat. When the monks rang the remaining bells the stolen one is supposed to have replied, then to have crashed through the ship's timbers - sending men, boat and bell to the bottom at a place afterwards known as Bell Hole. It is said that the lost bell still rings in response to the church bells. *3 miles SW of Chichester.*

BURPHAM

Harrow Hill. FAIRIES. On top of the hill is a small prehistoric fort, together with around 160 depressions which were Neolithic flint mines; here, the locals believed, was the last home in England of the fairies, who left when the mines were excavated early this century. Interestingly, in the tunnels the excavators found soot from the miners' lamps on the walls and roofs, and scratch marks which may have been records of the amounts of flint they had removed. This all dates back four to six thousand years! The 'fairies' may be a vague memory of the Neolithic people who mined flint on the hill. *2½ miles NE of Burpham and 5 miles NW of Worthing; footpaths cross hill from N and S.*

FINDON

Cissbury Ring. UNDERGROUND PASSAGE; TREASURE; FAIRIES. An underground passage was said to run from Offington Hall (now demolished) to Cissbury Ring, and tradition has it that treasure guarded by large snakes was hidden inside it. The hill is capped by a fine hillfort whose ramparts are still well defined, and the craters at the western end are Neolithic flint mines. As at Harrow Hill (see *Burpham*), excavations produced some fascinating relics of these activities from long ago: underground galleries and tunnels may have given rise to the tradition of an underground passage. Using radiocarbon methods, antler picks found in the tunnels have been dated to around 3500 BC. The mines predated the Iron Age hillfort by over three thousand years - more than the length of time from the building of the fort in *c.* 350 BC until today.

It was believed that fairies could be seen dancing on Cissbury at midnight on Midsummer Eve. *1 mile along road E from Findon, itself 4 miles N of Worthing.*

GOODWOOD

The Trundle. TREASURE. There was a strong local belief that treasure in the form of Aaron's golden calf was hidden somewhere in this hill, and when the prehistoric remains were excavated in 1928 there was great public interest - but nothing so exciting was found. Another version of the story speaks of a hoard of Viking treasure, hidden in the hill and guarded by a ghostly calf, which can sometimes be heard bleating. The hill was obviously of importance in prehistoric times, for remains of both a Neolithic causewayed camp and an Iron Age hillfort have been identified here. *W of Goodwood racecourse, itself 4 miles N of Chichester; path crosses hilltop from W to NE.*

HARTING

Torberry Hill. FAIRIES; TREASURE. The fairies would dance on the hill at midnight on Midsummer Eve, it was believed; also gold was supposed to have been hidden underground. Little trace remains of the Iron Age hillfort on the summit. *3 miles SE of Petersfield; minor road runs along base of hill.*

HORSHAM

St Leonard's Forest. DRAGON. A pamphlet published in 1614 gave graphic details of a 9-foot-long 'monstrous Serpent (or Dragon)' seen in the forest, especially in the Faygate area. The description of the creature doesn't immediately suggest a rational identification, though it may have been some large exotic reptile escaped from captivity; alternatively it may have been a 'real' dragon (if there ever were such things outside of folklore). This particular specimen was said to live on rabbits, but could kill people and dogs with its venom, though it did not eat them. *Forest lies E of Horsham, with Faygate at N end, and crossed by several minor roads.*

LYMINSTER

Knucker Hole. DRAGON. A deep pool near the church supposedly housed a monster or dragon, who would come out and steal cattle, sheep and men. He was eventually slain by a knight who received as his reward the King of Sussex's daughter in marriage. The hero's tombstone can be seen in the church. There are several variations on this tale, for the dragon tradition was very strong in the area. *Just N of Littlehampton; pool 150 yards NW of church along footpath.*

POYNINGS

Devil's Dyke. DEVIL. A deep channel in the hillside was said to have been dug by the Devil, who was trying to drown the local people in anger at their religious enthusiasm. He was hurrying to dig as far as the sea before daybreak, but a cock crowed - the Devil, hearing that sound and seeing an old woman's candle, thought the sun was rising and abandoned his task. He is said to be buried along with his wife in two mounds on the hill (it's hard to imagine the Devil as a married man! His wife appears rarely in British legend). *On Downs S of Poynings, 5 miles NW of Brighton; easily reached by road and path from village.*

STOUGHTON

Kingley Vale. WARRIORS' GRAVES; DEVIL; GHOSTS. The fine yew trees are said to mark the graves of warriors killed in a battle fought here between the Saxon and Viking invaders; the *Anglo-Saxon Chronicle* records such a battle in AD 894. The Viking chieftains were buried in four round barrows known as the Kings' Graves or the Devil's Humps, and the Devil could supposedly be raised by running round the barrows six or seven times. Ghosts of the warriors, or maybe of druids, haunt the area. *Stoughton 5 miles NW of Chichester; Kingley Vale can be reached along footpaths from village to NW, and from other directions.*

TREYFORD

Devil's Jumps. DEVIL. Five well-preserved round barrows in a line on Treyford Hill got their name from a tale telling how the Devil met his match in the pagan god Thor. Thor was resting on Treyford Hill when the Devil came by and began to amuse himself jumping from one barrow to the next. The noise woke the god, who angrily told him to clear off. When the Devil started to taunted Thor, saying he was too old to jump like that himself, the irritated god scored a direct hit with a stone just as his unwelcome visitor was in mid-jump. The Devil took off yelling, never to return. *Treyford 6 miles SE of Petersfield; Devil's Jumps on Downs ¾ mile to S (SU 825173).*

WASHINGTON

★ **Chanctonbury Ring.** DEVIL; UNCOUNTABLE TREES; GHOSTS. The atmosphere can be decidedly eerie on this tree-covered hilltop where prehistoric man built a fort and dykes and left a now-destroyed burial mound, and where the Romans built a temple. Consequently numerous traditions have grown up, such as that the Devil will appear if you run backwards seven times round the clump of trees at midnight on Midsummer Eve; he will offer you a bowl of milk (or soup, or porridge). The trees are said to be uncountable (though here, as in other woodlands, enormous damage and destruction were caused by the 1987 hurricane); but anyone landing on the right number will raise the ghosts of Julius Caesar and his army. The ghost of an old white-bearded man, perhaps a druid, searches for the treasure buried in the hill; and the hooves of invisible horses have been heard. Altogether not a place for the faint-hearted! *Washington 6 miles N of Worthing; hillfort 1 mile to SE, reached by path from village.*

Eerie Chanctonbury Ring, site of a prehistoric hillfort

A34
OXFORD
A40
M40
M5
A38
M4
READING
BRISTOL
A4
BATH
M25
A36
A30
SALISBURY

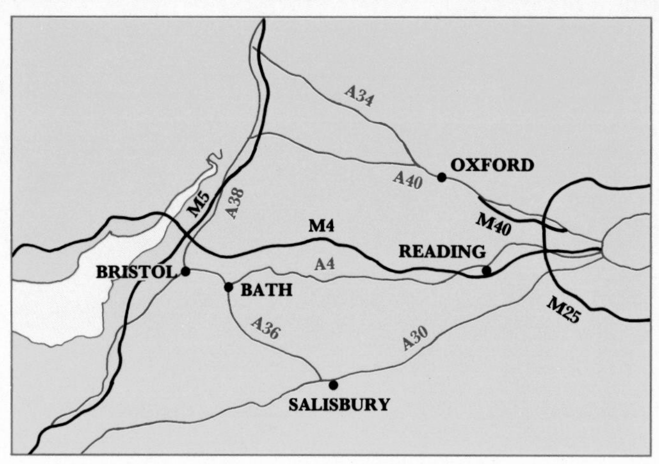

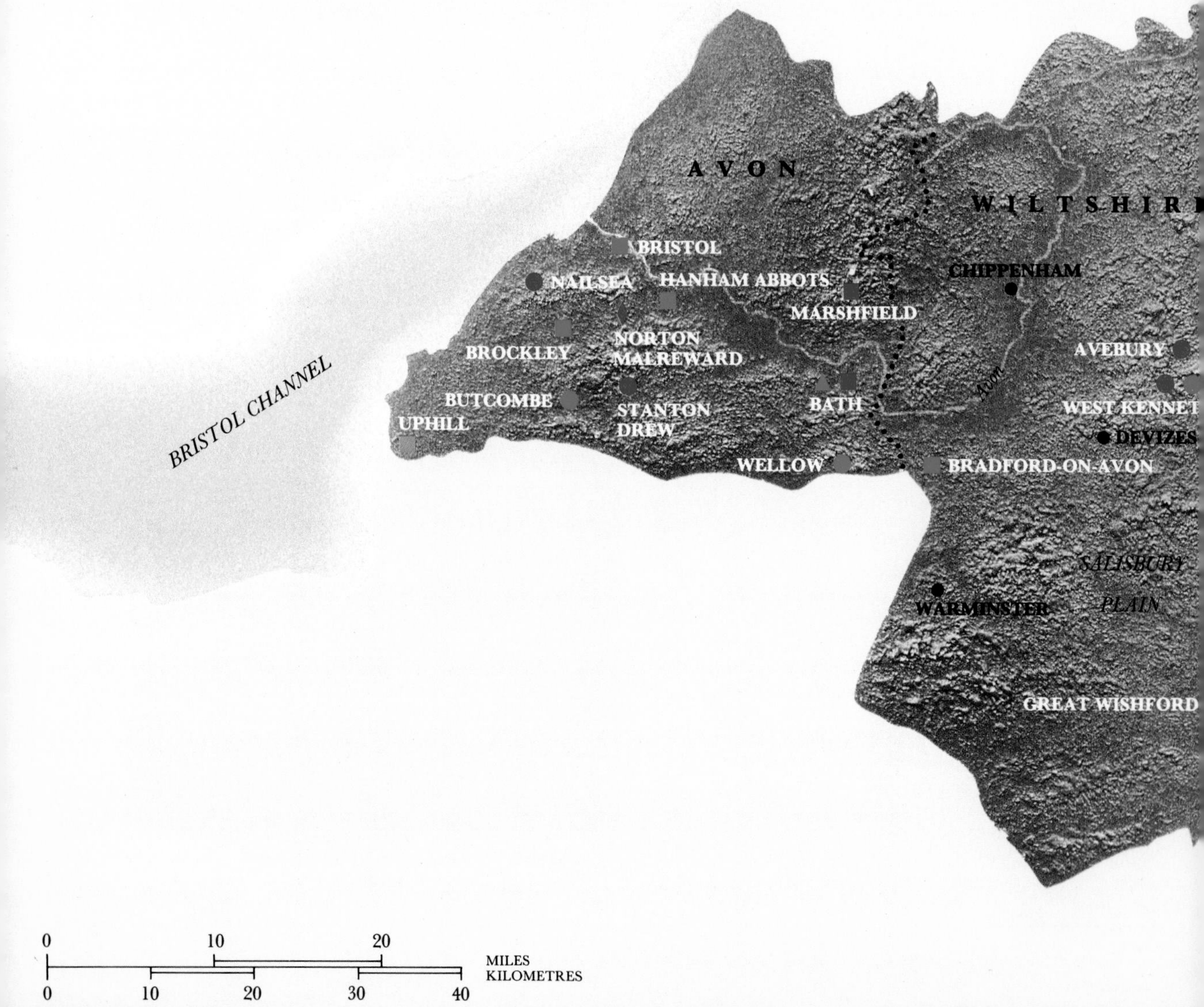

AVON
WILTSHIRE
BRISTOL CHANNEL
BRISTOL
NAILSEA
HANHAM ABBOTS
MARSHFIELD
CHIPPENHAM
BROCKLEY
NORTON MALREWARD
AVEBURY
BUTCOMBE
STANTON DREW
BATH
Avon
WEST KENNET
UPHILL
DEVIZES
WELLOW
BRADFORD-ON-AVON
SALISBURY PLAIN
WARMINSTER
GREAT WISHFORD
0
10
20
MILES
KILOMETRES
0
10
20
30
40

AVON BERKSHIRE OXFORDSHIRE AND WILTSHIRE

AVON

BATH

★ Roman Baths and Victoria Park. HEALING WATERS; ARTHURIAN LEGEND; GHOST. The healing properties of Bath's mineral springs are said to have been discovered by Prince Bladud around 900 BC. Banished from court because of his leprosy, he became a swineherd. When the pigs were suffering from cracked skins, he took them down to a marsh where the warm water gave off steam which healed them so completely that Bladud immersed himself and cured his leprosy. In fact, the Romans built a large baths complex round the shrine of the goddess Sulis in about AD 76, and Bath was known in Roman times as Aquae Sulis - though the Roman structure could have succeeded the water's use and worship by earlier pagans. The Roman baths have been well restored, and the atmosphere of the sacred site can be recaptured if you visit out of the busy holiday season. Many Roman votive offerings, and lead sheets inscribed with curses, have been recovered from the still-steaming waters.

The Roman Baths at Bath, whose healing properties were known many centuries earlier

It is possible that Bath was also Badon, the place where King Arthur was victorious in battle against the Saxons.

Finally, while walking in 1976 along a route designated as a Ghost Tour, a schoolboy saw a tall man with white hair whom no one else could see. This was on the Gravel Walk in Victoria Park, and other sightings of the ghost were made during the 1970s.

BRISTOL

Bristol Cathedral. GHOST. The cathedral is haunted by a monk in grey robes.

BROCKLEY

Church and Brockley Combe. GHOSTS; PHANTOM COACH. A little lady in brown has been seen on several occasions hurrying down the aisle to the altar or into the vestry, vanishing when approached or spoken to. The combe, a valley in Brockley Wood, is traditionally haunted by three phantoms: a coach driven at speed and causing fatal road accidents; a clergyman; and an old woman, seen rarely but causing death or madness to the witness. *7 miles SW of Bristol; minor road runs through Combe from Brockley to Lulsgate.*

BUTCOMBE

Fairy's Toot. FAIRIES; GHOSTS. This damaged burial chamber was said to be the home of fairies and goblins, and to be haunted - strange noises have been heard here. *8 miles SW of Bristol; Fairy's Toot ½ mile E of village (ST 520618).*

HANHAM ABBOTS

Church. GHOST. One night about midnight a man was cycling home after an urgent visit to the doctor in Bitton. On the road past Hanham Court and the church he felt a 'cold and clammy' atmosphere. Then he saw a ghostly woman in white - and fell off his bicycle; when he got up, she had disappeared. He learned later that a ghostly nun had been seen before in this area. *In E outskirts of Bristol, between A431 and A4.*

NAILSEA

Cadbury Camp. ARTHURIAN LEGEND; WITCHCRAFT. There is rumoured to be a cavern in the hillfort where King Arthur and his knights lie sleeping, waiting to be called out to help England face her enemies. Black magic and witchcraft were said to have been practised here, with dancing around a thorn tree on May Eve and Midsummer Eve. *7 miles W of Bristol; Camp on Tickenham Hill 1½ miles to NW, reached by footpath.*

CALENDAR OF EVENTS

Easter: second Tuesday following
HUNGERFORD, Berkshire. *Hocktide:* An old festival now only remembered here. Town officers are elected, including Tutti-men who go through the town with decorated poles to collect their dues (a penny or a kiss) and hand out oranges. Other events also take place, all deriving from pagan springtime rites.

May: Spring Bank Holiday
BAMPTON, Oxfordshire. *Morris Dancing:* Possibly the oldest morris team in England, going back at least 500 years, dances in the streets; the sword-bearer carries a cake on his sword and people buy slices to gain fertility and good luck.

29 May (Oak Apple Day)
GREAT WISHFORD, Wiltshire. *Grovely Rights Day:* Villagers maintain their right to gather wood in an annual custom, now combined with local Oak Apple Day celebrations, which commemorate the return of King Charles II from exile in 1660.

Early September
OXFORD. *St Giles Fair:* One of England's largest and oldest fairs, established in the 11th century; now mainly a funfair, although it used to be a trading fair.

26 December (Boxing Day)
MARSHFIELD, Avon. *'Paper Boys' Mumming Play:* England's best-known mumming play, performed in costumes of newspaper strips.

Hocktide Tutti-men at Hungerford

NORTON MALREWARD

Maes Knoll. GIANT. The story goes that a giant, Gorm by name and gormless by nature, was wandering around with a load of earth on his spade. Not remembering what it was for, he dumped it and thus made Maes Knoll, on which a hillfort was later built. *5 miles S of Bristol centre: Maes Knoll N of village, reached by footpath from lane to S.*

STANTON DREW

Stone Circles. UNCOUNTABLE STONES; PETRIFACTION LEGEND; DEVIL. Although not so visually spectacular as Stonehenge and Avebury, the Stanton Drew megaliths form an important Neolithic monument, with three circles and an avenue in the fields, and three more stones in a group called the Cove, which is in the village near the Druid's Arms.

The stones in the circles were believed to be uncountable. As John Wood wrote in his *Particular Description of Bath* (1750): 'No one, say the country people about Stantondrue, was ever able to reckon the number of these metamorphosed stones, or to take a draught of them, though several have attempted to do both, and proceeded till they were either struck dead upon the spot, or with such an illness as soon carried them off.'

Once the circles were called the Wedding, because of a long-standing belief that they were a wedding party turned to stone. The revels were continuing into the night, but when midnight came the harper refused to play into

Interior of Stoney Littleton burial chamber at Wellow

Sunday. A piper appeared and offered his services, and he played faster and faster. Too late the dancers realized he was the Devil - by that time they couldn't stop dancing. They shouted and cursed in vain, and when daylight came there was nothing to be seen but three rings of standing stones. *6 miles S of Bristol centre.*

UPHILL

Church. SITING LEGEND. The church is on a hilltop, but it is said it was originally intended to be at the foot of the hill. During the night, the day's building materials were mysteriously carried uphill and the builders could not gather enough material together at the foot of the hill to build the church there - so they gave in and built it on the hilltop. *2 miles S of Weston-super-Mare.*

WELLOW

Stoney Littleton Long Barrow. FAIRIES. This is a fine Neolithic burial chamber, with the interior still intact - a torch is essential to see it properly. It was traditionally supposed to be a fairy haunt, and it is not hard to imagine that the fairies might still be living here. *5 miles S of Bath; tomb reached from Stoney Littleton Farm, where key held, then ½-mile walk across fields (signposted) (ST 735572).*

BERKSHIRE

BEEDON

Beedon Barrow/Burrow Hill. TREASURE; FAIRIES; DIGGING PROHIBITION. A man named Burrow was buried here in a gold or silver coffin, according to legend. It is also supposed to be a fairy dwelling, and a ploughman who broke his ploughshare found it had been mended by them while he was away fetching tools. It was believed that the barrow could not be ploughed away; it would always remain the same. Desecration of the barrow by digging would bring on a thunderstorm, as did apparently happen in the mid-19th century; this event confirmed the truth of the legend in the minds of the local people. *1 mile NW of Beedon, itself 6 miles N of Newbury, in field off Stanmore–Peasemore lane (SU 467786).*

COOKHAM DEAN

Church and Common. GHOSTS. The wife of a temporary vicar saw a 'vague shadow', man-sized, in the church in 1979 and felt suddenly cold. Her husband later felt he was being watched. They learned that the ghost of a previous vicar had been seen more than once in the church.

One summer evening in the 1920s, a woman walking on the common saw a man wearing antlers coming out of the undergrowth. She followed him and watched him disappear into an oak tree. Cookham Dean lies on the northern edge of Windsor Forest, and she may have seen Herne the Hunter (see *Windsor: Windsor Great Park*). *2 miles N of Maidenhead.*

EASTHAMPSTEAD

Caesar's Camp. GHOSTS. The Camp is an Iron Age hillfort sited in woodland, and the course of the Roman road known as the Devil's Highway runs east–west half a mile to the south. This might be the source of the phantom footsteps heard at the Camp one night during the Second World War by two women who lived in a house that has now been demolished. They were aware of what sounded like voices and soldiers marching, but there was nothing to be seen. One of the women also saw, on another occasion, the ghost of a red-haired man standing by her bed. *Easthampstead now part of south Bracknell; Camp 1 mile to S, touching Ninemile Ride at its junction with minor road from Easthampstead (SU 863657).*

HERMITAGE

Grimsbury Castle Hillfort. TREASURE. Grim is a nickname given to Woden, an Anglo-Saxon god, and the awe in which he was held is shown by the number of ancient sites given his name. Somewhere in the woods nearby is a supposedly bottomless pond in which, according to tradition, lies a golden calf. *Hermitage 4 miles NE of Newbury; fort in woods S of village, crossed by minor road (SU 512723).*

KINTBURY

Church. GHOST. A ghost in a black cloak and wearing a wide-brimmed hat has been seen by several witnesses, who reported that he faded away as they watched. *3 miles SE of Hungerford.*

Windsor Castle, haunted by royalty

WINDSOR

Windsor Castle. GHOSTS. Many royal figures haunt this fine building. Elizabeth I has been seen in the library, Henry VIII haunts the cloisters, Charles I has been seen in a canon's house in the precincts, and George III was seen looking out of a window in his old rooms. Other ghosts include William of Wykeham, the architect of the 14th-century building work, who stands on the Round Tower at night. In the Horseshoe Cloisters, one house had a ghostly woman in white who appeared daily at 6 p.m., and in another house a boy saw a man lead a horse through the room and into a wall. Ghostly footsteps were heard in the Mary Tudor Tower, and the Norman Tower is also haunted. Unfortunately not all the castle is open to the public, and with so many visitors the atmosphere during opening hours is hardly calm and peaceful. Any self-respecting ghost is likely to keep well away from the tourist influx!

One of the strangest ghost stories from Windsor Castle concerns men on guard duty. In 1927 a young sentry shot himself while patrolling the Long Walk. A few weeks later, another guardsman was alone there on a bright moonlit night when he saw a guardsman walking towards him. It was a ghost, with the face of the man who had shot himself; the man who had taken the previous turn of guard duty had also seen the ghost. There have been other instances of sentries at Windsor seeing ghosts, for example in 1906 and 1976. In the most recent instance, the guardsman said a statue had come to life. Was this a manifestation of Herne the Hunter, another famous Windsor ghost? (See below, *Windsor Great Park*)

Windsor Great Park. HERNE THE HUNTER; GHOSTS. The figure known as Herne the Hunter, said to haunt the park, is probably Cernunnos, the Celtic god of the underworld, who is identified by his stag's antlers; it may be that the still-current legends recall the time when this god was worshipped in the park, or forest as it then was. The story told to explain the presence of this figure, who has been around for at least five hundred years, is that Herne was a royal forest keeper in King Richard II's time. While the King was out hunting he was attacked by a wounded stag, but Herne saved his life by stabbing the animal. A mysterious stranger appeared and told how the life of Herne, badly injured in the struggle, could be saved: the dead stag's antlers must be bound to Herne's head. He duly recovered, but lost all his knowledge of the forest, was sacked and hanged himself. Thereafter he has haunted the park, appearing close to the oak which replaced the one on which he hanged himself, especially at times when disaster threatens the nation. Also seen elsewhere in the Great Park, he is usually on horseback and accompanied by a pack of phantom hounds. Sometimes only the baying hounds and galloping horses are heard. Other ghosts seen in the Great Park include a headless poacher and a man in a long black cape and a large-brimmed hat. *S of Windsor; public access allowed.*

OXFORDSHIRE

ASHBURY

Wayland's Smithy. INVISIBLE SMITH; WITCHCRAFT. A well-preserved Neolithic chambered long barrow, Wayland's Smithy derives its unusual name from a belief that Wayland, an invisible smith, would shoe the horse of any traveller along the prehistoric trackway known as the Ridgeway if he left a coin or other payment. Relics found near the barrow suggest that witchcraft was once practised here. *1 mile E of Ashbury and 1 mile SW of Uffington White Horse (see Uffington); reached off B4507 via Ridgeway (SU 281854).*

BANBURY

Crouch Hill. DEVIL. Traditionally, the Devil in disguise was helping to build the churches of Adderbury, Bloxham and King's Sutton. He was a very skilful worker, but was recognized when one day he stumbled and dropped his load of mortar. This became Crouch Hill. *Just SW of Banbury between B4035 and A361; footpath passes close to hill, linking these roads.*

BURFORD

Burford Bridge and Nunnery. BOTTLED SPIRIT; GHOSTS. In the 18th century the spirit of Lady Tanfield was so troublesome, riding over the rooftops in a fiery chariot and prophesying misfortune, that the clergy used magic to entice her into a bottle, which was corked and thrown into the River Windrush beneath the first arch of Burford Bridge. It was said that if the river were ever to dry up under that arch, Lady Tanfield would again be free.

The ancient priory, now a nunnery, is haunted by a brown monk, and a ghostly gamekeeper has also been seen. Auditory phantoms include mystery footsteps, a phantom bell, and singing in the garden. *6 miles NW of Witney.*

ENSTONE

Hoar Stone. MOVING STONES. Said to be a memorial to a Civil War general named Hoar, this site is in fact the remains of a prehistoric burial chamber. The stones were said to return if taken away; and the main stone, the Old Soldier, was reputed to go to the village to drink on Midsummer Eve. *S of Enstone $4\frac{1}{2}$ miles SE of Chipping Norton, in woods off B4022 (SP 378236).*

GREAT ROLLRIGHT

★ **Rollright Stones.** PETRIFACTION LEGEND; WITCHES; UNCOUNTABLE STONES; FAIRIES; EARTH ENERGIES. The prehistoric stones here comprise a stone circle called the King's Men, a burial chamber known as the Whispering Knights, and a standing stone (just over the border in Warwickshire) called the King Stone; together they have generated a wide variety of folklore beliefs. Their names give a hint of the main legend: that the stones were men turned to stone. The King and his army were supposed to have been turned to stone by a witch, and the Whispering Knights were conspirators against him.The witch herself turned into an elder tree. When it bloomed, people would gather by the King Stone on Midsummer Eve and cut into the tree. As the sap bled, the king would move his head. It is said that modern witches continue to perform their rites at the Rollright Stones.

It was said that the stones of the King's Men could not

be counted; also that the stones were believed to go down to a brook on New Year's Eve to drink. When taken away to make a footbridge across a stream, the biggest stone was soon returned because the person who took it could not rest, and the return journey uphill needed only one horse as against the two needed to drag it downhill. Bits of stone were regularly chipped off the King Stone in particular, as good luck charms to keep the Devil away and by soldiers going into battle. Fairies were said to dance at midnight around the King Stone; they lived in the mound on which the stone stands. There was also an annual celebration held close to the stone, with dancing, feasting and drinking.

Beginning in 1978, the Rollright Stones were the focus of the Dragon Project, a long-term attempt to measure and identify energies emanating from the stones, using ultrasonic detectors, geiger counters, dowsing and mediums. Some of the intriguing results were published in *Circles of Silence* by Don Robins. *Beside lane between Great and Little Rollright, off A34 2 miles NW of Chipping Norton; on private land, but admission allowed.*

KINGSTON LISLE

Blowing Stone. KING ALFRED. When blown, this stone in a cottage garden makes a loud noise like a siren, said to be audible around 2 miles away in certain conditions. It is said to have been blown by King Alfred to summon his Saxon troops into battle. *In cottage garden on Blowingstone Hill off B4507 4 miles W of Wantage (SU 324871).*

UFFINGTON

★ **White Horse and Dragon Hill.** DRAGON; TREASURE. Probably cut into the chalk during the Iron Age, this 'horse' may in fact be a dragon. Just below the figure is a flat-topped hill known as Dragon Hill, with a bare patch where grass never grows. Here St George is said to have killed the dragon: the bare chalk is where the dragon's blood fell, poisoning the earth. In past centuries, the cleaning of the horse's outline every seven years was accompanied by feasting, merry-making and sports, one of the races being in pursuit of a cheese which was rolled down the Manger, a combe below the white horse.

Above the figure, and emphasizing the antiquity of this site, is the Iron Age hillfort known as Uffington Castle. South of that is the prehistoric trackway known as the Ridgeway, and a walk of just over a mile to the south-west leads to Wayland's Smithy (see *Ashbury*). A golden coffin is supposed to lie buried somewhere between the two sites. *Uffington village in Vale of White Horse, 6 miles NW of Wantage; Horse on Downs $1\frac{1}{2}$ miles S of village, reached along lane off B4507.*

The chalk-carved White Horse of Uffington

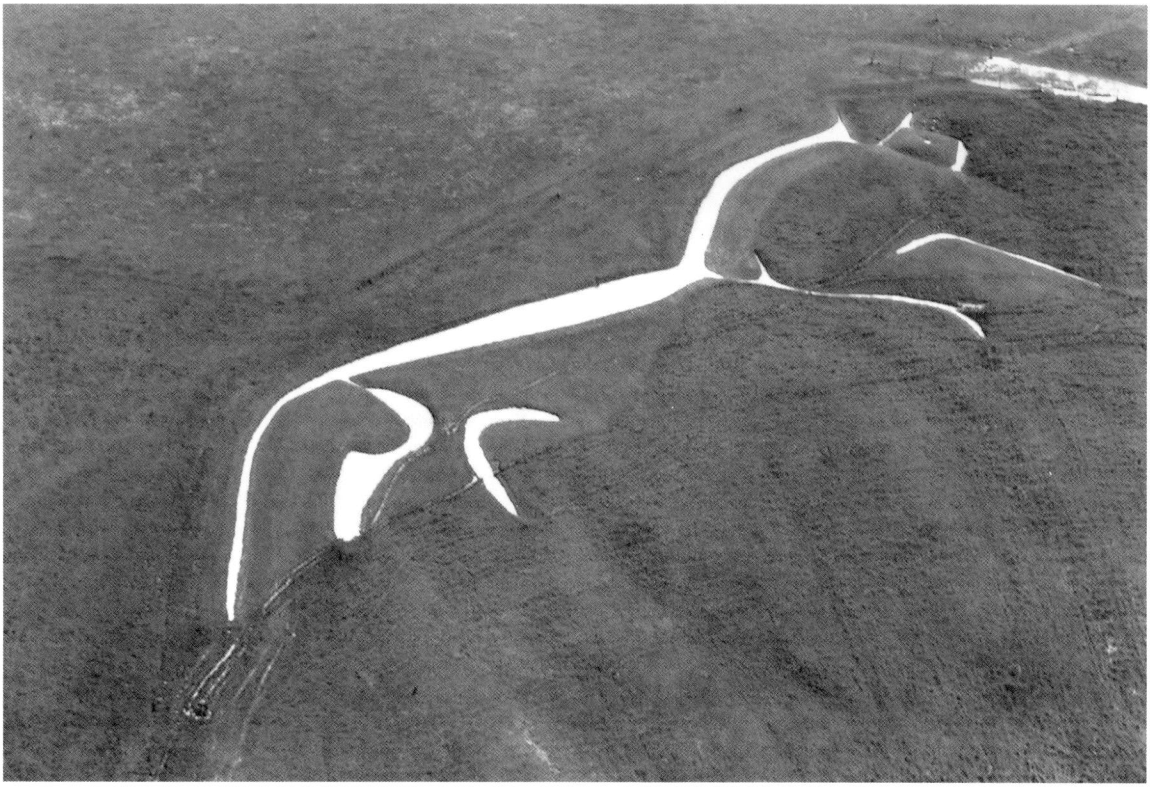

WILTSHIRE

ALTON PRIORS

Adam's Grave Long Barrow. GIANT. Known as Woden's Barrow in Saxon times and Old Adam in the 19th century, this barrow, around 60 yards long, is said to be a giant's resting place. If you run around it seven times the giant is supposed to come out. *On Walker's Hill ¾ mile N of Alton Priors, itself 3 miles NW of Pewsey; reached by footpath from nearby lane (SU 112634).*

Silbury Hill, one of Wiltshire's wealth of prehistoric sites

AMESBURY

★ **Stonehenge.** MAGIC; HEALING STONES; DEVIL; GIANTS. Stonehenge must be the most famous prehistoric monument in Europe, perhaps even in the whole Western world, but not many people know the details of its legendary history. According to Geoffrey of Monmouth, writing in his *History of the Kings of Britain* (*c.*1136), Aurelius Ambrosius, who was King of the Britons in the 5th century AD, wanted a monument to commemorate a battle. He asked the advice of Merlin the magician, who told him to fetch a famous circle of stones from Killare, an Irish mountain. This circle, said Merlin, had been brought to Ireland from Africa by giants. An army led by Uther Pendragon went to Ireland to fetch the stones, but they were unable to move them until Merlin used his magic powers to bring them to Wiltshire.

Of course, Stonehenge has stood on Salisbury Plain for much longer than the fifteen hundred years suggested by Geoffrey's story. The stones were erected in their present form around four thousand years ago, and there is no evidence to link them with Ireland. However, there may be a grain of truth in Geoffrey's story, because it has been conclusively proved that the bluestones (the inner ring of smaller standing stones) came originally from the Preseli Hills in south-west Wales. In Geoffrey's time there may still have been some memory of the transportation of the stones by water from the west, an event which had taken place some 2500 years before. They were brought along the Bristol Channel, which since the Bronze Age had also been a traveller's route from Ireland.

Geoffrey also told of the healing properties of the stones:

> For in these stones is a mystery, and a healing virtue against many ailments ... for they washed the stones and poured the water into baths, whereby those who were sick were cured. Moreover, they mixed confections of herbs with the water, whereby those who were wounded were healed, for not a stone is there that is wanting in virtue or leechcraft.

Even in the 18th century, local people still believed that stone scrapings from Stonehenge, when soaked in water, could be used to heal wounds.

There was also another tradition that Stonehenge was built by the Devil; and the alternative name, Giant's Dance, suggests a belief that the stones were giants who sometimes danced. This century, computers have been used to try to prove that Stonehenge was used as an astronomical observatory, but its true purpose is as obscure now as in the days when Merlin and the Devil were invoked to explain its presence on the wide expanse of Salisbury Plain. *Beside A344 2 miles NW of Amesbury, itself 7 miles N of Salisbury.*

AVEBURY

★ **Henge and Manor.** PREHISTORIC RITUALS; DEVIL; MOVING STONE; GHOSTS. Avebury village was built inside a prehistoric monument: a circular area of 28 acres, bounded by a deep ditch, inside which are three circles of stones, some of them destroyed, buried or used for house-building in the village. Enough survives to give a good impression of the henge as it originally was, and it is an extraordinary site. Although no one has any idea what went on here, other than rituals of some kind, its importance is emphasized by the existence of an avenue of a hundred pairs of standing stones leading from Avebury for 1½ miles towards a small stone circle known as the Sanctuary, and evidence of another avenue of stones (now lost) leading to Beckhampton. This was a vast structure, entailing thousands of man-hours of work, set close to other sites equally important and puzzling: Windmill Hill causewayed camp, Silbury Hill and West Kennet long barrow (see *West Kennet*). Archaeologists have estimated that Avebury was a sacred site in use for around a thousand years, from the Neolithic into the Bronze Age.

Europe's most famous prehistoric monument, Stonehenge, was erected on Salisbury Plain four thousand years ago

That is almost the same length of time that our oldest Norman churches have been in existence (it will be the one thousandth anniversary of the Norman Conquest in 2066).

Strangely, little folklore survives that relates to Avebury henge. The structure now called the Cove was in the 18th century known as the Devil's Brand Irons; and the large Diamond Stone close to the main road on the north side of the village is said to cross the road when it hears the clock strike midnight.

Not surprisingly, perhaps, the henge is said to be haunted. Lights and music were seen and heard among the stones at night during the First World War - a possible ghostly rerun of the annual fair which had stopped 50 years before. Another witness recently saw small figures among the stones on a moonlit night.

The fine old manor house is also haunted: a monk was seen in the library, and a Cavalier in the garden. A ghostly lady dressed in white has also been noticed in the village by several witnesses. *6 miles W of Marlborough; henge and manor both open to public.*

The haunted Saxon church at Bradford-on-Avon

BRADFORD-ON-AVON

Church of St Laurence. GHOSTS. This little 10th-century church was 'lost' until 1856, having been used as a cottage, but some fine Saxon details have survived, like the carved angel above the chancel arch. The atmospheric interior is haunted: a priest taking Communion saw a group of people in medieval costume standing by the altar rail; and in 1932 the American medium Eileen Garrett went into an involuntary trance inside the church and saw a group of grim-looking people taking Communion - possibly lepers, she felt. *4 miles SE of Bath; church N of river, opposite Holy Trinity church.*

FYFIELD

Devil's Den. DEVIL; IMMOVABLE STONES; PHANTOM DOG. A mixture of folklore has grown up around this Neolithic burial chamber which comprises a large capstone on top of two uprights. The Devil is said to try to move the stones at night, helped by four white oxen; but he is unsuccessful, for the stones are known to be immovable, and whenever people tried to do so the chains holding them broke. Overnight a fiend or demon will drink any water that is poured into hollows on the capstone; and the tomb is haunted by a dog with large fiery eyes. *2 miles W of Marlborough; approached along track from A4 E of Fyfield (SU 152696).*

HIGHWORTH

Church. GHOSTS. There have been numerous sightings of ghostly figures here, though whether they are all of the same ghost is not clear. In 1907 the Master of Balliol and three others saw a man whose face was 'a featureless grey blank' with 'sunken dark shadows' instead of eyes. They saw it from close to the organ, but a woman by the font saw nothing and said no one had entered the church. In 1936 the then verger saw a figure in a long white robe gliding up the centre aisle. *5 miles NE of Swindon.*

SALISBURY

Old Sarum and Salisbury Cathedral. SITING LEGENDS; LEY. The original cathedral was built at Old Sarum just outside Salisbury, on a raised plateau where there was formerly an Iron Age hillfort. The cathedral outline can still be seen, as can the hillfort ramparts and the remains of a Norman castle. A medieval town was also built here, but the site was not satisfactory, with problems like shortage of water, wind damage to the cathedral, and quarrels between the priests and soldiers at the castle. So it was decided that the cathedral should be rebuilt elsewhere. Legend gives two reasons for the final choice: either Bishop Poore dreamed of a site near the merging of two rivers, or an archer on the ramparts shot an arrow and the cathedral was built where it landed. These tales hint at some mystical method of divination being used to determine the cathedral's new site.

Both Old Sarum and Salisbury Cathedral are on a ley which was first discovered a hundred years ago: Stonehenge, Old Sarum, Salisbury Cathedral and the hillfort Clearbury Ring are in alignment. *Old Sarum just N of Salisbury, reached from A345.*

UPAVON

Casterley Camp. TREASURE; SITING LEGEND. When the place was excavated, four human burials and fourteen red deer antlers were found in this Iron Age hillfort,

Old Sarum, on a ley which also includes Salisbury Cathedral, Clearbury Ring hillfort (both seen here) and Stonehenge

suggesting that it may have been a religious cult centre as well as a defensive site. There was a belief that a gold chair was buried in the ramparts. Another old story says that Upavon village was originally sited at Casterley Camp. *Upavon 4 miles SW of Pewsey, and Camp 1½ miles to SW, reached along track from A342 (SU 115535).*

WEST KENNET

Silbury Hill. PREHISTORIC ASTRONOMY; TREASURE; DEVIL; ANCIENT CUSTOMS. This impressive man-made mound (the largest prehistoric mound in Europe) continues to baffle archaeologists. They cannot be certain it was a burial mound, for attempts to find traces of graves inside it have been unsuccessful. Numerous theories have been put forward to explain it: a gigantic sundial; a representation of the winter goddess; a structure for astronomical calculations.

Legend too has some answers: the grave of King Sil, buried there upright on horseback, wearing golden armour, or in a golden coffin; or a load of soil dumped by the Devil on his way to bury Avebury or Devizes, and told by a man that he had worn out a sackful of shoes while coming from there.

At one time it was the custom for local people to gather on top of the hill on Palm Sunday, and there to eat fig cakes and drink sugared water. Whatever its intended function, Silbury was clearly part of a great complex of prehistoric sites which included nearby Avebury henge and West Kennet long barrow. *1 mile S of Avebury, beside A4.*

West Kennet Long Barrow. GHOST; PHANTOM DOG. One of the finest of Britain's chambered long barrows, this Neolithic tomb is also well sited overlooking Silbury Hill and Avebury henge a mile further on. It may have been in use for up to a thousand years, just like our cathedrals, and archaeologists have found bones (human and animal), pottery, flints, stone tools and beads. Unfortunately, in 1685 a Marlborough doctor took away 'many bushells' of human bones to make medicines. Surprisingly, the long use of this important site has resulted in very little folklore, the only recorded belief being that the ghost of a priest enters the barrow at sunrise on Midsummer Day, followed by a ghostly white dog with red ears. *S of Avebury, reached by footpath off A4 almost opposite Silbury Hill.*

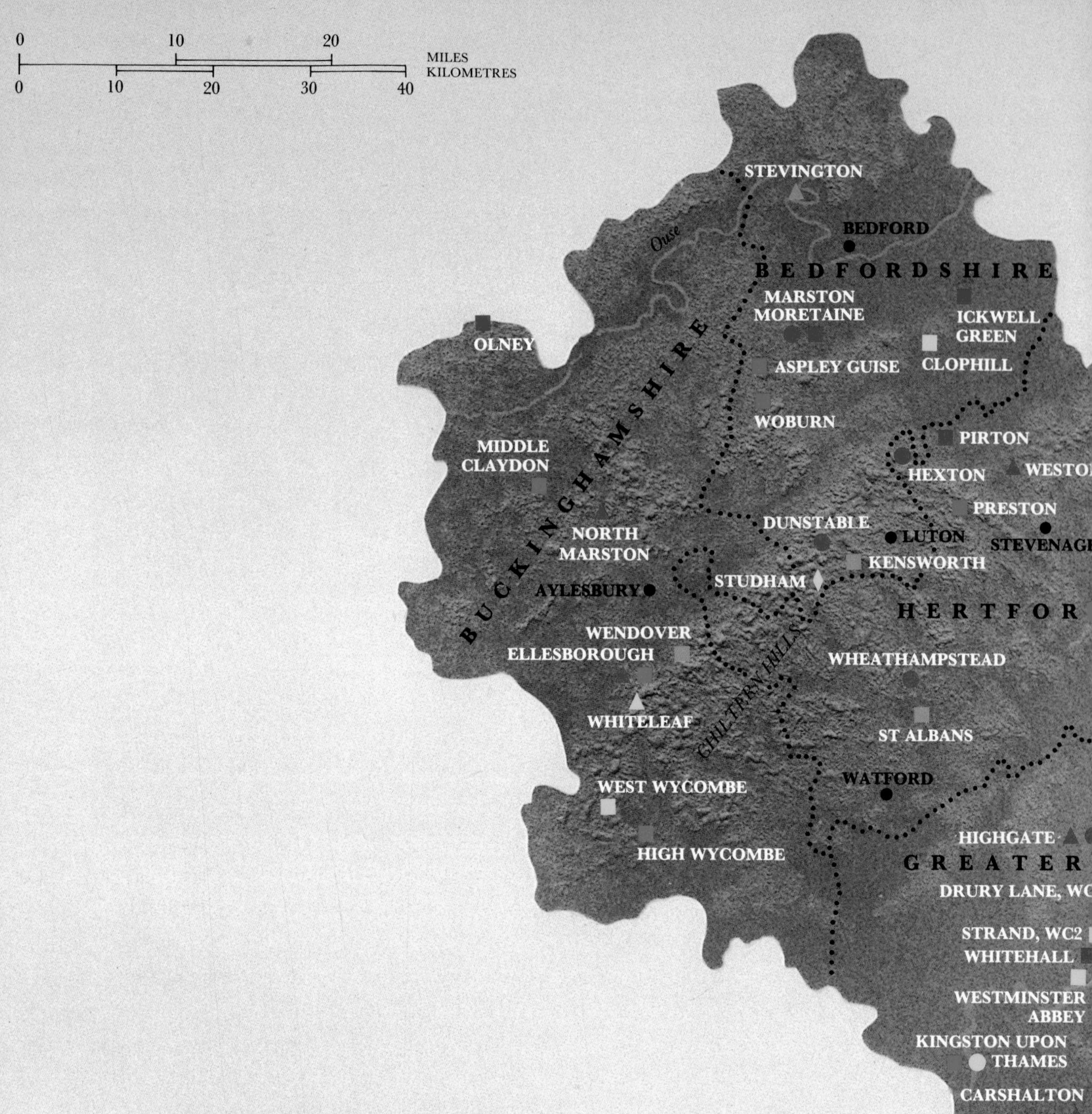

BEDFORDSHIRE BUCKINGHAMSHIRE ESSEX GREATER LONDON AND HERTFORDSHIRE

OYSTON
HADSTOCK
BORLEY
Stour
ANSTEY
SAFFRON WALDEN
Blackwater
BRENT PELHAM
MANNINGTREE
COLCHESTER
BISHOP'S STORTFORD
E S S E X
ST OSYTH
CLACTON
HIRE
Chelmer
WALTHAM ABBEY
CHELMSFORD
ENFIELD
THEYDON BOIS
EPPING FOREST
Crouch
BRENTWOOD
CANEWDON
LONDON
SOUTHEND-ON-SEA
UILDHALL, EC2
TOWER OF LONDON
GRAYS
Thames
A1
A6
M1
BEDFORD
A41
A5
COLCHESTER
A1(M)
M11
LUTON
A10
A12
A40
CLACTON
CHELMSFORD
M40
HIGH WYCOMBE
GREATER LONDON
M4
A4
M25

BEDFORDSHIRE

ASPLEY GUISE

Weathercock Lane. GHOST. Highwayman Dick Turpin is said to have used the wine cellar of the old manor house as a hideaway, and his ghost still rides along Weathercock Lane. One witness saw him enter the courtyard and fade away into the wall of the house; the sighting was accompanied by the sound of his horse's hooves *1 mile E of Woburn Sands; Weathercock Lane at N end of village.*

St Mary's church at Clophill, site of alleged black magic activities in recent years

CLOPHILL

St Mary's Church, Dead Man's Hill. BLACK MAGIC. It was alleged that black magic rituals were being performed at this ruined church during the 1960s and 1970s, with graves being opened and bones taken out. When we visited we felt an overwhelming evil atmosphere emanating from the whole area of church and graveyard. We hurriedly took a few photographs and then left as quickly as we could. *4 miles E of Ampthill; church to N, up lane from village street.*

DUNSTABLE

Five Knolls. ROYAL BURIALS; WITCHCRAFT. Five kings or chiefs were said to be buried in these prehistoric round barrows. In fact, when the most northerly barrow was excavated in 1928 a crouched female skeleton with a late Neolithic knife at her shoulder was found. In Saxon times about 30 bodies were buried here, hands behind their backs, and people hung on the gallows were also buried here later. A 17th-century witch claimed to have practised witchcraft here. *1 mile SW of Dunstable centre, between B489 and B4541 at N end of Dunstable Downs (TL 007210).*

Maiden Bower. SITING LEGEND. It was said that this hillfort's location and configuration were determined by a queen who cut a bull's hide into narrow strips and laid them out in a circle. Her king then ordered his men to dig the ditch and bank along this circle. The hillfort was constructed on the site of an earlier Neolithic enclosure. *1 mile W of Dunstable, reached along track from Sewell to N or Totternhoe to S (SP 997225).*

KENSWORTH

Church. SITING LEGEND; GHOSTS. The church was planned for Kensworth Common, but at night the stones were supernaturally moved a mile away to the area of Bury Hill, where the church was finally built. The path over Bury Hill to the church is said to be haunted by a witch and a headless milkmaid. *2 miles SE of Dunstable.*

MARSTON MORETAINE

Church. DEVIL. The church tower is separate from the church itself, and it is said that this division happened when the Devil was trying to steal it. It was too heavy for him, so he put it down and left it. *3 miles NW of Ampthill.*

Devil's Jump Stone. DEVIL. Although only 2 feet high and therefore not an impressive standing stone, it is unusual because standing stones are rare in this part of Britain. There used to be three stones here, marking the place where traditionally the Devil jumped on a landowner playing leapfrog on the Sabbath. *Close to lane running S from Marston Moretaine to Lidlington (SP 999409).*

STEVINGTON

Church. HOLY WELL. Churches were often built very close to holy wells, and the obvious reason seems to be that water would be immediately available for baptisms. However, the answer may be more esoteric. Water sources were worshipped in Celtic and prehistoric times, and were often considered to be sacred sites. Flowing water may mark lines of subtle earth energy, making the places where it broke free of the ground especially powerful. Whatever the reason, churches were often sited near wells and springs, and dowsers have located underground water courses beneath the buildings themselves. Anyone with moderate sensitivity can easily sense that ancient churches are built on atmospheric sites. At Stevington, the well issues from a limestone rock on which the church is built, and has never been known to run dry or freeze.*5 miles NW of Bedford; well reached by following path to right of church gate.*

STUDHAM

Studham Common. LITTLE MAN. On 28 January 1967, seven boys aged 10 and 11 were playing on the common at lunchtime, on their way back to school, when Alex Butler suddenly saw a 'little blue man with a tall hat and beard'. He was about 3 feet tall, surrounded by a greyish blue glow; his tall hat was like a brimless bowler, and his legs and feet were not clearly seen. Alex called the others and they ran towards the little man, who disappeared in a puff of yellowish blue mist. They saw him again, and once more he vanished as they approached.The third time they caught sight of him, they didn't run towards him; this time they could also hear voices, foreign-sounding and babbling.

Their teacher's whistle called them back to school, where they told what they had seen. As well as the strange hat, they also described a black box on his broad black belt. This and the puff of mist suggest a space-age connection, so perhaps he was a UFO entity - but no UFO was seen. In other respects he sounds like a 20th-century version of the Little People or fairies seen in earlier times. *Studham 4 miles S of Dunstable; common not far from village school.*

WOBURN

Woburn Abbey. GHOSTS. Apart from being plagued by mysteriously opening doors - possibly caused by some psychic manifestation - ghosts have been seen in the house, which is the seat of the Dukes of Bedford. A tall man in a top hat was seen to walk through the antique market; a summer-house is haunted by an unhappy ghost, perhaps the present Duke's grandmother; and a monk in a brown habit has been seen in several parts of the house. *6 miles SE of Milton Keynes; open to public.*

BUCKINGHAMSHIRE

ELLESBOROUGH

Church. GHOST. Occasionally the ghost of a man in medieval costume is seen in the church. The organist saw him just after the Second World War; a lady arranging altar flowers was a witness a few years later; and in 1970 a visitor saw him. *4 miles S of Aylesbury.*

Cymbeline's Castle. DEVIL. Cunobelinus (or Cymbeline, as Shakespeare called him) was a king who controlled most of south-east England by his death around AD 40. A small motte-and-bailey earthwork now known as Cymbeline's Castle was traditionally said to have been his home. If you run round it seven times, the Devil will appear - perhaps. *Castle, in woods, can be seen from footpath through Chequers Park which starts nearly opposite Ellesborough church (SP 832064).*

HIGH WYCOMBE

Hughenden Manor. GHOST. Prime minister Benjamin Disraeli lived here until his death in 1881, and it is now a museum dedicated to his life. His ghost has been seen in the house by several visitors - near the main stairs, by the study doorway, and at the bottom of the stairs to the cellar. *Just N of High Wycombe, by A4128; open to public.*

MIDDLE CLAYDON

Claydon House. GHOSTS. The home of the Verney family since 1620, the house is haunted by Sir Edmund Verney, who carried the King's Standard at the Battle of Edgehill in 1642. It is said that he is looking for his hand, which was cut off after his death because the Roundheads could not unfasten his grip from the Standard. The hand was eventually sent home for burial, but his body lies elsewhere. Towards the end of the last century, Miss Ruth Verney saw the ghost of a man on the Red Stairs. He wore a long black cloak, the tip of a sword showing beneath its hem, and carried a 'black hat with a white feather gracefully curled round the crown'.

Florence Nightingale was the sister of a 19th-century Lady Verney, and there is a Florence Nightingale museum at the house. The ghost of a woman in a long grey gown seen in the Rose Room and close to a room where Miss Nightingale slept may be the famous nurse. Ghostly footsteps have also been heard in the house. *5 miles SE of Buckingham; open to public.*

NORTH MARSTON

Schorne Well. HEALING WELL. Traditionally the well was created by Sir John Schorne, who was rector of North Marston from 1290 to 1314. During a drought he struck the ground with his staff, and a spring began to flow. Pilgrims visited the well seeking cures for ague, gout and sore eyes, and after his death they also visited Sir John's tomb in the church. This was such a popular pilgrimage in the 15th century that his bones were moved in 1480 to the newly built St George's Chapel at Windsor, where they were one of the main attractions until overshadowed by King Henry VI's remains. *6 miles NW of Aylesbury; well in centre of village, in Schorne Lane off Church Street, with wooden cover and pump beside it.*

WENDOVER

Church. SITING LEGEND. The church was intended to be built in a field called Witches' Meadow, but the building materials were mysteriously moved every night, so the location was changed to its present one. *5 miles SE of Aylesbury.*

WEST WYCOMBE

West Wycombe Park and Church. BLACK MAGIC. Sir Francis Dashwood, who lived at West Wycombe Park in the 18th century, founded in about 1755 a society called the Knights of St Francis. His select band of 24 men of high social standing became known as the Hellfire Club, and gained a bad reputation because of lurid tales of black magic and orgies. Dashwood rebuilt West Wycombe church, which has on top of its tower a golden ball seating several people - here, it was said, the Hellfire Club sometimes met. The church is inside an Iron Age earthwork, which suggests that the site may have been chosen for a church because it was already a sacred place. To add to the air of mystery, Dashwood also built on the hill a fantastic mausoleum, in which he was buried in 1781. *2½ miles NW of High Wycombe centre; Park (open to public) to S of A40, church to N.*

WHITELEAF

Whiteleaf Cross. CHALK HILL CARVING. No date is known for the cutting of this cross on a triangle, but a boundary mark known as Wayland's Stock was mentioned in a charter of AD 903. This was a phallic symbol, and it has been suggested that monks reshaped it into a cross. Periodically the cross is 'scoured' or cleaned, and this task was once accompanied by festivities. There is another cross at Bledlow, and both crosses are close to the Icknield Way, an ancient long-distance trackway; the siting tends to confirm that they were first cut more than a thousand years ago. *On steep W-facing slope of Chiltern Hills 6 miles S of Aylesbury; best seen from valley (e.g. Princes Risborough–Thame road) or can be approached up steep lane from Whiteleaf (SP 822040).*

ESSEX

BORLEY

Church and Rectory. GHOSTS. Dubbed 'The Most Haunted House in England', Borley rectory was destroyed by fire in 1939, but before then the house and grounds were allegedly a hotbed of psychic manifestations. Handwritten messages appeared on the rectory walls; mysterious lights were seen in the windows; stones were unaccountably thrown and strange noises heard; and in the grounds ghosts were seen, including a phantom coach and horses. Many books have been written on Borley, for example *The Ghosts of Borley* by Paul Tabori and Peter Underwood (1973).

The rectory ghosts have tended to overshadow those at the church, but strange events have also occurred both inside and outside the church. A phantom girl with a nun's veil was seen in the churchyard by a visiting clergyman in 1949, and in later years by others; sometimes she has appeared across the road by the old rectory garden. Footsteps have been heard approaching the church and going inside; sometimes ghostly chanting has been heard from inside the locked church, sometimes organ music. *2 miles NW of Sudbury; site of Borley rectory, now built over, opposite church.*

CANEWDON

Church. WITCHCRAFT; GHOST. Canewdon was once a stronghold of witchcraft, and its reputation persists. Whether there are still witches practising there in secret is impossible to say, but according to an old tradition there will always be nine witches living in the village. Many stories were told about the Wise Man of Canewdon, George Pickingill, who died in 1909. It was said that he summoned imps to do his work in the harvest field while he sat and smoked his pipe, and he was so much feared by the local people that they would do his bidding to avoid being bewitched by him.

The church, and especially the fine early 15th-century tower, features in some of the legends. It was believed that every time a stone fell from the tower, one witch would die and another take her place. So long as the tower stands, there will be witches in Canewdon.

The churchyard also houses a ghost, a woman who on moonless nights is said to rise from her grave and wander through the west gate down to the river. One man who claimed to have seen her said that she wore a crinoline and poke bonnet, and floated quickly above the road. When she reached him he was thrown to the ground by a mysterious force - but not before he saw with horror that she had no face. She was believed to be the ghost of a witch who had been executed. *5 miles N of Southend-on-Sea.*

HADSTOCK

Church. GHOST; MAZE. The church, a late Saxon building with a very old door, possibly also late Saxon, is haunted by a 'pleasant old gentleman', seen several times over the last 50 years.

In the churchyard is buried the writer and artist Michael Ayrton, who died in 1975. A maze on his tombstone commemorates his work with the labyrinth theme and the story of Daedalus, the figure in Greek mythology who built the Cretan labyrinth to house the

Borley Rectory, 'The Most Haunted House in England', photographed in the 1920s

Minotaur – half bull, half man. Ayrton wrote a 'life' of Daedalus, a novel entitled *The Maze Maker. 4 miles NW of Saffron Walden.*

MANNINGTREE

Manningtree. WITCHCRAFT. The town was the home of Matthew Hopkins, the notorious witchfinder-general in the 17th century. As a result of his activities, so-called witches were brought to trial and executed. Witchcraft was allegedly rife throughout Essex, and other places where witches were tried and executed include Chelmsford and Colchester. The old witchcraft practices may have survived into the present century in some remote corners of the county (see *Canewdon*).

SAFFRON WALDEN

Common. MAZE; GIANTS. The largest surviving turf maze in England can be seen here, with a pathway 1650 yards long. Only eight ancient turf mazes survive in England, though there were many more in the Middle Ages. If not attended, they soon become overgrown and lost.

On the exterior of the old houses in the town, there are

some fine examples of the decorative plasterwork known as pargetting. Above a doorway of the old Sun Inn can be seen two giants, known as Gog and Magog (for another depiction, see *Guildhall*, Greater London). Alternatively, the figures shown are Tom Hickathrift the giant-killer, and the Wisbech giant he killed.

Matthew Hopkins, witchfinder-general from Manningtree, with witches and their familiars

ST OSYTH

St Osyth's Priory. HOLY WELL; GHOSTS. Today the gatehouse is the most impressive part of the 12th-century priory. A nunnery was founded nearby by St Osyth, daughter of the first Christian king of East Anglia. She was beheaded by the pagan Danes in AD 653; where her head fell a spring flowed, which became a healing well visited by pilgrims seeking cures. This well may be one in Nun's Wood. It is said that, after the beheading, St Osyth picked up her head and walked a third of a mile to the church of St Peter and St Paul, where she struck the church door and then fell dead. One night a year she is said to return to the scene of her martyrdom, walking with her head in her hands.

In more recent years, when the priory was a convalescent home, a patient saw a ghostly monk in brown. Outdoors, a ghost in a white robe has been seen near the ruins. *3 miles W of Clacton; gatehouse and grounds open to public in summer.*

THEYDON BOIS

Ambersbury Banks. GHOSTS. In Epping Forest, a rampart and ditch enclose an Iron Age hillfort where the ghosts of Queen Boadicea and her daughters are said to have been seen. *Easily accessible from B1393 SW of Epping (TL 438004).*

WALTHAM ABBEY

Abbey Church. ROYAL BURIAL; GHOST. A cross found in Somerset was brought here (see *Montacute*, Somerset), and in 1060 the large new church was consecrated in its honour. Thereafter the abbey church of the Holy Cross was visited by many pilgrims. A stone in the abbey gardens marks the possible burial place of King Harold, killed at the Battle of Hastings in 1066.

In the 1970s a ghostly monk was seen in the graveyard.

GREATER LONDON

CANNON STREET, EC4

London Stone. SACRED CENTRE. Only a fragment of the original stone survives, though it is amazing that even this has survived so long. It was once used to make proclamations from, and in 1450 when Jack Cade, leader of a rebellion against King Henry VI, entered the city he struck it with his sword and said, 'Now is Mortimer [the name Cade had assumed] lord of this city.' The stone was said to have been brought there by Brutus all the way from Troy; he was supposed to have set it up in his New Troy (i.e. London) as an altar to Diana. Whatever its real origins (and it may have been part of a prehistoric sacred site), the London Stone has always had a special significance, marking the sacred centre of London. *Set behind railings in wall of Bank of China, opposite Cannon Street Station.*

CARSHALTON

Anne Boleyn's Well. SITING LEGEND. The belief was that a spring began to flow where the horse of Anne Boleyn, Henry VIII's second wife, struck its hoof on the ground when she was riding here with the King. An alternative name is Queen Anne's Well, and it was probably originally named for St Anne, the Anne Boleyn connection arising later. *3 miles W of Croydon; well near old churchyard where Church Hill joins High Street.*

DRURY LANE, WC2

Theatre Royal. GHOSTS. Many people have seen the ghost of a man in grey, the first recorded sighting being in

1750. In 1848, during alterations, the skeleton of a man with a dagger stocking in his ribs was found, and as the ghost appears very close to where the skeleton was found the two are very likely linked. The ghost, in powdered wig, three-cornered hat and long grey riding cloak, always follows the same route through the auditorium and into an ante-room where he dissolves into the wall. The ghost of the music hall star Dan Leno is also said to haunt the theatre.

ENFIELD

Nags Head Road Area. PHANTOM COACH. Numerous witnesses have seen Enfield's phantom coach, including three Ponder's End factory workers who were walking home in 1899. It seemed to rise out of the ground, and as the girls watched it moved in the Brimsdon direction before disappearing; they saw the driver and another man leaning out of the window. Other witnesses saw two women in large hats, and again the coach was moving just above the ground. Once it even passed through a house! In 1961 a boy cycling along Bell Lane saw two lights bearing down on him. He couldn't get out of the way in time, and the apparition passed right through him. He saw a jet-black, four-wheeled vehicle drawn by four horses and travelling 6 feet above the ground.

GUILDHALL, EC2

Guildhall. GIANTS. Statues of the giants Gog and Magog can be seen inside the Guildhall, though these are modern figures made to replace the 18th-century ones destroyed by bombing in 1940. They were said to be the last of the British giants. Originally the first figures, erected in the 15th century, were of the giant Gogmagog and the Trojan general Corineus, who according to folklore tackled the giant in a wrestling bout and threw him into the sea.

HIGHGATE

Boadicea's Grave, Parliament Hill Fields. TREASURE. As well as being the legendary grave of the warrior queen, this tumulus was said to contain buried treasure in the form of a golden coffin or table. *TQ 274865.*

Highgate Cemetery. VAMPIRES. With its wealth of ornate Victorian statuary, its vaults, mausoleums and catacombs, all overgrown following decades of neglect, it is perhaps inevitable that rumours of vampires should have arisen - fortunately they are unfounded rumours. But even though the cemetery has recently been tidied up and the vampires banished, it is still one of the most atmospheric places in London. *W cemetery most interesting part, off Swain's Lane; open to public spring and summer afternoons.*

Fountain Court at Hampton Court, Kingston upon Thames

CALENDAR OF EVENTS

30 January
WHITEHALL, London. *King Charles I Ceremony:* Procession gathers at the statue of the King, wreaths are laid, and a ceremony is then held at the spot where he was executed in 1649.

February/March: Shrove Tuesday
OLNEY, Buckinghamshire. *Pancake Day Race:* In a ceremony dating back to 1445, local ladies race down the High Street with pans and pancakes.

April/May/June (Ascension Day)
TOWER OF LONDON. *Beating the Bounds:* 31 boundary landmarks beaten every third year (1987, 1990 etc.) with willow wands carried by choirboys accompanied by Yeoman Warders.

May Day Bank Holiday
ICKWELL GREEN, Bedfordshire. *May Day Celebrations:* Maypole dancing, May Queen, morris dancing. Two 'Moggies' are present - a man dressed as a woman, and 'her' husband, in rags and with blackened faces, who collect money.

Late September
SOUTHEND-ON-SEA, Essex. *Blessing of the Fishes Ceremony:* A special service is followed by a fish banquet.

26 December (Boxing Day)
ST ALBANS, Hertfordshire. *Mumming Play:* Traditional Christmas celebration, still widely performed.

Beating the Bounds at the Tower of London

KINGSTON UPON THAMES

★ **Hampton Court Palace.** GHOSTS. Catherine Howard, one of King Henry VIII's wives, is perhaps the most famous ghost in the fine 16th-century palace. She ran screaming to the King, who was in the chapel, when she heard she had been charged with adultery. Her pleas were ignored and she was dragged away to be executed, but her screams are still heard echoing down the Long Gallery, and her running ghost has also been seen.

Other royal ghosts include Jane Seymour, Henry's third wife, who walks in Clock Court and Silver Stick Gallery; Anne Boleyn, his second wife; and King Henry himself. Cardinal Wolsey, who built the palace, was seen in 1966 during a Son et Lumière performance; and Sybil Penn, who was Edward VI's nurse, is sometimes seen sitting spinning in one of the apartments.

There are almost too many other reported ghosts in the palace to mention! Those seen in the grounds include a White Lady near the landing stage, a group of men and women who were observed to vanish by a policeman, and a grey, misty figure in Tudor costume who appeared to actor Leslie Finch. The many tragic and dramatic events which Hampton Court has seen have certainly left strong after-shocks echoing down the centuries. *Palace and grounds open to public.*

King Stone. CORONATION STONE. This ancient stone, possibly originally part of a prehistoric structure, gave Kingston its name. It was here that several Saxon kings were crowned, including Athelstan in AD 924, Eadmund in 939, Eadred in 946 and Eadwig in 955. *Near Kingston market and Guildhall.*

STRAND, WC2

St Clement Danes Church. LEYS. Two leys pass through this ancient sacred site, on which a church has stood since the 9th century. The leys were both discovered by the father of ley hunting, Alfred Watkins, and further researched by Paul Devereux and Ian Thomson for their book *The Ley Hunter's Companion.* A $3\frac{1}{4}$-mile ley links up St Clement Danes, the Temple church, St Paul's Cathedral, St Helen's Bishopsgate and St Dunstan's Stepney; while a $2\frac{1}{2}$-mile ley links St Martin-in-the-Fields, St Mary-le-Strand, St Clement Danes, St Dunstan's in Fleet Street, and Arnold Circus where there was once an ancient mound. The latter ley follows the line of the present Strand, and it is likely that this road, and the church sites, are all ancient in origin. Certainly many of the present churches are known to incorporate the remains of much earlier churches. Although the city is constantly being changed and rebuilt, it is intriguing to see that careful research can reveal so many traces of its early history.

TOWER OF LONDON

★ **Tower of London.** LEGENDARY GUARDIANS; GHOSTS. Brutus, legendary founder of the capital city and first king of Britain, is said to be buried in the White Mound on which the Tower now stands. Also buried here was the head of Bran the Blessed, king of Britain, brought here at his command, with a promise that while it was buried here Britain would not be invaded. King Arthur did not approve: he had the head dug up, not wishing anyone but himself to be responsible for guarding this island. These legends suggest that the mound was once a sacred site. The name 'Bran' also means crow, rook or raven in Welsh, and there is a long-standing custom of keeping ravens on Tower Hill to protect the country from invasion.

The Tower is one of Britain's most haunted places, and its many ghosts include the Earl of Northumberland in Martin Tower, Sir Walter Raleigh near the Bloody Tower, and the Countess of Salisbury, whose execution is said to be re-enacted on its anniversary. Anne Boleyn, executed here in 1536, has been seen in several places around the Tower. In 1933 a sentry saw her headless body floating towards him and instantly deserted his post; because of the place's reputation, he was only reprimanded. Other sentries have reported similar experiences. She has also been seen in the Chapel of St Peter-ad-Vincula, where she is buried. When strange lights were seen in the chapel, an officer looked in through a window and saw a procession of people in Elizabethan dress, with Anne Boleyn at their head.

Catacombs at Highgate Cemetery

WESTMINSTER ABBEY

★ **Westminster Abbey.** CORONATION STONE; GHOSTS. The Stone of Scone beneath the Coronation Chair has a long legendary history. In 1296 it was brought from Scone in Scotland where it had been used for the coronations of Scottish kings, but before that it may have come from Ireland where it was the Stone of Destiny, used to crown Irish kings and groaning aloud if someone other than a rightful heir to the throne sat on it. In legend it was taken to Scotland by Joseph of Arimathea, or it came from the Temple of Jerusalem, or was Jacob's pillow: there are many alternative versions of its early history. Since the late 13th century it has been used as the Coronation Stone for British monarchs, an interesting survival of an ancient practice, similar to the use of inauguration stones (see *Kilmichael Glassary*, Strathclyde).

The abbey is built on an earlier sacred site, and is said to have replaced an earlier pagan temple and a Saxon church. The present abbey replaced a church built in the 11th century by King Edward the Confessor, attaining its present form in 1745. The building claims several ghosts, including the man who signed King Charles I's death warrant, a khaki-clad soldier near the Tomb of the Unknown Warrior, and a Benedictine monk who walks above the present ground level, the floor having been lowered during restorations. In 1932 he appeared to three people and spoke in what sounded like Elizabethan English, saying he had been killed in the time of Henry VIII.

HERTFORDSHIRE

ANSTEY

Anstey Castle. UNDERGROUND PASSAGE; DEVIL. Demons were said to live in a cave from where a mile-long underground passage led to Anstey Castle, and no one who entered would emerge alive. A blind fiddler poohpoohed this story and agreed to walk the length of the tunnel, beginning at Devil's Hole (or Cave Gate, in another version). He played his fiddle as he entered, accompanied by his dog, and the watchers heard the music moving underground. Suddenly a scream was heard, then silence – then the dog reappeared, with his hair singed off (presumably having encountered the Devil), but the fiddler was never seen again. *6 miles SE of Royston; castle mound close to church.*

St Alban's Abbey, dedicated to the 4th-century martyr

BRENT PELHAM

Church. DRAGON; DEVIL. According to tradition, lord of the manor Piers Shonks set out to kill a dragon which lived in a cave under a yew tree close to the village. As he thrust his spear down the dragon's throat, the Devil appeared and vowed to have Shonks' body and soul, whether he was buried inside or outside the church. When Shonks lay dying, some years later, he shot an arrow from his bow, saying his body would lie where the arrow fell. It hit the north wall of the nave in the church, and today the 11th-century tomb of Piers Shonks can still be seen there in the wall - neither inside nor outside the church. *7 miles NW of Bishop's Stortford.*

HEXTON

Wayting Hill. SLEEPING WARRIOR; FAIRIES. The hill is a round barrow, where a warrior is said to lie sleeping until needed for battle. There was formerly a famous holy well and shrine, St Faith's, adjoining the churchyard in Hexton, but they were destroyed so thoroughly in the 17th century by the lord of the manor that the site cannot be found.

Just south of the village is a fine hillfort, Ravensburgh Castle, which may have been the stronghold of the British chieftain Cassivellaunus when attacked in 54 BC by Julius Caesar. 'Fairy Hole' on the Ordnance Survey map also suggests that this same wooded hilltop was a haunt of the Little People. *5 miles W of Hitchin; Wayting Hill in woods just S of main street (TL 102299); Ravensburgh Fort 1 mile S of village. Private property, but sites can be viewed from track across Barton Hills to W, leaving B655 W of village.*

PIRTON

Church. SITING LEGEND; TREASURE; LEY. This church was originally intended to be built on Toot Hill close to the churchyard, which was a castle mound in Norman times. But the Devil removed the stones to the bottom of the hill every night, so it is said, and the church was built on the present site.

There is said to be gold and treasure in the pond near the church and castle mound.

Pirton church is on an 8½-mile ley which also takes in Waulud's Bank, Dray's Ditches, Galley Hill, Deacon Hill, a moat and Holwell church. Our book *Mysterious Britain* gives details of other alignments on the Hertfordshire-Bedfordshire border. *2 miles NW of Hitchin.*

PRESTON

Minsden Chapel. GHOST. A long-ruined chapel in woods on a lonely hilltop is said to be haunted by a monk, who appears on All Hallows' Eve (Hallowe'en); ghostly bells ring before his arrival. *3 miles S of Hitchin; Minsden Chapel 1 mile to E, reached by footpath from Royal Oak public house on B656 to N, or from B651 to S.*

ST ALBANS

★ **St Albans Abbey.** SAINT'S SHRINE; UNDERGROUND PASSAGE; GHOSTS. Although famous for its Roman remains - for St Albans was once the great city of Verulamium - the cathedral church or abbey is equally interesting, housing the shrine of St Alban who was martyred here in the early 4th century. It is thought that the abbey was built on the hilltop where St Alban died. There is also a legend that when he prayed for water to drink just before his death a spring began to flow at his feet, but the site of this holy well is now lost. The saint's shrine survives, however, having been restored in the 19th century along with the rest of the abbey. The holes at the base are where pilgrims put their hands while seeking cures, for miracles were believed to occur here.

Tunnels under the abbey, known as Monk's Holes and possibly intended as bolt-holes for use when the monks were in danger due to civil disorder, were said to run across-country - to the friary at King's Langley 5 miles away, and to Gorhambury House 2 miles away, the latter (open to the public) being the home of Sir Francis Bacon, to whom Shakespeare's plays are attributed by some people.

St Albans Abbey is also said to be haunted by phantom monks, who can sometimes be heard singing matins at the old time of 2 a.m.

WESTON

Churchyard. GIANT. Jack o' Legs, who lived in a wood near Weston, was supposed to be a giant who robbed the rich to feed the poor. Various places were called Jack's Hill or Jack's Cave, and were associated with tales of his exploits. Finally he was hanged for his misdeeds, his final request being that he be allowed to shoot an arrow, and to be buried where it fell. The arrow landed in Weston churchyard, and his grave can still be seen there, marked by two tombstones 14 feet apart. *4 miles NE of Stevenage.*

WHEATHAMPSTEAD

Devil's Dyke. DEVIL. The ditch, 500 yards long and 40 feet deep, was dug out by the Devil, according to legend. In fact it was made by deepening a natural valley, and the area protected by this and another earthwork to the east may have been occupied by Cassivellaunus after the attack by Julius Caesar. *5 miles N of St Albans; Devil's Dyke lies beside minor road running S from W-E village road (TL 186133).*

CAMBRIDGESHIRE NORFOLK AND SUFFOLK

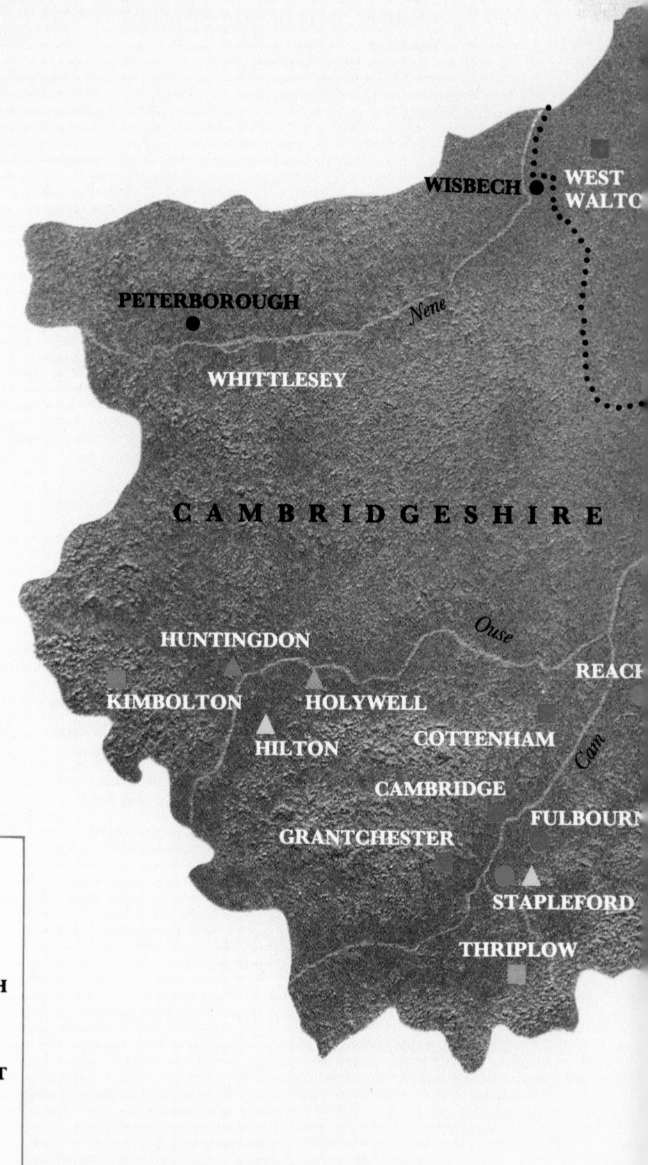

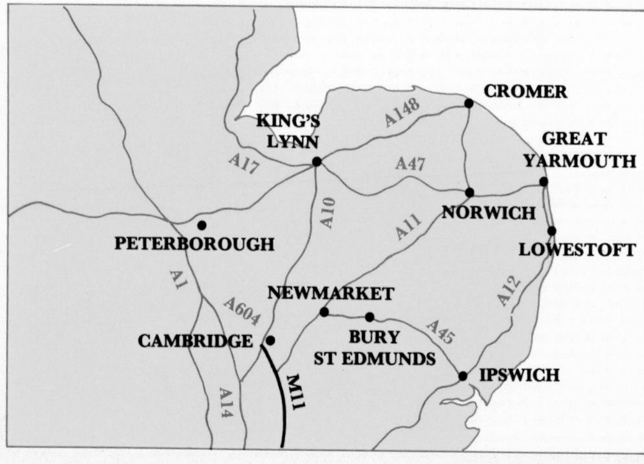

NORTH SEA

HUNSTANTON

BINHAM

CROMER

LITTLE WALSINGHAM

BLICKLING

GREAT SNORING

KING'S LYNN

GREAT MASSINGHAM

CAWSTON

Bure

TILNEY ALL SAINTS

HICKLING

EAST DEREHAM

NORWICH

LUDHAM

GREAT YARMOUTH

SWAFFHAM

BAWBURGH

Yare

NORFOLK

GELDESTON

LOWESTOFT

QUIDENHAM

BUNGAY

THETFORD

THORPE ABBOTTS

Waveney

SOUTHWOLD

Y

BLYTHBURGH

MILDENHALL

WALBERSWICK

WICKEN

HOXNE

DUNWICH

BURY ST EDMUNDS

DENNINGTON

NEWMARKET

WESTLETON

WOOLPIT

SUFFOLK

LEISTON

WITHERSFIELD

Deben

HADLEIGH

IPSWICH

SUDBURY

LITTLE CORNARD

WISSINGTON

Stour

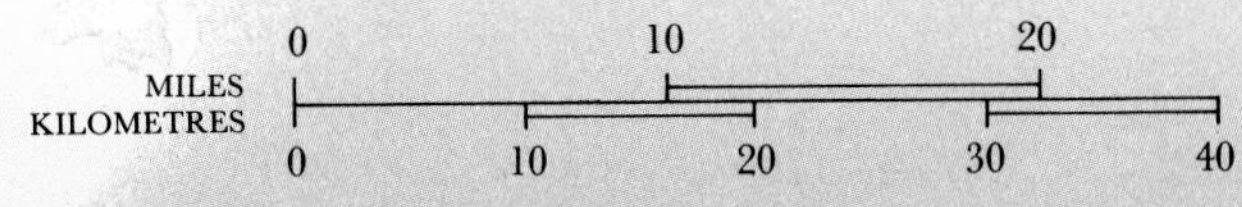

CAMBRIDGESHIRE

COTTENHAM

Church. SITING LEGEND. The church is at one end of this long village. According to tradition, the villagers tried to rebuild it nearer the centre, but the stones were mysteriously transported back again. *5 miles N of Cambridge.*

FULBOURN

Mutlow Hill. TREASURE. A golden chariot is said to be buried in this prehistoric barrow. Judging from its name (moot-low) it was probably used as a meeting place in Saxon times. *2 miles SE of Fulbourn, itself 5 miles SE of Cambridge centre, on footpath following Fleam Dyke just NW of A11 (TL 547544).*

GRANTCHESTER

Manor House. UNDERGROUND PASSAGE. From the cellars of the old house run two tunnels, one of which extends a long way with the roof getting lower all the way. No one knows where it goes to, but it is rumoured to reach King's College Chapel. A fiddler who offered to follow the passage set off playing his fiddle; the music became fainter and finally could no longer be heard. The fiddler was never seen again. On a 17th-century map of Grantchester, one of the fields is named Fiddler's Close. *2 miles SW of Cambridge centre.*

HILTON

Village Green. MAZE. One of Britain's few surviving turf mazes can be seen in Hilton, on the village green not far from the church. The message on the central obelisk states that it was laid out in 1660 by 19-year-old William Sparrow; but maybe he only recut a neglected maze. Nothing more is known of its history. *5 miles SE of Huntingdon.*

HOLYWELL

Church and Ferry Boat Inn. HOLY WELL; GHOST. The holy well from which the village gets its name is tucked away behind the church. A well-dressing ceremony is now held there every year.

A girl who committed suicide after an unhappy love affair was buried on the bank of the River Ouse, and later

The turf maze on the village green at Hilton

the Ferry Boat Inn was built on the site. On 17 March, the anniversary of her death according to tradition, she sometimes appears in ghostly form and moves towards the river bank. *1 mile E of St Ives; church at W end of village, inn at E.*

HUNTINGDON

Nun's Bridge. GHOST. Hinchingbroke House was once a convent, and it is thought that the ghost which haunts the bridge over the Alconbury Brook is a nun; she is accompanied by another ghost looking like a nurse. The nun may have had a lover who was a monk, and they were murdered: that is one tale told to explain the sightings. A woman and her husband driving across the bridge in 1965 saw the ghosts, and when they returned the same way shortly afterwards they saw them again. *1 mile SW of Huntingdon centre; old, haunted bridge bypassed by modern road bridge carrying A141 into Huntingdon.*

KIMBOLTON

Kimbolton Castle. GHOST. Catherine of Aragon, one of the wives of Henry VIII, died here in 1536, and her ghost is said to haunt the gallery. *9 miles SW of Huntingdon; open to public.*

REACH

Devil's Ditch. DEVIL. One of several Saxon dykes in the county, the Devil's Ditch earthwork was thrown up as protection against the Britons to the west; though in legend it was built by the Devil. *7 miles long, from Reach to Woodditton SW of Newmarket; footpath runs along its length.*

STAPLEFORD

Wandlebury Hillfort. GIANTS; HILL FIGURE; TREASURE; GHOSTS; PHANTOM DOGS. The hillfort is situated in the Gog Magog Hills, Gog and Magog being either one or two legendary giants (see *Guildhall*, Greater London) said to be buried at Wandlebury. There was once a giant figure cut into the turf on the hill slope, still visible in the 18th century but now overgrown. In 1954 archaeologist T.C. Lethbridge attempted to relocate its outline by using soundings, and found that there had been a group of figures which he interpreted as Magog the Earth Goddess, walking beside her chariot, preceded by the Spirit of Darkness poised for flight, and followed by the giant Gog. It is intriguing that a golden chariot is said to be buried under Mutlow Hill not far away (see *Fulbourn*), and that there was also said to be a giant horse buried under Little Trees Hill to the west. Are these legends perhaps distorted memories of the ancient hill figure?

There is also another tradition, recorded in Gervase of

CALENDAR OF EVENTS

January: Saturday before Plough Monday
WHITTLESEY, Cambridgeshire. *Straw Bear Festival:* Straw Bear (formerly an unemployed ploughboy covered in straw) dances through the streets collecting money for charity.

Late January (Plough Sunday)
CAWSTON, Norfolk. *Blessing of the Plough:* Church service on the day before Plough Monday, in past times a day of festivity before farm work recommenced after Christmas.

February/March: Shrove Tuesday
THORPE ABBOTTS, Norfolk. *Pancake Races:* Originally pancakes were made to use up fats before Lenten fast began.

May Day Week
CAMBRIDGE. *May Day Revels:* Spring celebrations held in city and Grantchester Meadows.

June: second week
SOUTHWOLD, Suffolk. *Trinity Fair:* Ancient charter fair begins with mayor riding on roundabouts.

June: Thursday nearest 28th
BURY ST EDMUNDS, Suffolk. *Cakes and Ale Ceremony:* Commemorates a town benefactor who died in 1481; ale is now replaced by sherry.

The Whittlesey Straw Bear

Windmill at Wicken Fen, where ghostly monks have been reported

Tilbury's *Otia Imperialia* (*c.*1211), 'that if a warrior enters this level space [on the hilltop] at the dead of night, when the moon is shining, and cries "Knight to knight, come forth", immediately he will be confronted by a warrior, armed for fight, who charging horse to horse, either dismounts his adversary or is dismounted.' He goes on to relate how one Osbert did as the legend said, met the knight, and was wounded in the thigh; his wound is said to have opened up on the anniversary of the contest every year.

Phantom black dogs also haunt this area: one runs over the Gog Magog Hills on winter nights, and another, the size of a small donkey, was seen about 60 years ago on the road 100 yards south of the earthworks. *Close to A1307 5 miles SE of Cambridge centre, and accessible by footpath.*

THRIPLOW

Church. SITING LEGEND. The hilltop church was to have been built in the hollow where the village lies, but the stones were moved uphill by night. Not wanting the labour of continually shifting the stones, the villagers gave in and built the church on the new site. *7 miles S of Cambridge centre.*

WICKEN

Wicken Fen. GHOSTS; PHANTOM DOG. The Fen is now a nature reserve, and of great interest to visit. To the north-west of Wicken is a farm called Spinney Abbey. Originally a priory stood here, and various strange happenings have been reported in its vicinity: chanting monks have been heard; ghostly figures seen; and a mysterious twinkling light, called a Will-o'-the-Wisp or Jack-o'-Lantern, has been seen drifting between the farm and Spinney Bank, a fen-bank leading to Wicken Fen. A phantom black dog, calf-sized and with 'eyes as big as bike lamps', is also reputed to haunt the area. It is said that anyone who sees it will die soon afterwards. *Wicken 6 miles NW of Newmarket; Fen (National Trust) easily accessible from A1123.*

NORFOLK

BAWBURGH

St Walstan's Well. HOLY WELL. St Walstan is the patron saint of agricultural workers and sick animals. Born in AD 965 at Bawburgh, he worked on a farm even though he was a king's son. In 1016 an angel warned him of his approaching death, but he worked with the animals until the end, telling his master to place his body in an ox-cart and let the animals go where they wished. They went from Taverham through Costessey Wood, and wherever they stopped to rest, springs began to flow. The third of these was at Bawburgh, where the saint was buried and a church and shrine were built. The well at Bawburgh became famous for curing sick animals, and at one time the water was sold in the Norwich streets. *5 miles W of Norwich centre; well on farm below church; shrine, formerly on N side of church, no longer survives, and church itself has been rebuilt and restored.*

BINHAM

Binham Priory. UNDERGROUND PASSAGE; GHOST. From the now-ruined priory a tunnel was said to run 3½ miles across-country to Walsingham. A ghostly monk in black used to walk along the route of the tunnel above ground, as if looking for something, but he was never seen again after a fiddler took his dog into the tunnel to explore it. He played his fiddle as he walked – until suddenly the music stopped. The dog reappeared, his tail between his legs, but of the fiddler there was no trace. It is believed that he had been carried off by the Black Monk. *7 miles NE of Fakenham; priory close to church, its Norman nave now forming part of church.*

BLICKLING

Blickling Hall. GHOSTS; PHANTOM COACH; PHANTOM DOG. Standing as it does on the site of the birthplace of Anne Boleyn, it is not surprising that her ghost is said to haunt the Hall. A phantom coach drawn by four headless horses carries the headless Anne, her head held in her hand, at midnight on the anniversary of her execution. They drive up to the Hall, she enters the house and moves unseen through the corridors. Her father, Sir Thomas Boleyn, is also said to haunt the surrounding area on the same night, condemned to drive over 40 Norfolk and Suffolk bridges before dawn. There was also a legend of a phantom black dog at the Hall. *1 mile NW of Aylsham; open to public (National Trust).*

CROMER

Cliff Paths. PHANTOM DOG. Black Shuck is one name given to the phantom black dog seen in many parts of East Anglia. It is usually calf-sized, with red glowing eyes, and is often considered to be an omen of death. For once this phantom is definitely more than a legend: there are many reliable first-hand accounts of people seeing this monstrous apparition. One of his local haunts is the cliff paths around Cromer: south-east to Overstrand and north-west to Sheringham. He was also said to haunt Overstrand churchyard.

EAST DEREHAM

★ **St Withburga's Well.** HOLY WELL. Withburga was a daughter of the Saxon king Annas. She was born around AD 630, and founded a convent at East Dereham which was destroyed by the Danes in 974. When Withburga died, she was buried in East Dereham churchyard and her tomb was visited for cures. The abbot of Ely had her body removed to Ely Cathedral during the 10th century, and at the spot where the saint had been buried a miraculous spring of pure healing water began to flow. It is still there, with the remains of a chapel, all enclosed by a small garden.

GELDESTON

Road to Bungay. PHANTOM COACH. A phantom coach drawn by four horses and with a headless coachman is said to follow the main road from Bungay, past the church, down Bigod's Hill and back to Bungay by the low road. It may be the same coach which haunts the road from Bungay to Ditchingham, seen one night by a man driving down to Bungay. Certain he would collide with it, he braked; then, as he accelerated in order to pass it, he saw it float away into a lay-by at a place known as Lion's Grave. The lay-by was probably part of the old road which the real coach would have followed.

GREAT MASSINGHAM

★ **Peddar's Way.** PHANTOM DOGS. The Roman road, which is now a green lane for much of its length, is haunted at several spots by the phantom black dog so familiar in East Anglia. One such place is Massingham Heath, where in October 1977 a man hiking along the Way saw a big black dog running fast towards him, jaws wide open and teeth 'very evident'. On reaching him, it leaped up at him and he raised his arm to protect himself. But the dog never struck him, and when the shocked man opened his eyes it had gone. A year later to the day, he suffered a severe road accident. Phantom black dogs have on numerous other occasions portended ill-fortune for the witness.

Another sighting, this time of a grey dog, 'with sparks and the sound of gravel', reportedly took place 2 miles north of Castle Acre; the dog was running along an old sheep-drove which crossed Peddar's Way.

At Roudham Cross, where the Way crosses the A11 north-east of Thetford, a man driving along the road early one morning in 1962 suddenly saw a huge black dog cross in front of him. He could not avoid hitting it - but it reappeared on the other side of his car, still following the line of the old road. *9 miles SW of Fakenham; Peddar's Way runs NW–SE just W of Great Massingham.*

GREAT SNORING

Road South. PHANTOM DOG. Just before the Second World War, a motorist ran over (or rather, through) a ghostly white dog which was in the habit of rushing across the road between Great and Little Snoring. The shocked driver left his car at the roadside. *3 miles NE of Fakenham.*

HICKLING

Hickling Broad. GHOSTS. A ghostly skater sometimes seen on the surface of the water is said to be a drummer who drowned while skating across the ice to meet his sweetheart in secret. This took place at the time of the Napoleonic Wars.

In more recent years, a couple holidaying in a cruiser on the Broad were moving their craft at night when they saw a woman in a white dress punting towards them. They shouted a warning but she took no notice, and they feared a collision. Then they saw her moving off into the darkness on the other side of their boat. While having a much-needed drink in the pub, they told their story and learned that they had seen a ghost. She was apparently well known for punting across from one mill to another. *10 miles NW of Great Yarmouth; Broad to S of village.*

Hickling Priory. GHOST; UNDERGROUND PASSAGE. A ghostly monk haunts the ruins of the priory; he is said to walk along an underground tunnel which runs from the ruins to a drain in the marshes half a mile to the north-east. *Priory ½ mile NE of Hickling.*

LITTLE WALSINGHAM

★ **Abbey Ruins and Walsingham Shrine.** VISION OF VIRGIN MARY; HOLY WELLS. Walsingham is one of the great holy places of England, where pilgrims have come to worship for nearly a thousand years. It all began in 1061, when the lady Richeldis de Faverches had a vision of the Virgin Mary, who told her to build a Holy House like that in Nazareth. This shrine was duly built and became famous for miracles. There were already two holy wells at Walsingham, and these too became famous for the healing power of their water, especially for headaches and stomach problems. Later they degenerated into wishing wells; the wisher knelt on a stone between them and dipped a hand into each well while making a silent wish, and finally took a sip of water from each well.

In 1931 it was decided to build a new shrine, and while the site was being excavated an ancient well was discovered. It was found to link directly to the two wells in the abbey ruins, and so was incorporated into the new shrine.

Today over a hundred thousand pilgrims visit Walsingham annually. The holy well is in the Anglican Shrine in the village; the original two wells can be visited in the abbey grounds, where they are close to a Norman archway. *4 miles N of Fakenham.*

LUDHAM

How Hill. DEVIL. Having dug out a load of gravel from a pit in Neatishead, legend has it, the Devil was wheeling it through Irstead when his barrow overturned and some of the spilled gravel formed Bunker's Hill. More was lost in the River Ant, and in Ludham two mounds called Great and Little Readhams were also formed from his load of gravel. When he lost the remainder, the Devil is supposed to have cried 'How!' in his anger as he kicked the barrow. Thus How Hill came into being. *10 miles NE of Norwich; How Hill 1 mile to NW, beside lane and E of River Ant.*

St Benet's Abbey. GHOST; DRAGON. The ruined abbey is haunted by Ethelwold, a monk who was hanged above the abbey gateway for letting in William the Conqueror's men so they could take the abbey - according to legend. It also became the refuge of a winged dragon, which lived near Ludham and came out of its lair at night to terrorize the villagers. Even though they filled up the entrance to its den with stones and bricks, it moved them away - until a man placed in the hole a single round stone which the dragon could not move. It then rushed across the fields to the ruined abbey where it disappeared through the gateway and into the vaults, never to be seen again. *Close to River Bure, 1½ miles S of Ludham, reached either by water or by footpath.*

QUIDENHAM

Viking's Mound. ROYAL BURIAL; LEY. In local lore this round barrow is said to be the burial place of Queen Boadicea. It was also found by Paul Devereux and Ian Thomson to lie on a possible ley which runs for 16½ miles from Bunwell church to a barrow on Elder Hill, passing also through a tumulus, an ancient moat and West Harling church. (See *The Ley Hunter's Companion* for more details.) *10 miles NE of Thetford; tree-covered Viking's Mound close to road NW of church (TM 027878).*

THETFORD

Castle Hill. DEVIL; TREASURE. An Iron Age hillfort before becoming a Norman castle site, the hill was in legend said to have been created by the Devil scraping mud off his shoes after digging the Devil's Ditch (see *Reach*, Cambridgeshire). A hollow in the hill was known as Devil's Hole, and if you walk round the hill seven times at midnight it is said you will see the Devil. A palace full of treasure is supposed to be hidden in the hill; another story has it that six silver or golden bells hidden at the Dissolution of the Monasteries in the 16th century are still there. *S of A1066 within Thetford.*

TILNEY ALL SAINTS

Churchyard. GIANT. Tom Hickathrift was a giant whose base was the Wisbech area of Cambridgeshire, and across the county boundary in Norfolk 6–8 miles to the north-east of Wisbech can be seen several memorials which are said to support the legend. In Tilney All Saints churchyard are two of his 'candlesticks' (the remains of old memorial crosses); the five indentations on top of the one by the south porch are said to be the marks of the giant's fingers and thumb. Close to the south side of the church is an oval stone nearly 8 feet long, said to be Tom's gravestone. He threw the stone from 3 miles away, saying that he would be buried where it fell - and it landed here. Carved on the outer north wall at Walpole St Peter church, in the corner of the chancel, is an effigy said to represent the giant. One of his exploits was to kill a Wisbech giant, an event depicted in *Saffron Walden* (see Essex). *Tilney All Saints 3 miles SW of King's Lynn; Walpole St Peter a further 4 miles SW.*

Peddar's Way near Little Massingham, haunt of phantom black dogs

WEST WALTON

Church. DEVIL. There are two versions of the story that explains why the church has a detached tower. According to one version, the Devil disliked the sound of the church bells and tried to carry the tower away, but it proved too heavy for him and he dropped it just south of the church, where it still stands. The other tells how the Devil hired several evil fenmen to carry the tower away. They had it on their shoulders but could not get it over the churchyard wall; they ran round and round with it until they found they could not get it out of consecrated ground at all, and so they left it inside. *2 miles N of Wisbech.*

The ruins of Bury St Edmunds Abbey

SUFFOLK

BLYTHBURGH

★ **Church.** DEVIL (PHANTOM DOG). The Devil in the form of a black dog is said to have disrupted the service on Sunday morning, 4 August 1577. As at *Bungay* church (see next entry), this event may be explained by the intrusion of rare ball lightning into the building during a thunderstorm, causing injury and damage. Black marks left on a door in Blythburgh church are said to be the Devil's finger-marks. They can still be seen, on a door at the back of the church. *4 miles W of Southwold.*

BUNGAY

St Mary's Church. DEVIL (PHANTOM DOG); UNDERGROUND PASSAGE. A black dog said to be the Devil wrought havoc in this town-centre church during a storm in 1577, when the people were attending Sunday morning service. The dog's passage through the building killed and injured some members of the congregation. It is probable that the phenomenon was ball lightning or some similar rare and inexplicable fiery event, but it is natural that it should have been interpreted as the Devil in the form of Black Shuck, the huge black dog well known and feared throughout East Anglia. His visit is now commemorated by a black dog weathervane in Bungay town centre.

In the churchyard of St Mary's is the Druid's Stone where the Devil can be summoned by following a certain ritual: either knock 12 times on the stone, or run around it 12 times.

There is also said to be an underground passage at Bungay, running from St Mary's church to the ruined castle.

BURY ST EDMUNDS

Bury St Edmunds Abbey. GHOSTS; LEY. Edmund, last king of the East Angles, was killed by the Danes in AD 869 and became a martyr and saint. According to legend his head was lost, until after 40 days of searching his officers heard Edmund calling from a wood, and found his head between the paws of a grey wolf (see *Hadleigh*). His tomb at 'St Edmondsbury' was an important shrine visited by many pilgrims. The abbey where he was buried is now in ruins, and several ghosts have reportedly been seen there. The abbey gateway is said to be particularly haunted, and phantom monks have been seen in buildings close to the abbey.

The long-distance alignment called the St Michael Line touches Bury St Edmunds (see *Marazion*, Cornwall).

DENNINGTON

Church. MYTHICAL BEAST. This fine Tudor church boasts around 70 beautiful 15th-century bench-ends. One shows a Sciapod, a fabulous creature which was said to live in the desert and to use its enormous foot as a sunshade. This is the only depiction of a Sciapod in Britain. *6 miles NW of Saxmundham.*

DUNWICH

North Sea. DROWNED TOWN; TREASURE. It is difficult to believe that the encroaching sea has swallowed whole towns and villages on the east coast of England during the past centuries. Coastal erosion on the Suffolk coast south

Door in Blythburgh church, showing marks said to have been made by the Devil in the form of a huge black dog

of Lowestoft has been particularly severe, with the major port of Dunwich, once the capital of East Anglia, almost completely overwhelmed. This happened gradually during the 14th to 20th centuries, during which time nine churches were lost. Now Dunwich is a quiet village, with the sea and sand dunes giving no clue as to the former presence of an important town. But it is said that the sunken church bells ring to warn of impending storms, and that the shadowy ghosts of Dunwich's former inhabitants can sometimes be seen close to the shore.

Dunwich also features in a tradition which tells of three holy crowns buried in East Anglia to protect England from invasion. One was said to have been buried at Dunwich, and lost when the town was inundated; the second was dug up at Rendlesham in the 18th century; the third has not yet been found. *4 miles SW of Southwold.*

HADLEIGH

Church. SAINT'S DEATH. A carved bench-end from the 14th century shows a wolf holding the head of the martyred King Edmund (see *Bury St Edmunds* and *Hoxne*). *8 miles W of Ipswich; carving in south chapel of parish church.*

17th-century oak dole cupboard in Bungay church; the figure below the initials may be the notorious black dog

HOXNE

Goldbrook Bridge. SAINT'S CURSE. King Edmund hid from the Danes under this bridge, but was betrayed by a newly married couple who saw his gilt spurs lit by the moonlight and reflected in the water. Thereafter couples would not cross the bridge on the way to be married, for fear of King Edmund's curse on them. It was said that Hoxne (pronounced Hoxen) was Haegelisdun, where Edmund was slain, and a monument in a field marks the alleged site of the tree to which he was tied before being killed (see *Bury St Edmunds*). *4 miles SE of Diss; Goldbrook Bridge on road to Cross Street, and monument in field beside same road (TM 183766).*

LEISTON

Churchyard. PHANTOM DOG. Earlier this century, Lady Rendlesham and a friend sat up in the churchyard to watch for the Gallytrot, a Suffolk name for the phantom black dog. They saw it at midnight, as it leaped over the churchyard wall and slipped down the dark lane to the sandhills. *4 miles E of Saxmundham.*

LITTLE CORNARD

Kedington Hill. DRAGONS. According to tradition two dragons, a black one living on Kedington Hill and a reddish spotted one living on Ballingdon Hill across the county boundary in Essex, met on 25 September 1449 in Sharpfight Meadow near Little Cornard to fight a battle. The Essex dragon won, and both returned to their respective hills. It has been suggested that this battle commemorates some inter-village rivalry of the 15th century; but it is also intriguing that the same field, now called Shalford Meadow, is said to be the place where Queen Boadicea defeated the Roman Ninth Legion from Colchester. *Little Cornard 2 miles SE of Sudbury; battle site close to River Stour.*

MILDENHALL

Three Hills. TREASURE. It was believed that Oliver Cromwell hid chests full of treasure in these round barrows. When one of them was excavated in 1866 local people came to look, following an unsubstantiated rumour that a chest had been found. *8 miles NE of Newmarket; Three Hills in woods N of A1101 2 miles SE of village (TL 743742).*

SUDBURY

St Gregory's Church. ARCHBISHOP'S DEATH; WATER DIVINER. Rebuilt in the 14th century on an old religious site, the church contains some unusual items, including a rare and magnificent telescopic font cover. Simon de Sudbury, Archbishop of Canterbury, was responsible for the 14th-century work. He was murdered in the Peasants' Revolt of 1381, and his skull is preserved in a glass case in the church.

Also to be seen is a screen painting of the water diviner John Schorne, who was said to have found the holy well at *North Marston*, Buckinghamshire (see entry) when he was rector there. *St Gregory's, one of three churches in Sudbury, is at W end of town.*

WALBERSWICK

Church and Common. GHOSTS; PHANTOM DOG. The ruined church is haunted by a man seen by numerous witnesses including the writer George Orwell, who saw him in the chancel in the mid-1930s, and a workman at the church nearly 50 years later. Other ghosts have been seen at Walberswick, especially on the common. A woman blackberrying there felt a cold wind and heard the sound of galloping hooves, but could see nothing. Another woman saw standing on the top of Squire's Hill a ghostly man, who vanished as she approached him; her dog was apprehensive and refused to go on. Two ladies saw a calf-sized phantom dog on Walberswick Common. *1 mile S of Southwold; common N of church.*

WESTLETON

Witch's Stone. RITUAL. Traditionally children would place a straw or handkerchief in the grating in the wall above the stone, which is in the grass close to the chancel door of Westleton church. Then they would run around the church three (or seven) times and look again at the grating. The object placed there should have disappeared; or else rattling chains would be heard. *5 miles NE of Saxmundham.*

WISSINGTON

Church. DRAGON. A fine wall-painting dating from the 13th century and depicting a dragon can be seen in the church. Since Wissington is not too many miles from *Little Cornard* (see entry), this may have inspired the tale of a dragon fight there. Other wall-paintings include the Magi asleep in bed, the Presentation in the Temple and the Nativity, St Francis preaching to the birds, and gossiping women encouraged by devils. Many country churches were similarly decorated originally, and the dramatic illustrations must have made a great impression on the illiterate country people. *7 miles SE of Sudbury.*

WITHERSFIELD

Church. DRAGON. A bench-end carving depicts a dragon being slain by a knight, perhaps St George. The dragon is particularly well portrayed, lying on its back in its death agony. *2 miles NW of Haverhill.*

WOOLPIT

Woolpit. PHANTOM WOLF; GREEN CHILDREN. Woolpit takes its name from wolf-pit, where the animals were once trapped and killed. In more recent times, a farmer saw what appeared to be a large calf emerging from a hole in the ground. In the moonlight he saw it was a wolf, and rushed out with his gun. But since he could find nothing, not even footprints, he realized he had seen a phantom wolf.

Two strange children came to Woolpit in the 12th century. They had green skins, and the villagers found them at the entrance to the wolf-pit. No one could understand their language, and they would not eat the food that was offered to them. But when they saw freshly cut beans they showed an interest, and then ate nothing but beans for a long time. The boy did not thrive and

Bench end from Withersfield church depicting a knight slaying a dragon

eventually died, but the girl adopted the local diet and lost her green colouring. When she had learnt English, people used to ask her about her former home. She said that all the people were green, and that they lived in a land without a sun, where the light was like our twilight. The two children had strayed into a cave while looking after flocks of sheep, and had been entranced by the sound of bells. After wandering for a time in the cave they had come out into bright sunlight, and had been unable to return before being captured. It is said that the girl lived for many years, and married a man from King's Lynn. This tale, for which there is no factual evidence, may stem from the medieval belief in fairyland. It is still remembered at Woolpit, where the children are depicted on the village signs. *7 miles E of Bury St Edmunds.*

A49
M5
M42
A46
M45
A6
NORTHAMPTON
WORCESTER
A44
HEREFORD
STRATFORD-
UPON-AVON
A5
M1
A38
A34
A41
GLOUCESTER
CHELTENHAM
A40
M25
LONDON
ROMSLEY
KIDDERMINSTER
HEREFORD
AND
WORCESTER
KINGTON
WORCESTER
WEOBLEY
BRINSOP
MARDEN
WIXFORD
MIDDLE LITTLETON
Avon
DORSTONE
HEREFORD
MALVERN
HILLS
STOKE
EDITH
BREDON
ACONBURY
CLODOCK
GARWAY
TEWKESBURY
Wye
DEERHURST
CHELTENHAM
GOODRICH
GLOUCESTER
CHURCHDOWN
WHITCHURCH
BIRDLIP
COTSWOLD
HILLS
Severn
BISLEY
DUNTISBOURNE
ABBOTS
MINCHINHAMPTON
CIRENCESTER
AVENING
RODMARTON
0
10
20
MILES
KILOMETRES
0
10
20
30
40

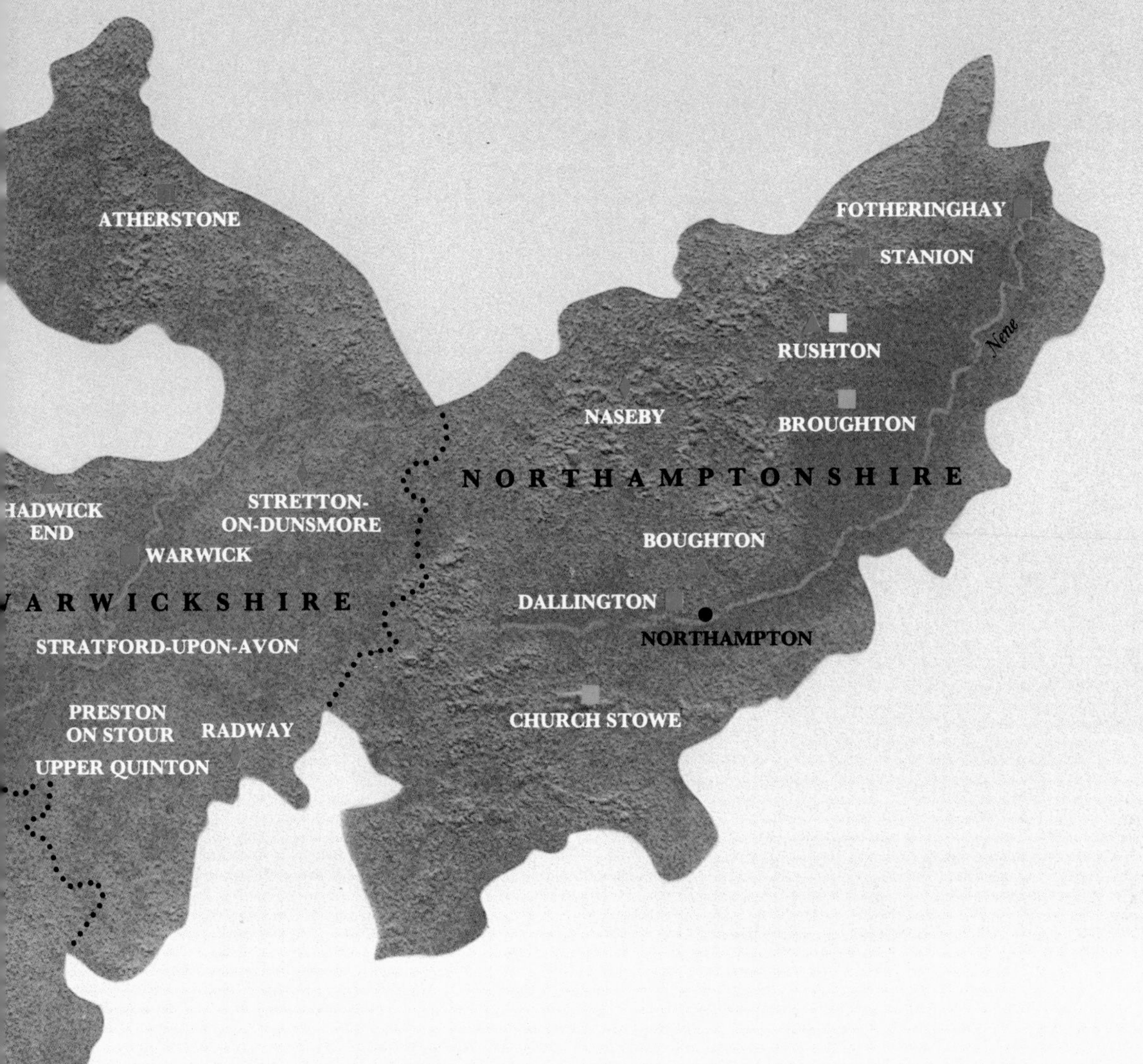

GLOUCESTERSHIRE HEREFORD AND WORCESTER NORTHAMPTONSHIRE AND WARWICKSHIRE

GLOUCESTERSHIRE

AVENING

Tingle Stone Long Cairn. MOVING STONE. When it hears the clock strike 12, the standing stone at the east end of this Neolithic chambered tomb is said to run round the field. *9 miles SW of Cirencester; Tingle Stone (tree-covered and inside stone wall) ½ mile N of village, W of lane leading N to Hampton Fields (ST 882990).*

BISLEY

Money Tump. TREASURE; GHOSTS. It was once believed that treasure was hidden in this prehistoric round barrow. It was also a haunted place: two men passing it at night saw a group of headless men. Headless men have also been seen at Giant's Stone chambered barrow not far away. *3 miles NE of Stroud; Money Tump ½ mile to S of village beside path (SO 903048); Giant's Stone ¾ mile to E, beside track (SO 918061).*

CHURCHDOWN

Church. SITING LEGEND. The church is built on the summit of a steep hill, though originally it was intended to be built in a more accessible place. However, the building materials were spirited away uphill every night, which was considered a sign that the church should be built on the hill. *3 miles NE of Gloucester centre; hill to S of village.*

DEERHURST

St Mary's Church. DRAGON; GHOST. Deerhurst has two fine Saxon churches, St Mary's church and Odda's Chapel not far away. A carving of a monster's head above the church door may have inspired the legend that a dragon terrorized Deerhurst until it was slain by a labourer, who fed it a huge trough of milk and then while it was sleeping in the sun struck off its head with his axe.

In 1968 a man went to look at the church while his wife waited in the car. She saw a woman dressed in clothes from earlier this century, who stood and gazed at her for 15 minutes before walking up the church path ahead of the organist, who had arrived by car. The husband returned before the two could have reached the church, saying he didn't like the atmosphere in the building. He had seen the organist on the path, but not the woman in old-fashioned clothes, and there was nowhere she could have hidden as she and the organist were only a few paces apart on the path when the woman in the car had last seen them. *2 miles SW of Tewkesbury.*

DUNTISBOURNE ABBOTS

Hoar Stone. MOVING STONES. The field where this prehistoric long barrow is located was once called Devil's Flights. The stones from the barrow were said to turn over or walk around the field at midnight. *5 miles NW of Cirencester; barrow beside lane 1 mile SW of village (SO 965066).*

MINCHINHAMPTON

Long Stone. HEALING STONE; IMMOVABLE STONE; PHANTOM DOG; TREASURE. It was once believed that this standing stone with two large and several small holes through it could cure children of rickets and whooping cough: they would be passed through one of the large holes. The stone was also believed to have the power of locomotion, moving round the field when it heard the clock strike midnight. On the other hand, when someone tried to pull the stone out of the ground using oxen, it could not be shifted.

A phantom black dog has been seen close to the Long Stone, while a tumulus at nearby Hyde was also haunted, and gold was said to be hidden in it.

There was formerly another healing stone at Minchinhampton, Ragged Jonathan or Holey Stone, where children could be cured of whooping cough. This stood on the common, but now seems to be lost. However there are several prehistoric earthworks still visible on the common, as well as pillow mounds which might have been artificial rabbit warrens constructed in medieval times. *3 miles SE of Stroud; Long Stone in field at Hampton Fields 1 mile SE of village (ST 884999); Hyde tumulus 1 mile NE (ST 890015); common (National Trust) to W and NW of village.*

RODMARTON

Windmill Tump. UNDERGROUND PASSAGE; TREASURE. A Neolithic cairn where the remains of adults and children were found buried, the Tump contains galleries and chambers (not now accessible), and it is from these that the belief in an underground passage probably developed. It was also said that a golden coffin was hidden in the cairn, but none was found on excavation. *5½ miles SW of Cirencester; cairn (tree-covered and enclosed in stone wall) in field S of road from Rodmarton to Cherington (ST 932973).*

TEDDINGTON

Tibble Stone. GIANT. It was the intention of this particular giant to destroy his enemy's house, and he selected a stone for the purpose. But as he was carrying it down the hill, his foot slipped and he dropped the stone. The marks of the giant's fingers are said to be visible

CALENDAR OF EVENTS

February/March: Shrove Tuesday
ATHERSTONE, Warwickshire. *Shrovetide Football:* Water-filled football used in a game going back to King John's reign in 13th century.

April/May/June (Ascension Day)
BISLEY, Gloucestershire. *Blessing of the Wells:* Seven wells dressed with flower garlands and blessed by vicar.

29 May
GUILDHALL, WORCESTER. *Oak Apple Day Ceremony:* Oak boughs decorate gates, and service is held to commemorate Charles II's return to London.

May: Spring Bank Holiday
COOPERS HILL, BIRDLIP, Gloucestershire. *Cheese Rolling:* Youths chase down steep hill after rolling cheese; originally done to maintain grazing rights.

12 October
STRATFORD-UPON-AVON, Warwickshire. *Mop Fair:* Traditionally a time for hiring labour. Whole ox roasted. Runaway Mop Fair was held on 26 October, when employees could change employer. Similar events held in WARWICK in October.

December: Sunday after 12th
BROUGHTON, Northamptonshire. *Tin Can Band:* Men parade around the village at midnight making noise to frighten off gypsies, whose magic powers were feared.

Shrovetide football at Atherstone

on it. *4 miles E of Tewkesbury; Tibble Stone in grass opposite Teddington Arms public house at crossroads of A435 and A438 NW of village.*

WINCHCOMBE

Cemetery. GHOSTS. A phantom monk has been seen walking 2 feet above the ground along the road near the cemetery. Ghostly music and chanting have also been heard from the site of the abbey church at night. *6 miles NE of Cheltenham.*

St Kenelm's Well. HOLY WELL; SAINT'S BURIAL. In Anglo-Saxon times Winchcombe was capital of the kingdom of Mercia, and an abbey was founded here by King Kenulf in AD 798. The child-king Kenelm, said to have been Kenulf's son, was murdered in the Clent Hills (see *Romsley*, Hereford and Worcester) and brought back to Winchcombe for burial. Where the bearers laid the body on the ground as they rested on the journey, a spring began to flow, and this became St Kenelm's Well. St Kenelm's Chapel was built nearby, and the saint's shrine at the abbey made Winchcombe famous, since miracles were said to occur there.

Nothing of the abbey can now be seen, as it was destroyed at the Dissolution. In 1815 two stone coffins were found near the site of the high altar, one containing the bones of a man, the other those of a child; possibly these were Kenulf and Kenelm. The relics were lost, but the coffins can still be seen in Winchcombe church. *Abbey was close to parish church, and cross marks centre of tower; not open to public. Well and chapel in hills 1 mile to SE along lane past Sudeley Castle (SP 044278).*

Sudeley Castle. GHOST. Katharine Parr, Henry VIII's last wife, once lived here and is buried here, but her ghost is not known to haunt the castle. Janet, a former housekeeper, is the identity of the ghost seen by visitors in various parts of the building. She wears a white blouse and long pink and white skirt, black shoes and a mob cap, and has been seen in the main bedroom, the 'needlework bedroom', and coming out of the Rupert Room. *SE of Winchcombe.*

HEREFORD AND WORCESTER

ACONBURY

Church. GHOST. A ghostly monk was thought to be Roger de Clifford, whose tomb is in the church. The clergy are said to have trapped his spirit in a bottle and buried it underneath the tomb, in the church wall, so that he is neither inside nor outside the church. However, it may not have immobilized him completely, since a tall, shadowy, hooded figure in flowing garments has been seen since the exorcism. *4 miles S of Hereford.*

BREDON

Bredon Hill. TREASURE; MOVING STONE; HOLY WELL. A fine hillfort from the Iron Age crowns this hill. Archaeological excavations have traced its history, and the most dramatic find was the remains of about 60 people by the gateway, the result of an attack on the fort early in the 1st century AD. A number of human skulls, probably battle trophies, had been set up on poles.

The Banbury Stone, near the tower on top of the hill (the 18th-century Parson's Folly), is said to have treasure hidden beneath it. Traditionally, when the stone hears the church clock strike 12 it goes down to the River Avon to drink. St Catherine's Well is also on the hilltop. *Bredon 3 miles NE of Tewkesbury, and Bredon Hill further 3 miles NE, crossed by footpaths from all surrounding villages.*

BRINSOP

Church. DRAGON. Brinsop is one of two places in England where St George is said to have slain the dragon (see also *Uffington*, Oxfordshire). This belief clearly arose from the fine 12th-century tympanum (carving over the doorway), which depicts the event. The dragon was said to live in Dragon's Well in a meadow south of the church. *6 miles NW of Hereford, off A480.*

CLODOCK

Church. SITING LEGEND; PHANTOM DOG. Clydawg was a local king, murdered near the River Monnow in the 6th century. While being taken away by ox-cart, the body suddenly began to weigh so heavily that the oxen could not pull it. So the saint was buried at that spot, and an oratory was built, followed later by a church.

A black dog was said to haunt a lane half a mile below the church. It would run alongside horses and vehicles before disappearing. *Close to Welsh border, 14 miles SW of Hereford.*

DORSTONE

★ **Arthur's Stone.** ARTHURIAN LEGEND; GIANT. A number of large stones which formed a Neolithic burial chamber still survive, in particular the huge capstone supported on nine uprights. Traditionally, King Arthur killed a giant here (or a king), and the giant or king, or even King Arthur himself, is buried here. A stone under the hedge, called the Quoit Stone, has hollows said to be the marks of the giant's elbows, or Arthur's knees where he knelt to pray, or quoits players' heel-marks. *5 miles E of Hay-on-Wye; Arthur's Stone in hills ¾ mile NE of Dorstone, beside lane (SO 318431).*

GARWAY

White Rocks. DEVIL. The story goes that the Devil was helping Jack o' Kent, a local 'mystery man' (who was perhaps the Welsh hero Owain Glyndŵr in hiding, or a wizard), to dam a weir on Orcop Hill with stones in order to make a fishpool. The Devil brought the stones in his apron, and while he was coming over Garway Hill the apron string broke and he dropped them all. He had to leave them, because the cock crew, and the Devil cannot stay out in daylight. *10 miles SW of Hereford; White Rocks lie on Garway Hill 2 miles to NW; hill crossed by footpaths.*

GOODRICH

Goodrich Castle. GHOSTS. In the 17th century Colonel Birch's niece Alice eloped, taking refuge in the castle. Her uncle besieged it, and as she attempted to escape with her lover, Charles Clifford, they both drowned in the River Wye. In stormy weather, it was said, their shrieks can be heard on the river, and their ghosts haunt the castle. *3 miles SW of Ross-on-Wye; open to public.*

HEREFORD

Hereford Cathedral. LEYS. Alfred Watkins, the man who in the twenties developed the theory of leys – alignments of prehistoric and other sites – was born in Hereford, and researched many leys in the county. His classic book is *The Old Straight Track* (first published 1925, and still available in paperback), in which many of his leys are described in detail. A sample alignment, linking Dinedor Camp, Hereford Cathedral and All Saints

Goodrich Castle, haunted by a pair of drowned lovers

church, Hereford, was extended by Paul Devereux and Ian Thomson to include Birley and Stretford churches (see *The Ley Guide* for details).

KIDDERMINSTER

St Mary's Church. SITING LEGEND. It was originally intended to build the parish church on rising ground on the Bewdley side of the River Stour, but every night the day's work was destroyed. So the builders moved across the river, and were able to build the church without hindrance. The old site was called Curst Field, which degenerated into Cussfield.

KINGTON

Church. GHOST; PHANTOM DOG. Thomas Vaughan, whose family home was Hergest Court, lies buried in Kington church with his wife, and their effigies can be seen in the Vaughan Chapel. Since Vaughan was traditionally believed to have been a wicked man, his ghost was troublesome after death, and many local mysteries were ascribed to 'Black Vaughan'. Twelve parsons with 12 candles met at Kington church and tried to entice him into a snuffbox, but all the candles bar one went out and the priests were afraid. The last priest continued until the spirit was in the box, having asked him before closing it where he wished to be buried. He answered, 'Anywhere, but not in the Red Sea!' So they buried him for a thousand years at the bottom of Hergest pool with a big stone on top. The real Thomas Vaughan was killed at the Battle of Banbury in 1469, and there is no evidence that he was the evil man he has become in folklore.

In the park at Hergest, two bare patches in the grass where he stood to watch the deer were called Vaughan's Footmarks. Hergest Court is said to be haunted by a phantom black dog, supposed to have been Vaughan's dog in life. The dog favoured a pond on the road from Kington - a place avoided by late-night travellers. *12 miles W of Leominster; Hergest Court 1¼ miles SW of Kington; not open to public.*

King Arthur's Cave, near Whitchurch

MARDEN

St Ethelbert's Well. HOLY WELL; MERMAID. In AD 794 King Ethelbert was murdered, allegedly on the orders of King Offa, and buried at Marden. This well, now inside the church, marks the spot where the body is said to have been buried before being taken to Hereford. In Hereford itself, the site of St Ethelbert's Well (now dry) is marked on Castle Green near the cathedral. King Offa erected a shrine to the memory of the dead king, and the cathedral now stands on the site. The well at Marden is one of the few holy wells to be found inside rather than outside a church.

It was said that a bell from a previous church at Marden fell into the nearby River Lugg, where it was seized by a mermaid who refused to return it. The parishioners tried to retrieve it while she was asleep, but one man spoke too loudly and she awoke. She hid the bell in a pool, where, it is said, it can still sometimes be heard tolling underwater. *On E bank of River Lugg, 4 miles N of Hereford.*

MIDDLE LITTLETON

Cleeve Hill Tumulus. DEVIL. A large stone atop the prehistoric tumulus is probably a cross base. It was said to have been thrown by the Devil from Meon Hill, when he was aiming at Evesham Abbey. The sound of the abbey bells apparently caused the stone to fly off course. *3 miles NE of Evesham; several footpaths cross Cleeve Hill to W, passing tumulus (SP 071470).*

ROMSLEY

St Kenelm's Well. HOLY WELL. This spring began to flow when the body of Kenelm, the boy-king of Mercia, was lifted from his hillside grave where he was murdered in the Clent Hills in AD 819. It was carried to *Winchcombe* (see Gloucestershire) for burial. St Kenelm's church, close to the well, dates from the 12th century, and is a good example of a church being built where a sacred spring was already in existence. The legend of King Kenelm is not based on fact. *Romsley church 1 mile NW of village, itself 5 miles N of Bromsgrove; footpath leads to well behind church.*

STOKE EDITH

St Edith's Well and Church. HOLY WELL; DEVIL. According to legend, St Edith was building the church and she prayed for water, as she had to carry it from a stream; a spring began to flow where she knelt. The water was for many centuries used for healing purposes. It was said that by walking slowly round the church seven times at midnight, and reciting the Lord's Prayer backwards, you could raise the Devil - you only had to look through the keyhole in the church door to see him. *6 miles E of Hereford; well can be seen in bank below church.*

WEOBLEY

Church. DEVIL. The tradition was that anyone walking slowly seven times round the preaching cross in the churchyard and saying the Lord's Prayer backwards would see the Devil. *8 miles SW of Leominster.*

WHITCHURCH

★ King Arthur's Cave. ARTHURIAN LEGEND; UNDERGROUND PASSAGE. Excavations have found the bones of late Ice Age animals in this cave, including mammoths and woolly rhinoceros. The cave was occupied from about 25,000 BC up until Roman times. It is unlikely that King Arthur ever came here, but in folklore it is said that when he was on the run from his enemies he hid his treasure here, and Merlin laid a spell on the cave so that the treasure would never be found. It was also believed that an underground passage ran from the cave to New Weir. *Whitchurch 4 miles NE of Monmouth; cave in woods 1 mile to S, on N side of River Wye, reached along footpath from NE (SO 545155).*

NORTHAMPTONSHIRE

BOUGHTON

St John's Church. GHOST; MAZE; HOLY WELL. A ghost which is said to haunt the ruined church at Christmas time has been identified as 'Captain Slash', an early 19th-century gang-leader. There used to be a turf maze on the green close to the church, and every June, when a three-day fair was held, people would follow the path of the 'Shepherd's Ring' or 'Shepherd's Race'. Sadly, the maze was destroyed during the First World War. But a holy well still survives in the churchyard: the water from St John's Spring was formerly used for baptisms in the church. *Boughton 3 miles N of Northampton; church at Boughton Green ¾ mile E of village, and well in steep bank at S corner of E end.*

CHURCH STOWE

Church. SITING LEGEND. Eight times the Saxon church builders tried to proceed, but each time the day's work was demolished. Finally they began building on a new site indicated by a supernatural creature 'summat bigger nor a hog', and they were left alone. The parish has the name of Stowe Nine Churches. *5 miles SE of Daventry.*

DALLINGTON

Church. GHOSTS. An unusual psychic manifestation occurred in this church in 1907, when two girls were visiting it at dusk. One girl went into the building, but

Fotheringhay church, where ghostly martial music from the Middle Ages has been heard

came out again immediately. The second girl went in to investigate, and saw a church full of kneeling people – but they were insubstantial, as if made of bubbles. *On NW outskirts of Northampton.*

The Triangular Lodge at Rushton

FOTHERINGHAY

★ Fotheringhay Castle and Church. GHOSTS. There was once a castle at Fotheringhay, though now all that can be seen is a grassy mound near the river. It is a place rich with memories, for here Mary Queen of Scots was beheaded in 1587. Close by is the stately building of Fotheringhay church, dating from the 15th century and with many interesting features. Not least of them is the ghostly music that has been heard here by many people: it sounds like drums and trumpets, and may date back to the time of Agincourt. Edward, Duke of York, was killed at Agincourt in 1415 and buried in Fotheringhay church. *9 miles SW of Peterborough.*

NASEBY

Battlefield. GHOSTS. Charles I suffered a severe defeat at the Battle of Naseby in 1645, but had he heeded the pleas of a ghost it could have been averted. He was staying at the Wheatsheaf Hotel in Daventry when the ghost of an old friend, the Earl of Strafford, appeared and pleaded with him not to fight the Roundheads but to continue his march northwards. Inclined personally to accept this advice, Charles instead gave in to his generals, with disastrous results. For about a century afterwards, the fighting was said to have been re-enacted in ghostly form in the sky above the battlefield. Although this no longer occurs, the area is said to be still haunted. Early in 1989 it was decided to build a new main road across the southern side of the battlefield, and the disturbance to this quiet rural area may well reactivate any quiescent spirits. *6 miles SW of Market Harborough; battlefield 1 mile N of village, along lane to Sibbertoft, and marked by monument.*

RUSHTON

The Mount and Barford Bridge. GHOST. Along the A6003 between Corby and Kettering, near Barford Bridge a mile east of Rushton, there was formerly an ancient burial mound called the Mount. When it was excavated before being flattened in 1964, skeletons were found. Between the site of the Mount and Barford Bridge numerous people have seen a ghostly monk who seems to be carrying something in his arms, and several have had to brake hard to avoid hitting the figure walking across the road.

Triangular Lodge. MAGIC; UNDERGROUND PASSAGE. This strange building in the grounds of Rushton Hall was built by Sir Thomas Tresham in 1597. It was all based on the number three, and has three sides, three floors, trefoil windows and so on, but it also incorporates much deeper occult and numerological themes. There was a legend of an underground passage starting at the Lodge, which was entered by a fiddler who accepted a payment of £50 to explore it. He disappeared, and searchers found a hat and candle beside a bottomless pit. Later his wife had a letter from her husband who said that he had fallen all the way to Australia. It turned out to be a plot to obtain more money, the fiddler having slipped out of the tunnel and gone into hiding. *By road to Desborough; open to public.*

The Civil War battlefield of Edge Hill, near Radway

STANION

Church. GIANT COW. A 6-foot bone in the church was said to be a rib from a gigantic dun cow which provided endless milk. But when a witch appeared with a sieve and ordered the cow to fill it, the valiant animal died of exhaustion. The bone is in all likelihood from a whale, brought back by a sailor. *2 miles SE of Corby.*

WARWICKSHIRE

ALCESTER

Church. GHOST. At the turn of the century, a woman cleaning in the church saw someone standing in the shadows by the tomb of Sir Fulke Greville. She thought it

Warwick Castle, scene of many hauntings

was a visitor, but as he stepped forward she was surprised to see him dressed in 16th-century clothes - and with the same sharply cut beard as Sir Fulke's effigy sported! As she gazed at him he began to dissolve, starting at the head, and the horrified witness fainted. *8 miles NW of Stratford-upon-Avon.*

CHADWICK END

A41 Road. GHOSTS. In the 1960s, police officers driving along the main road in the small hours saw several nuns walking along the road, and they nearly ran into them because their black habits made them difficult to see. The police stopped, intending to go back and speak to them. The men saw the nuns walk into the grounds of Chadwick Manor, and followed them, but at the entrance to the house they had gone. Other officers called in to assist also saw the nuns walking along the road, a mile south of the Manor, and on returning along the road they too found no sign of them. *On Warwickshire-West Midlands border, 7 miles NW of Warwick.*

HASELOR

Alcock's Arbour. TREASURE; DEVIL. A robber named Alcock was said to have lived in a cave at the base of this conical hill, and he kept his riches inside the cave in an iron-bound chest with three locks, guarded by a fierce cockerel. An Oxford scholar managed to open two of the locks, but the cockerel attacked him as he worked on the third. So the chest still lies in the cave, accessible only to the person who can bring one of Alcock's bones.

An alternative name for the hill, the Devil's Bag of Nuts, came from the story that on 21 September, Devil's Nutting Day, he collected a sackful and was returning home when the Virgin Mary suddenly appeared and told him to drop the sack. He did so, and it became a hill. *2 miles E of Alcester; hill ½ mile to S, S of A422, inside copse.*

PRESTON ON STOUR

Alscot Park. GHOSTS. A man is said to haunt the main road by the entrance to Alscot Park; he appears at midnight, walking across the road and disappearing into a wall. The novelist Ursula Bloom saw him when she was a young girl cycling home from Stratford with her mother. She nearly ran over him, but didn't realize until later that he had been a ghost. He was said to be a local farmer who died in 1882 when swept from his horse by a low branch while riding at a gallop past the park. Alscot House itself is also haunted. *Entrance to Alscot Park beside A34, 3 miles S of Stratford-upon-Avon.*

RADWAY

Edge Hill Battlefield. GHOSTS; PHANTOM DOG. A Civil War battle was fought here on 23 October 1642, and two months later, on Christmas Eve, shepherds on the hill saw a ghostly battle in the sky. It was repeated on following nights, but not in subsequent years, though some people have reported hearing the sounds of battle on 23 October. Phantom horses, and other ghosts possibly connected with the battle, have been seen in the area in recent years.

A calf-sized black dog also haunts the area of Radway Grange. *Edge Hill 6 miles NW of Banbury; battlefield (Ministry of Defence property) in valley below, between Kineton and Radway, and best seen from hill.*

STRETTON-ON-DUNSMORE

Dunsmore Heath. GIANT COW; PHANTOM LORRY. The Dun Cow milked dry by a witch at Mitchells Fold stone circle (see *Priestweston*, Shropshire) came east to Warwickshire, where it was killed by Guy, Earl of Warwick, on Dunsmore Heath some time in the 10th century. In some respects the cow was similar to a dragon, for it terrorized the countryside, killing men and animals. The hero Guy shot at it with arrows first of all, but they could not penetrate its thick hide, so he took his axe and, locating its weak point under the ear, managed to dispatch it. There is still a Dun Cow inn at Dunchurch, and other place-names commemorate the legend. Later Guy became a hermit and lived in a cave at Guy's Cliffe; an 8-foot statue of him, hewn out of the living rock and thought to be six hundred years old, still stands in the chapel of the now-ruined Guy's Cliffe house.

A 3-mile stretch of the A45 road crossing Dunsmore Heath and centring on Knightlow Hill was said to be haunted by a phantom lorry, which caused accidents when vehicles swerved to avoid it. One witness was an ex-policeman who lived nearby, and on that particular winter's night in the early 1950s he was helping at a traffic accident. Bonfires had been lit to warn approaching vehicles, but one lorry drove straight past, and as the witness turned he saw that the fires were visible through it. Nor did the lorry crash into the vehicle pile-up. *Guy's Cliffe 1 mile N of Warwick centre, beside road to Kenilworth; Dunsmore Heath 6–8 miles SE of Coventry centre, crossed by A45.*

UPPER QUINTON

Meon Hill. DEVIL; WITCHCRAFT; PHANTOM DOG; GHOSTS; PHANTOM COW. A lump of earth said to have been thrown by the Devil at Evesham Abbey was deflected by the prayers of the Bishop of Worcester: it fell short and formed Meon Hill. It was here on the lower slopes of the hill on St Valentine's Day 1945 that a farm labourer called Charles Walton was murdered, impaled by his hayfork and with a cross slashed on his chest and throat. The mystery was never solved, but a ritual murder was suspected. In 1929 Walton saw the black dog of Meon Hill eight times; on the ninth occasion he saw the ghost of a headless woman, and next day he heard of his sister's death. The hill was also said to be haunted by the Mickleton Hooter, a ghostly cow so-called because of the noise it made, and said to be somehow related to the Dun Cow killed by Guy of Warwick (see *Stretton-on-Dunsmore*). *Meon Hill 9 miles E of Evesham; clearly visible from surrounding lanes, and footpaths from Upper Quinton and Mickleton cross lower slopes.*

WARWICK

★ Warwick Castle. GHOSTS. It is not surprising to learn that the fine castle is haunted, for so many dramatic events must have occurred there since William the Conqueror built the first motte-and-bailey castle in 1068. Sir Fulke Greville, Lord Brooke, was granted the castle in 1604, and having spent thousands of pounds restoring it came back to haunt it, especially his rooms in the Water Gate Tower. His ghost has also been seen in the church where he is buried (see *Alcester*). Mysterious footsteps have been heard in the Japanese corridor.

WIXFORD

George's Elm. SAINT'S BURIAL. St George was said locally to have been buried here with an elm stake through his heart (the usual fate of suicides, not saints!). An elm tree grew from the stake, and when cut it would bleed. The tree is now gone, but the site remains. *8 miles W of Stratford-upon-Avon; site is in George's Elm Lane, between Wixford and Bidford.*

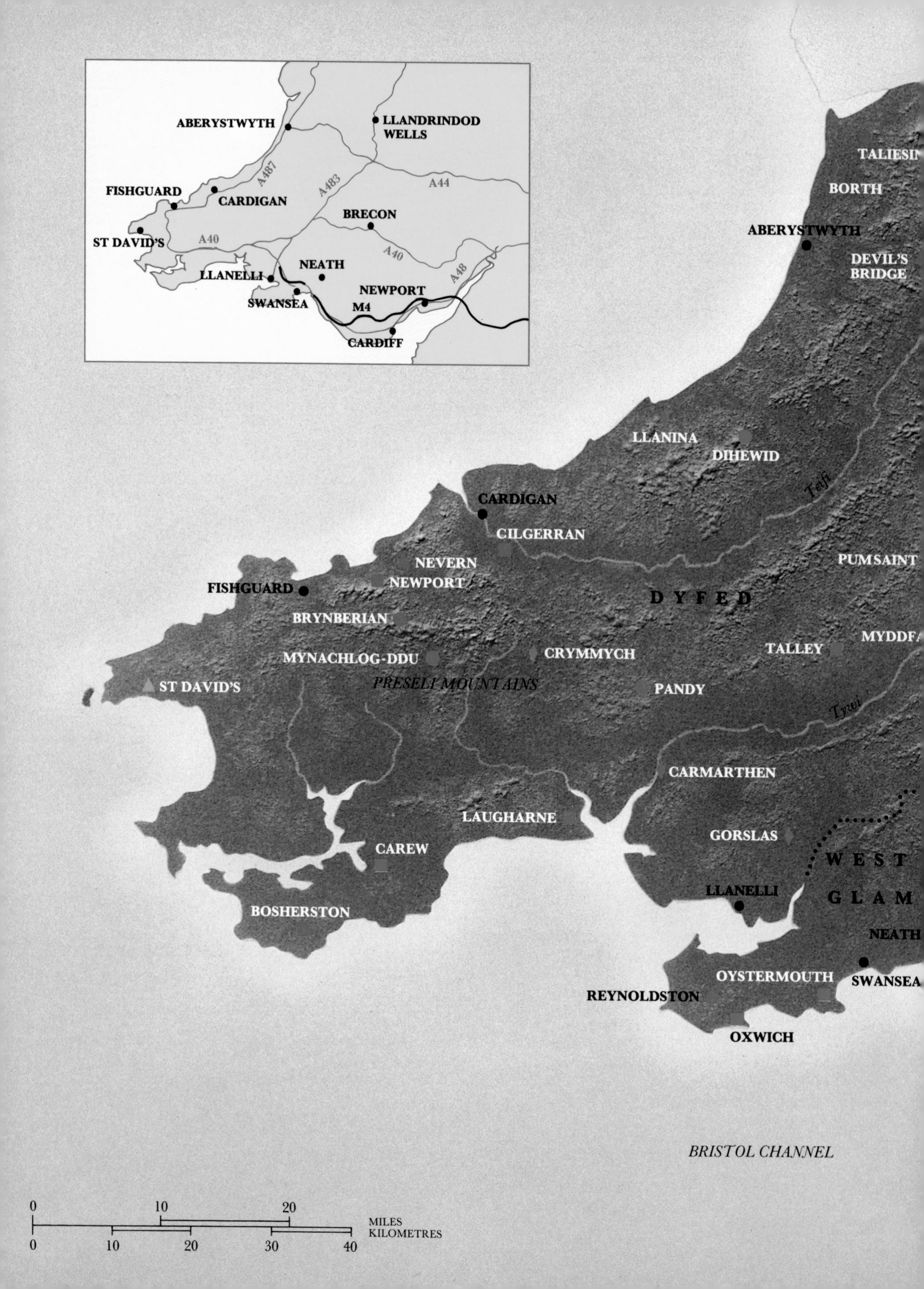

ABERYSTWYTH
LLANDRINDOD WELLS
A487
A483
A44
FISHGUARD
CARDIGAN
BRECON
ST DAVID'S
A40
A40
NEATH
A48
LLANELLI
NEWPORT
SWANSEA
M4
CARDIFF
TALIESIN
BORTH
ABERYSTWYTH
DEVIL'S BRIDGE
LLANINA
DIHEWID
Teifi
CARDIGAN
CILGERRAN
NEVERN
NEWPORT
FISHGUARD
PUMSAINT
DYFED
BRYNBERIAN
MYDDFA
TALLEY
CRYMMYCH
MYNACHLOG-DDU
PRESELI MOUNTAINS
ST DAVID'S
PANDY
Tywi
CARMARTHEN
LAUGHARNE
GORSLAS
CAREW
WEST
GLAM
LLANELLI
BOSHERSTON
NEATH
OYSTERMOUTH
SWANSEA
REYNOLDSTON
OXWICH
BRISTOL CHANNEL
0
10
20
MILES
KILOMETRES
0
10
20
30
40

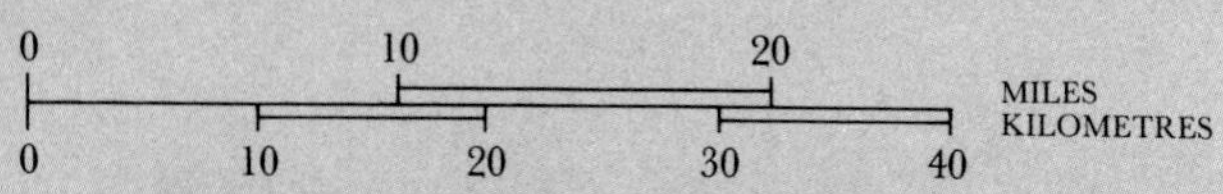

SOUTH WALES

ELAN VILLAGE
OLD RADNOR
LLANDRINDOD WELLS
Wye
LLANDEILO GRABAN
POWYS (SOUTH)
LLOWES
BRECON
GROSMONT
LLANGORSE
BRECON BEACONS
LLANGUA
ABERGAVENNY
TRELLECH
GWENT
GLYN-NEATH
GAN
MID GLAMORGAN
ABERTILLERY
TINTERN
KILGWRRWG
RISCA
ARGAM
CILFYNYDD
PENHOW
NEWPORT
CAERLEON
LLANGYNWYD
CAERPHILLY
PENCOED
Severn
KENFIG
TONGWYNLAIS
OGMORE
ST LYTHANS
CARDIFF
PENTRE MEYRICK
SOUTH GLAMORGAN

DYFED

BORTH

Cors Fochno. HAG. The marshy land at the mouth of the River Dovey was said to be the home of a hag known as Yr Hen Wrach (the Old Hag). An old woman who saw her eating her supper of bog beans and toadstools said she was 7 feet tall, thin and bony, with yellow skin and long black hair; her teeth were also black. When the old woman wished the hag goodnight, she jumped up, hissed and vanished. She was believed to be responsible for bringing sickness to people living nearby, by blowing into their faces on misty nights. *NE of Borth as far as A487; B4353 crosses N side of bog; footpath on S side.*

BOSHERSTON

★ **St Govan's Chapel and Well.** ARTHURIAN LEGEND; HOLY WELL. Sir Gawain's adventures with the Green Knight form one of the tales in the Arthurian tradition, and it is possible that 'Govan' is in fact Gawain. At any rate, nothing is known of any saint named Govan. Gawain was believed to have been buried on the Pembrokeshire coast, and a possible location for his tomb is in the tiny chapel at St Govan's Head, underneath the altar. There may have been a religious building here as early as the 5th century, although the present chapel is 13th-century. A flight of steps cut into the rock leads down to the chapel in a cleft in the rocks; the steps are said to be uncountable. Inside the chapel the legendary St Govan concealed himself in a vertical cleft in the rock, which closed around him while his enemies searched for him. A wish made while standing in the cleft facing the wall will be granted if you do not change your mind before turning round. The saint's well is below the chapel. *Bosherston 4 miles S of Pembroke; chapel 1 mile further S at St Govan's Head.*

BRYNBERIAN

Bedd-yr-Afanc (Water Monster's Grave). MONSTER. The monster was said to have been caught in a pool near Brynberian bridge and taken up the mountain for burial. His grave is in fact a prehistoric chambered tomb. *9 miles E of Fishguard; grave ¼ mile SE of Brynberian (SN 109345) on open moorland.*

CAREW

Carew Castle. GHOST. A woman in white seen wandering in the ruins by visitors may be the ghost of Nest, daughter of the last king of South Wales, who was abducted from her husband and her home here in the 11th century. *4 miles NE of Pembroke; open to public.*

CARMARTHEN

Merlin's Hill (Bryn Myrddin). ARTHURIAN LEGEND. Merlin the wizard, who lived in the 6th century and played a part in the stories of King Arthur, was said to have been born in Carmarthen. An old oak tree in the town was known as Merlin's Oak and could not be cut down because of the belief that, when it was destroyed, Carmarthen would fall down too. However in 1978 the dead tree's stump was removed because it was a traffic hazard, and fortunately Carmarthen is still there. North-east of the town is Merlin's Hill, where the wizard is said to lie sleeping in a cave. If you listen with your ear to the ground at twilight, you might hear his groans and the rattling of his chains. *3 miles NE of Carmarthen, N of A40.*

CRYMYCH

Freni-Fawr. FAIRIES. A boy tending sheep on the hill called Freni-Fach is said to have looked across to the higher mountain of Freni-Fawr and seen fairies dancing there. They beckoned to him to join them, so he went over and cautiously stepped inside their circle. Then he heard the most beautiful music and was give wonderful food to eat. He could do whatever he liked in fairyland, except drink from a certain well in the garden. But his curiosity proved too much for him, and one day he dipped his hand into the well and drank the water. The fairy palace vanished and he found himself alone and shivering on the cold mountainside. *8 miles S of Cardigan and 1½ miles NE of Crymych; crossed by footpath from NW.*

DEVIL'S BRIDGE

Devil's Bridge. DEVIL. Famous for the River Mynach waterfalls and rocky gorges, Devil's Bridge also has three bridges, one of which gives the village its name. The bridges were built one above the other, the lowest by monks possibly in the 12th century, the middle one in 1753 and the upper one in 1901. The legend of the Devil's Bridge dates back to the time before there were any bridges here. A country girl lost her cow and saw it on the other side of the gorge. A dark man said he would build her a bridge overnight if he could have the first living creature that crossed it. He was the Devil, and he thought the girl would be the first across, going to fetch her cow. She agreed to his terms, and the bridge was duly built, whereupon the girl took out a bread crust, showed it to her dog and threw it across the bridge. The dog raced after it and the Devil realized he had been outwitted. (For a very similar tale, see *Kirkby Lonsdale*, Cumbria.) *10 miles SE of Aberystwyth; 3 bridges viewed from steep steps down to Mynach gorge; pay to enter.*

DIHEWID

Castell Moeddyn. FAIRIES. The Little People or Tylwyth Teg were believed to visit this prehistoric hillfort in May, dressed in green. *Dihewid 4 miles SE of Aberaeron, and Castell Moeddyn 2 miles S; track from lane to Cribyn passes through Moyddin Fawr just N of hillfort (SN 484520).*

GORSLAS

Llyn Llech Owen. DROWNED LAND. The story is that a man called Owen used to get water from a well which he kept covered with a large flagstone. He was always careful to replace it, but one day he forgot. After he had ridden some distance towards his home, he looked back and saw that the well had overflowed and was covering the land with water. He quickly rode around the edge of the flood and this stopped the well overflowing any further. Had he not done so, a much greater area would have been flooded. The lake called Llyn Llech Owen (the Lake of Owen's Flagstone) was the lasting result of his forgetfulness. *Gorslas 7 miles SW of Llandeilo; lake ¾ mile N, and lane to W passes close to lake shore.*

LLANINA

Cerrig Ina. ANCIENT CHURCH; MERMAID. The present church on the cliff only dates from the last century, but offshore is a group of rocks, Cerrig Ina or Ina's Stones, which mark the place where the original Llanina (Ina's church) stood. The story is that it was built by King Ina of England in thanksgiving for being rescued from drowning in the 8th century by a local fisherman and his daughter.

Traditionally, a mermaid used to sit on the rocks. One day she got entangled in the nets of some fishermen, and after being rescued by them she warned them of an approaching storm. They were able to get back safely to shore, but others were drowned. *1 mile E of New Quay.*

MYDDFAI

Llyn-y-Fan-Fach. FAIRIES. A farmer's son who used to graze his cattle on the hills around the lake is said to have seen a beautiful girl sitting on the water combing her long hair. She agreed to marry him, but said that if he were to strike her a total of three times the marriage would end.

St Govan's Chapel, among the rocks at Bosherston

They lived together happily for many years in a farm just outside Myddfai. Then, one day, he tapped her jokingly on the shoulder; she reminded him of the marriage condition, but in future years it happened twice more, so she took her cattle and disappeared with them under the waters of Llyn-y-Fan-Fach. Although she never saw her husband again, she did reappear to her three sons, who would go to the lake and gaze into its depths. She told them of herbal remedies using local plants, and they became famous physicians in Wales. The skills were handed down from generation to generation until the last descendant died a hundred years ago. *Llyn-y-Fan-Fach 5 miles S of Myddfai, itself 3 miles SE of Llandovery, and in wild mountain country not easily accessible by road; but possible with care to drive along lane from Llanddeusant village as far as Blaenau Farm, and then walk remaining 1¼ miles.*

The 'bleeding' yew tree in Nevern churchyard

MYNACHLOG-DDU

Bedd Arthur. ARTHURIAN LEGEND. A prehistoric hilltop cairn in the Preseli Mountains is named Arthur's Grave, though there is no explanation why he should have been buried here. A natural rock outcrop a short way to the east is called Carn Arthur, and also here is Carn Meini, from where the Stonehenge bluestones are said to have come. *11 miles SE of Fishguard; cairn 1½ miles NW of Mynachlog-Ddu, with W–E footpath passing close by (SN 130325).*

NEVERN

★ **Churchyard.** CUCKOO LEGEND; BLEEDING TREE. Close to the church stands a fine carved Celtic cross, St Brynach's Cross. On 7 April, the saint's day, the first cuckoo of spring was said to perch on the cross and sing. Mass was delayed until the bird arrived, and one year, after much waiting, it appeared and had scarcely landed on the cross before it dropped dead of exhaustion. One of the yew trees in the churchyard exudes a reddish sap which has led to the belief that it bleeds. The explanation is said to be that a monk executed in the churchyard swore that he was innocent, and that the tree would bleed in proof of his innocence. *8 miles NE of Fishguard.*

PANDY

Crug-y-dyrn (Crug Ederyn). DRAGON. Traditionally said to be the burial place of the prince or chieftain Ederyn, this barrow was also home to a winged serpent or dragon, which used to be seen on or near to it. *Village 7 miles NW of Carmarthen; barrow 1 mile NW of Pandy beside lane E of B4299 (SN 293250).*

PUMSAINT

Dolaucothi Gold Mines. SLEEPING SAINTS. Archaeological excavation has revealed much evidence of gold mining on this site during Roman times, and these early workings can still be seen. Most impressive are the entrances to the mining tunnels, where, according to legend, five saints are sleeping. The Five Sleepers were the sons of Cynyr Fârfdrwch, whose brother worked for King Arthur. The men sheltered in the tunnels during a thunderstorm, lay down and fell asleep. Their first 'pillow' is a stone that now stands upright near the lane. It has four hollows in it, said to have been worn by the pressure of their heads (where did the fifth saint rest?). They will not awaken until King Arthur reappears, or the throne of St David (in Dyfed) is filled by a genuine and faithful apostolic bishop. One day the Devil led a local girl, Gwen of Dolaucothi, into the tunnels to see the Five Sleepers, but she was not a welcome visitor and in punishment the sleepers have kept her imprisoned with them. In stormy weather she is allowed to roam free; then her shape can be seen near the tunnel entrances, and her cries heard echoing around the crags. *1 mile E of Pumsaint, itself 8 miles NW of Llandovery; open to public (National Trust); Five Saints' Stone beside lane between two car parks.*

ST DAVID'S

St David's Cathedral, Ruined Chapel and St Non's Well. SPEAKING STONE; SAINT'S CHAPEL; HOLY WELL. The River Alun passes close to the cathedral and is crossed by small bridges. One of these near the west front replaced a stone called Llechllafar (Speaking Stone), across which no dead bodies could be carried; once, when this was about to happen, the stone spoke out and split in two. Merlin prophesied that a king of England, returning from conquering Ireland, would die on this stone, wounded by a red-haired man. The king was believed to

Devil's Bridge, where, according to legend, a local girl outwitted the Devil

be Henry II, but he spoke solemnly to the stone and was able to cross it safely.

Wales's patron saint, St David, was reputedly born close to the town that bears his name, at the site of a now-ruined chapel by the sea, dedicated to his mother, St Non or Nonna. There are slight remains of a stone circle in the chapel field, and a holy well close by, showing that this was an early sacred site. The well water was used for centuries for its healing properties, and the well is still venerated today. Ghostly hymn-singing is said to be heard in the chapel ruins on the nights before and after St David's Day (1 March). *Well and chapel ½ mile S of St David's, at end of lane to St Non's Bay; chapel in field to W of well.*

CALENDAR OF EVENTS

May: Spring Bank Holiday
LAUGHARNE, Dyfed. *Common Walk:* Held every third year (1987, 1990 etc.), this is a 'Beating the Bounds' walk taking about 8 hours and covering about 26 miles.

May: last week, during spring festival
NEWPORT, Dyfed. *Cnapan:* Ancient ball game played between teams from Newport and Nevern.

August: third Friday
NEWPORT, Dyfed. *Beating the Bounds:* Children forgetting correct names of boundary stones are beaten (lightly).

End August
CILGERRAN, Dyfed. *Coracle Races:* This ancient design of boat, used since the Bronze Age, is now rarely seen, but a few fishermen still use coracles on the Teifi, Taf and Tywi rivers, and annual races are held on the Teifi.

24 December until 6 January
LLANGYNWYD and PENCOED, Mid Glamorgan. *Mari Lwyd:* Once a well-known custom in South Wales, but now seen only in a few places. A decorated horse's head is carried from house to house, with singing and dancing, food and drink, and battles in Welsh verse.

Mari Lwyd at Llangynwyd

TALIESIN

Bedd Taliesin (Taliesin's Grave). LEGENDARY GRAVE. The 6th-century poet Taliesin was said to be buried in this prehistoric cairn, and anyone sleeping on it for a night would either go mad or become a poet. *Taliesin 8 miles NE of Aberystwyth; Bedd Taliesin ¾ mile E, beside junction of two lanes (SN 672912).*

TALLEY

Talley Abbey. UNDERGROUND PASSAGE; GHOST. According to legend, an underground passage links the ruined abbey with the manor house, Talley House. A ghost of a cloaked man seen in Talley House may be a monk from the abbey. *6 miles N of Llandeilo; open to public.*

GWENT

ABERGAVENNY

Skirrid Mountain (Ysgyryd Fawr). HOLY PLACE. This was believed to be a holy mountain, and until the 17th century on Michaelmas Eve pilgrims would visit the chapel dedicated to St Michael which stood on the summit. A hollow with two upright stones is all that remains of the chapel. At the northern end of the mountain is a notch or cleft said to be the result of an earthquake at the Crucifixion. Soil from the area near the chapel was taken to sprinkle on coffins up until the early 19th century, and scattered on farmland to bring good luck. *3 miles NE of Abergavenny; accessible by footpath (National Trust).*

ABERTILLERY

Llanhilleth Mountain. GHOST (WITCH). The Old Woman of the Mountain was once feared in these parts. She wore a four-cornered hat and ash-coloured clothes with an apron thrown across her shoulder, and carried a pot or wooden can. Anyone who heard her cry, 'Wow up!', knew she was about. She was thought to have been a witch who led travellers astray even when they knew the road. *1 mile SE of Abertillery, crossed by lanes linking Llanhilleth and Abersychan.*

CAERLEON

★ **Roman Amphitheatre.** ARTHURIAN LEGEND. It was the 12th-century Geoffrey of Monmouth, in his *History of the Kings of Britain*, who located King Arthur's court at Caerleon – probably because there were impressive remains of ancient buildings there. In his day, the Roman amphitheatre was covered with earth and sometimes

Tintern Abbey

called the Round Table. Now it has been excavated, and is the best example in Britain. *2 miles NE of Newport centre.*

GROSMONT

Church. JACK O'KENT; DEVIL. Jack o'Kent was a famous local hero with magical skills who sold his soul to the Devil. He lived in the Grosmont area, and when he died they buried him under the south wall of the church so that he would be neither inside nor outside the church, and so the Devil would not be able to claim him. An old effigy in the church was said to be that of Jack o'Kent. Before he died, he directed that his liver and lights should be stuck on three iron spikes on the church tower, and he prophesied that a raven and a dove would fight over them. If the dove won, it would show that his soul was saved. *10 miles NW of Monmouth.*

KILGWRRWG

Church. SITING LEGEND. The little church, very isolated in the middle of a field a long way from any settlement, owes its location to a sign given to the builders, who sited it where two white heifers lay on a mound. It is very likely that this was a pagan sacred site. *5 miles NW of Chepstow and 1¼ miles SW of Devauden (ST 463984).*

LLANGUA

Church. FAIRIES. Two people passing the church at night heard music and saw dozens of fairies dancing in the meadows behind the church. After the dance they went over a bridge into a wood. *On Gwent–Hereford and Worcester border, 11 miles NW of Monmouth.*

Caerleon's Roman amphitheatre, associated in legend with King Arthur

PENHOW

Penhow Castle. GHOST. Privately inhabited and recently restored, the fortified house has a ghost, a young girl wearing a blue-grey apron who has been seen scurrying from the Great Hall as if she were a maid on an urgent errand. Several visitors have seen her. *Beside A48 between Newport and Chepstow, 7 miles E of Newport; open to public.*

RISCA

Twm Barlwm. GHOSTLY MUSIC; BURIED MANSION. A castle mound and earthworks of a prehistoric fort show that this 1400-foot mountain was occupied at various times. Sounds like organ music have been heard on the summit by many people. On the eastern slope, not far from the reservoir, is the Pool of Avarice, a deep pool in winter and a damp hollow in summer. It was said that a great house which stood here was buried in a landslip after the mistress of the house refused food to a starving relative. *5 miles NW of Newport; accessible by footpath from Cwrt Henllys or from Cwmcarn scenic forest drive.*

TINTERN

Tintern Abbey. UNDERGROUND PASSAGE; GHOST. The impressive ruins dominate the Wye Valley at Tintern. An underground passage was said to extend from the abbey to Trellech, 3 miles to the north-west, and the story is that nuns used it to go to bathe in a medicinal pool, presumably St Anne's Well (see *Trellech*). It is an unlikely tale, as there were no nuns at Tintern! A ghostly monk is sometimes seen kneeling near one of the western arches; he vanishes when people approach. *4 miles N of Chepstow; open to public.*

TRELLECH

Harold's Stones. JACK O' KENT; DEVIL; BATTLE. Jack o'Kent (see *Grosmont*) is said to have thrown these stones, from Beacon Hill to the east, in a throwing match with the Devil. Another story is that they commemorate a battle against the Welsh won by Harold Godwinson, King of England, in the 11th century; all the men killed in the battle are said to have been buried in the huge mound called Tump Terret, in a farmyard in the village. Of course the stones were here long before that, but their original purpose is unknown. A 17th-century sundial now inside the church depicts the legend with carvings of the stones, the tump and the holy well (see below). *5 miles S of Monmouth; stones in field to SW of village beside B4293.*

St Anne's Well/Virtuous Well. HOLY WELL. Still in fine condition, this well was once one of nine in the area, each curing different illnesses. Wishes were also made at St Anne's Well: when a pebble was dropped into the water, a plentiful uprush of bubbles signified that the wish would be granted; a few bubbles meant a delay; none meant a failed wish. *In field beside lane just SE of village (SO 503051).*

MID GLAMORGAN

CAERPHILLY

Caerphilly Castle. GHOSTS; HAG. A Green Lady, with goggle eyes in a large head, wearing green robes and a long floating green veil, was said to haunt the ramparts, sometimes accompanied by ghostly soldiers in chainmail. The pools close to the castle were frequented by the Gwrach-y-Rhibyn, a hag with bat-like wings and long black hair, who could be heard moaning and wailing. *Open to public.*

CILFYNYDD

Cwmheldeg. GHOST. The wooded slopes above the Nant Caedudwg brook are said to be haunted by a White Lady. In 1968 the editor of a local newspaper saw what appeared to be a figure on horseback, and in recent years people have seen 'a white form in front of a tree', a 'white figure' moving in the trees, 'the shape of a head against a tree', and a luminous being in a white cloak. *2 miles NE of Pontypridd; woods N of village reached along lane E off A470 and then footpath along stream.*

KENFIG

Kenfig Burrows and Kenfig Pool. DROWNED FOREST; BURIED TOWN. There have been considerable changes to the coastline of Glamorgan over the centuries, and at Kenfig storms are said to have caused tidal waves which submerged a forest stretching from Kenfig to Mumbles - in other words, Swansea Bay was once dry land. There was a town at Kenfig, but it is now covered with sand following storms in the 16th and early 17th centuries. According to legend, Kenfig is submerged in Kenfig Pool as supernatural vengeance for a murder. *3 miles NW of Porthcawl; footpaths W from present Kenfig village cross Burrows, passing Kenfig Pool.*

OGMORE

Ogmore Castle. TREASURE; GHOST. Treasure was said to be hidden in the castle ruins, guarded by a White Lady ghost. She once showed it to a man who spoke to her, and gave him half the guineas in the old crock. Later, he thought he might as well go back and fetch the rest, but she caught him and scratched him with her talons. Afterwards he wasted away and died, killed by what people called 'the White Lady's revenge'. *On bank of Ewenny River, 2 miles SW of Bridgend.*

SOUTH GLAMORGAN

CARDIFF

Cardiff Castle. GHOST. A tall man in a red cloak has been seen by visitors and staff in various parts of the castle, including the stairs, the chapel doorway and the hall. The second Marquess of Bute died in the chapel, and the ghost looked similar to a portrait of him. *Open to public.*

PENTRE MEYRICK

Crack Hill. DEVIL. The A48 at this point follows an old Roman road, and the stretch known as Crack Hill had a strange reputation. There were tales of travellers being weighted down on their journey, and of seeing a 'great bundle' like a 'fat, short man' rolling downhill into a disused quarry, there exploding in a shower of sparks. This strange phenomenon was attributed to the Devil. *3 miles NW of Cowbridge.*

ST LYTHANS

St Lythans Chambered Tomb. MOVING STONES. An old name for this prehistoric burial chamber is Gwâl-y-Filiast or the Greyhound Bitch's Lair, which may come from a tale in the old Welsh *Mabinogion.* A 14-foot capstone is balanced on three upright stones, and only slight traces survive of the earth mound which once covered this structure. On Midsummer Eve, so it was believed, the capstone would whirl round three times, and all the stones would go down to the river to bathe. The field was said to be cursed, but nevertheless the stones would grant wishes made there on Hallowe'en. *3 miles N of Barry; tomb in field close to lane between St Lythans and Dyffryn (ST 101722).*

TONGWYNLAIS

Castell Coch. TREASURE; UNDERGROUND PASSAGE. Although the present castle is Victorian, it stands on the site of a 12th-century castle, and treasure dating from those times is believed to be still concealed in a cavern at the end of a tunnel leading to Cardiff Castle – guarded, legend has it, by three huge eagles. Parties searching for the treasure are said to have been unable to kill the eagles, despite battles lasting several hours. *Off A470 N of village and just NW of Cardiff; open to public.*

POWYS (SOUTH)

BRECON BEACONS

Llyn Cwm Llwch. FAIRIES; ARTHURIAN LEGEND. This small lake in the heart of the mountains had an eerie reputation. It was believed that there was an invisible island in the lake where the fairies had a garden; it could be reached on May Day through a door which would open in a certain rock by the shore. But the door failed to open again after a visitor took a flower back from the island. When an attempt was made to drain the lake by cutting a channel through the natural rock dam, a man in a red coat sitting in an armchair appeared on the water and threatened the workmen, telling them that if they continued they would release enough water to drown Brecon. Birds and animals were said to avoid the lake.

The mountain peaks close by have vague Arthurian connections. One hilltop was called Moel Arthur or Bann Arthur, and a dip between two peaks was known as Arthur's Chair. *Lake 5 miles SW of Brecon, only accessible by footpath (SO 002220).*

Maen Llia. MOVING STONE. This fine, tall standing stone overlooking a valley is said to visit the Neath River when it hears the cock crow. *3½ miles N of Ystradfellte beside lane N to Heol Senni (SN 924192).*

ELAN VILLAGE

Carn Cafall. ARTHURIAN LEGEND; MOVING STONE. On a stone lying on one of the cairns in a group on the mountain Corngafallt was said to be the imprint of the foot of Cafall, King Arthur's horse or dog, which was left there when Arthur was hunting the boar Twrch Trwyth. The stone is roughly 2 feet by 1 foot, and the hollow representing the footmark is 4 inches by 3 inches by 2 inches deep. If the stone was taken away, it was believed it would come back of its own accord by the next morning. *3 miles SW of Rhayader: approached by footpath either from Elan Village, or from N (SN 943644).*

LLANDEILO GRABAN

Church. DRAGON. The dragon slept on the church tower at night after having terrorized the locals by day, until it was killed by a ploughboy who made a dummy man which he dressed in red and fixed on the tower. It was covered with sharp hooks, and when the dragon attacked it and wound himself around it he was wounded so badly that he bled to death. *5 miles SE of Builth Wells.*

LLANGORSE

Llangorse Lake. DROWNED TOWN. An earthquake is said to have caused the deluge which, according to legend, swallowed up a thriving town without warning. An alternative explanation is that the catastrophe was an act of vengeance against a poor man who wished to marry a princess. She said she would only marry him if he were rich, and so he committed a murder for money. In stormy weather, it is said, the church bells can be heard ringing underwater. *5 miles SE of Brecon; many footpaths to lake shore from Llangorse village and from W and S.*

LLOWES

Mol Walbee's Stone. GIANTESS. Mol was the giantess who in legend built Hay-on-Wye Castle in one night. The carved Celtic cross which now bears her name was said to be either a pebble she found in her shoe and threw here from Hay, or a stone which fell from her apron as she was carrying building materials to Hay. *Inside Llowes church, 2 miles SW of Hay-on-Wye.*

OLD RADNOR

Four Stones. KINGS' GRAVES; MOVING STONES. The four standing stones are said to mark the graves of four kings killed in a nearby battle. They are believed to go down to Hindwell Pool to drink when they hear Old Radnor church bells. *3 miles NW of Kington; stones 1 mile N of Old Radnor, in field beside lane to Kinnerton (SO 246607).*

Maen Llia standing stone in the Brecon Beacons

WEST GLAMORGAN

GLYN-NEATH

Craig-y-Ddinas. ARTHURIAN LEGEND; TREASURE; FAIRIES. King Arthur is said to be sleeping in a cave at Craig-y-Ddinas, along with his warriors and a treasure hoard. Traditionally, a magician showed the cave to a man who was allowed to take some of the gold, and told that if he rang the bell, one of the knights would awake and ask if it was day. He was to answer, 'No, sleep on'. When he accidentally knocked the bell, it rang and the knight awoke, but the treasure-seeker gave the right answer. On a later visit, when he came back for more gold, he again rang the bell but this time forgot the correct answer; he was savagedly beaten by the warriors, who also took back the gold. The man was never able to find the cave again. Craig-y-Ddinas is also supposed to be one of the last places in Wales where the Little People lived. *Where borders of West Glamorgan, Mid Glamorgan and Powys meet, 2 miles NE of Glyn-Neath; footpaths cross hillside (SN 916081).*

MARGAM

Margam Abbey. GHOST. The abbey ruins are haunted by a monk, seen by many visitors in recent decades. Also of interest are the church, the ruined castle, and especially the carved Celtic stones in the museum by the church. *3 miles SE of Port Talbot in Margam Country Park.*

OXWICH

Church. PHANTOM HORSE. Early in the last century a boy and his father, walking by the churchyard at midnight after an evening's fishing in the bay, saw a white horse walking on its hind legs along the path to the church gate. It passed easily over the stile into the churchyard, and then disappeared. Later in the century, other people claimed to have seen a white form gliding over the gravestones around midnight. *10 miles SW of Swansea.*

OYSTERMOUTH

Oystermouth Castle. GHOST. Many witnesses have seen the White Lady in the 11th-century ruins. Her back bleeding, she stands crying by a tree close to the old castle wall. *N of the Mumbles on W side of Swansea Bay; open to public.*

REYNOLDSTON

★ Coetan Arthur (Arthur's Quoit). ARTHURIAN LEGEND; GHOST; MOVING STONES; RITUALS. Also known as Maen Ceti (Stone of Ceti), this well-sited prehistoric chambered tomb commands fine views over the Gower peninsula. The 25-ton capstone was said to be a pebble from the giant Arthur's shoe which he threw here from Carmarthenshire while walking to Camlann. When the moon is full Arthur's ghost walks down to the sea, dressed in glowing armour.

Sometimes, especially on Midsummer Eve and All Hallows' Eve, the stones themselves are said to go down to the sea to drink or bathe. Young girls used to come to Coetan Arthur to discover if their lovers were faithful. They would crawl around the stones three or seven times, and leave offerings of barley and honey cakes; the best time to come was at midnight when the moon was full. *11 miles W of Swansea and ½ mile NE of Reynoldston, on open land reached by footpath N from Reynoldston–Llethrid road (SS 491905).*

IRISH SEA
BODEWRYD
VALLEY
ANGLESEY
PENMAENMAWR
Menai Bridge
ROEWEN
LLANSANNA
NEWBOROUGH
CAERNARFON
LLANDWROG
BETWS-Y-COED
LLANFIHANGE
GLYN MYFY
BEDDGELERT
GWYNEDD
BALA
PENNA
MELANGE
DYFFRYN
ARDUDWY
BARDSEY
LLANWDDYN
MALLWYD
CARDIGAN BAY
CADER IDRIS
POWYS
(NORTH)
TYWYN
CLATTER
0
10
20
MILES
KILOMETRES
0
10
20
30
40

NORTH WALES

RELAWNYD
HOLYWELL
LLANGWYFAN
C L W Y D
RUTHIN
LLANFAIR
DYFFRYN
CLWYD
Dee
LLANGOLLEN
CORWEN
LLANRHAEADR-
YM-MOCHNANT
LLANFAIR
AEREINION
WELSHPOOL
TRELYSTAN
MONTGOMERY
HYSSINGTON
Severn

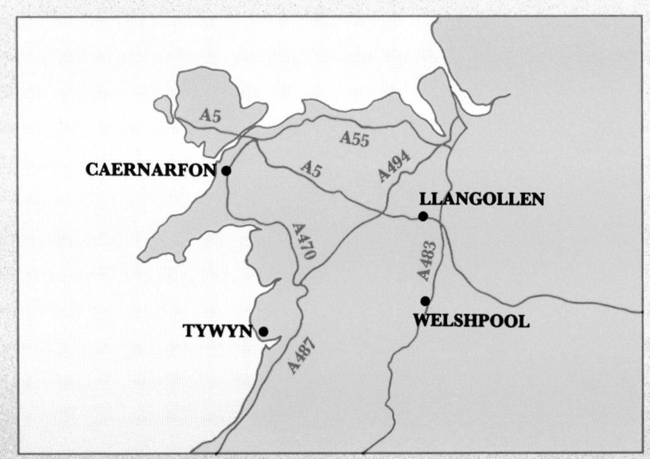

CLWYD

CORWEN

Caer Drewyn. FAIRIES; GIANT. The name of this Iron Age hillfort derives from *Tref Wyn* (Gwyn's settlement), Gwyn ap Nudd being King of the Fairies. Later Drewyn was said to be a giant's name, and the fort was a cattle enclosure used by his wife to milk her cows. Owain Glyndŵr (see below) may also have used the fort as an encampment during his rebellion. *1 mile NE of Corwen, on N side of River Dee; accessible along gravel track.*

Church. SITING LEGEND; OWAIN GLYNDŴR. There are many indications that this was an early church site, and possibly a pagan sacred site before being christianized. According to legend, the site for the church was changed when the original building work was repeatedly demolished. Two pointers to the place's antiquity are that the churchyard is practically circular, and that it contains a standing stone. There was also once a holy well just above the churchyard. The standing stone is called Carreg y Big yn y Fach Rhewllyd (the Pointed Stone in the Icy Corner). It originally stood in the churchyard but is now incorporated in the porch wall, and is visible from the outside.The priest's door on the south side has a lintel stone which was a 7th-9th-century cross stone, and it bears an incised cross said to be the mark of Owain Glyndŵr's dagger which he threw here from a nearby hill.

Owain Glyndŵr, the 14th-15th-century Welsh prince, had strong connections with Corwen, which was his headquarters where he assembled his forces before the Battle of Shrewsbury. He is commemorated by the large hotel which bears his name in the town centre; and Owain Glyndŵr's Mount, a large mound beside the A5 3½ miles east, is said to have been one of his strongholds, or his burial place, but was probably a Norman motte-and-bailey castle site.

Llangar Old Church. SITING LEGEND. The church was originally to be built by the bridge over the River Dee at Cynwyd, but the Devil is supposed to have moved the stones each night. A wise man told the masons to build where they saw a white stag, and so the church was built a mile further along the Dee valley; it was called Llangarw Gwyn - Church of the White Stag. Inside are unusual medieval wall-paintings, including a large skeleton representing Death. During excavations in 1974, 170 skeletons were found buried beneath the church floor. The legend, the atmosphere and the setting, approached along a sunken lane, all suggest that this was a pre-Christian sacred site. The medieval church is no longer used, but has been preserved. *1 mile SW of Corwen, off B4401 (SJ 063425).*

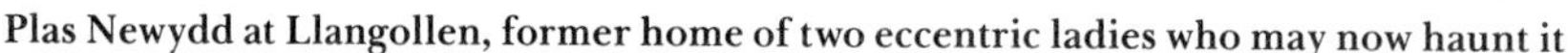

Plas Newydd at Llangollen, former home of two eccentric ladies who may now haunt it

HOLYWELL

Basingwerk Abbey. SPELLBOUND MONK. A monk was said to be so entranced by the sound of a nightingale that he somehow 'lost' several hundred years of time, and when he returned to the abbey it was in ruins. He was offered food by villagers, but crumbled to dust when he touched it. *In Greenfield valley 1 mile NE of Holywell centre; open to public.*

St Winefride's Well. HOLY WELL. One of the few holy wells in Britain still regularly visited by thousands of pilgrims annually, St Winefride's Well traditionally dates back to the 7th century when the saint Gwenfrewi (her Welsh name) was a young girl whom Caradog, a local chieftain, wanted as his mistress. She refused, and in anger he cut off her head. Her uncle, St Beuno, put her head back on again and she survived to become abbess of Gwytherin in the far west of the county. Where her head fell a spring began to flow, and the water was said to have magical healing properties. Today the water rises in a chapel and flows into a large bathing pool. Stones in the well are stained with red, said to be Gwenfrewi's blood, and the stone called Maen Beuno is also stained with her blood. Moss growing by the well, said to become red on the anniversary of the saint's beheading (22 June), is called St Winefride's Hair. In addition to the daily visitors, there is an annual pilgrimage to the well in June. This is led by a procession through the town, headed by a relic, the saint's thumb-bone. After a Catholic mass at the well, the pilgrims file past the reliquary and venerate it with a kiss. *Well at N end of town beside B5121 to Greenfield.*

LLANFAIR DYFFRYN CLWYD

Church. SITING LEGEND. The original site for the church was at or near Jesus Chapel, but nightly a phantom in the shape of a sow's head destroyed the previous day's work so that the builders moved the church to its present site. A farm later built on the original site was called Llanbenwch (Church of the Sow's Head). *Jesus Chapel 1 mile SE of village, itself 2 miles SE of Ruthin.*

LLANFIHANGEL GLYN MYFYR

Clocaenog Forest. FAIRY COW. Conifers now cover the wild hills where Y Fuwch Frech (the Freckled Cow) used to roam. Like her counterpart in Shropshire (see *Priestweston*) she gave endless quantities of milk to all, until one day she was milked into a sieve by a witch, after which she left the area and was never seen again. The farm called Cefn Bannog is close to the cow's grazing pastures, and there used to be places called the Freckled Cow's Crib, Meadow and Well. The nearest landmark today is the visitor centre at Pont Petrual, three-quarters of a mile east of Cefn Bannog. *Llanfihangel GM 10 miles SW of Ruthin, and Pont Petrual 3 miles NE of Llanfihangel GM just off B5105 which passes through Clocaenog Forest.*

CALENDAR OF EVENTS

April/May (Rogationtide)
LLANFAIR CAEREINION, Powys. *Blessing the Crops:* Performed by a priest from a train on the Welshpool and Llanfair Light Railway.

Early July
LLANGOLLEN, Clwyd. *International Eisteddfod:* Local *eisteddfodau* (competitions in all aspects of Welsh culture) are held throughout Wales, culminating in the National Eisteddfod held in the summer, one year in the north, next year in the south. Every July an international version is held in Llangollen, with thousands of competitors from all over the world.

December and into January
MALLWYD, Gwynedd. *Plygain:* Traditional Welsh impromptu singing of carols held during Christmas and January evening church services, once practised all over Wales, now confined to Mid-Wales (e.g. Llanymawddwy, Llanerfyl, Llanrhaeadr-ym-Mochnant).

LLANGOLLEN

★ **Castell Dinas Bran.** ARTHURIAN LEGEND; TREASURE; FAIRIES. At Llangollen the valley of the River Dee is dominated by a 1000-foot conical hill crowned by the ruins of a 13th-century castle. It is well worth exploring on foot – the views in all directions are breathtaking, and this impressive site has been suggested as the possible location of the Grail Castle. Whether or not Dinas Bran was the castle where the mystical Holy Grail was kept, there was a local tradition that great treasure was hidden in a cave beneath the castle, but that this treasure could only be found by a boy followed by a white dog with silver eyes; such dogs were said to be able to see the wind. The name Castell Dinas Bran links the site to Arthurian legend, because Bran (meaning, in Welsh, 'raven') was a Celtic god-king whose severed head King Arthur recklessly dug out from its burial place on Tower Hill in London. While buried, the head had ensured that no enemies could invade and conquer Britain (see *Tower of London*, Greater London).

Castell Dinas Bran at Llangollen, one of the places where the Holy Grail is supposed to have been hidden

While watching sheep on the castle hill, a man named Tudur encountered the Tylwyth Teg (fairies) in a hollow called Nant y Ellyllon. He could not resist joining in with their dance, and cried out 'Play away, old devil!' - whereupon they all changed into animals dancing around the Devil. Tudur was found next day by his master, still dancing - alone - on the hill. On another occasion a man passing Eglwyseg Rocks one summer night also saw the Tylwyth Teg. *Path from N end of town, by school, leads to summit; very steep in places.*

Plas Newydd. GHOSTS. The interesting 'black and white' house was the home of the 'Ladies of Llangollen' in the 18th and early 19th centuries. Lady Eleanor Butler and Miss Sarah Ponsonby transformed the original small stone cottage with romantic Gothic additions, and with their eccentric ways became a legend in their lifetime. It may well be their ghosts which have been seen in the house. Visitors have felt cold in the state bedroom, and some have seen little old ladies dressed in old-fashioned clothes. *Signposted in town; open to public.*

LLANGWYFAN

Moel Arthur. TREASURE. An iron treasure chest with a ring-handle was said to be buried in the hillfort, and at night a supernatural light would shine from it and reveal its location. But no one has been able to retrieve the treasure. When people grasp the handle, the legend goes, a fierce storm knocks them senseless, for a charm laid on the fort prevents treasure-seeker and antiquary alike from digging there. *5 miles E of Denbigh, in Clwydian Hills and on route of Offa's Dyke Path; can be reached from lanes to NW or SE (SJ 145660).*

LLANRHAEADR-YM-MOCHNANT

Post Coch. DRAGON. Red Pillar, also known as Pillar of the Viper (Post-y-Wiber), gets its names from the tradition that it was draped in red cloth, hiding spikes beneath, in order to entice a flying dragon to attack the stone and impale itself. Welsh dragons apparently have the same reaction to the colour red as bulls are supposed to show. *10 miles SW of Oswestry; stone 1 mile SE, in field beside B4580 (SJ 137248).*

LLANSANNAN

Bedd Robin Hood (Robin Hood's Grave). ROBIN HOOD; GHOST. One of a number of contenders for the folk hero's burial place (see also *Crosby Ravensworth*, Cumbria, and *Mirfield*, West Yorkshire), this damaged tumulus was said to be haunted, and people did not like to pass it at night. It is curious that a site named for Robin Hood is not far from one linked to King Arthur's name (see next entry). *Llansannan 6 miles NW of Denbigh; tumulus 2 miles SE of village, by lane (SH 968649).*

Bwrdd Arthur (Arthur's Table). ARTHURIAN LEGEND. A rocky outcrop with rough indentations around the edge was seen as King Arthur's Round Table. John Leland wrote in the 16th century of '24 holes or places in a roundel for men to sit in, but some less, and some bigger, cut out of the main rock by man's hand'. *From B5382 2 miles NE of Llansannan, follow lane SE from Bryn Rhyd-yr-Arian hamlet, and ¼ mile from junction take footpath up through woods; Bwrdd Arthur on left after ¼ mile (SH 961673).*

RUTHIN

Maen Huail. ARTHURIAN LEGEND. A block of limestone in the town centre was said to be the place where Huail, a local ruler, was beheaded. This came about after Huail began to show an interest in one of King Arthur's mistresses. The two men fought over the woman and Arthur was wounded in the knee. He said that there would be peace between them so long as Huail did not mention Arthur's wound. But shortly afterwards Arthur went in female disguise to Ruthin to visit another lady; while he was dancing Huail recognized him from his limp and commented: 'You would be a good dancer if it was not for your clumsy knee.' Whereupon Arthur had him arrested and beheaded. *14 miles NW of Wrexham; stone in St Peter's Square.*

TRELAWNYD

Gop Cairn. GHOSTS. Also known as Gop-y-Goleuni, this 40-foot-high cairn is an impressive prehistoric monument, but its original purpose is not yet known. It may well have been a burial mound, and tradition says that a Roman centurion is buried here. A local man, walking by the cairn one moonlit night, is said to have seen Roman soldiers in the fields, headed by a centurion on a white horse. They were lost to view when clouds hid the moon, and when it cleared the soldiers had gone. *2 miles S of Prestatyn; cairn on Gop Hill ¼ mile NW of village, reached by footpath from new houses at N of village (SJ 086802).*

The annual pilgrimage to St Winefride's Well at Holywell

GWYNEDD

BALA

Bala Lake (Llyn Tegid). DROWNED TOWN; MONSTER. The old town of Bala stood where the lake now is; it was drowned, according to legend, when someone forgot to put the lid on the well at Llangower, and during the night

Cader Idris, reputed home of a giant

the water overflowed and covered the valley and town. A new town was built at the north-east end of the lake, but it was said that some day that would be drowned too, the water extending as far as Llanfor. In another version of the tale, a fine palace was drowned in vengeance for the oppression and cruelty of the prince who lived there. In recent years there have been reports of a monster (identity unknown) seen in the lake; and a rare species of fish, the gwyniad, also lives in the deeps.

BARDSEY ISLAND (YNYS ENLLI)

Bardsey Island. GHOSTS; ARTHURIAN LEGEND. Ghosts of some of the twenty thousand monks said to be buried here have been seen from time to time wandering along the shore. The island was an important centre of pilgrimage. Merlin, the wizard in the Arthurian legends, is said to be sleeping in an underground cave, surrounded by the 13 Treasures of Britain. In another version he lives in an invisible house of glass with nine companions; this may be a memory of an ancient Celtic story. *2 miles off tip of Lleyn peninsula, reached by boat from Aberdaron.*

BEDDGELERT

Dinas Emrys. DRAGONS; ARTHURIAN LEGEND; TREASURE. The Iron Age hillfort on the hill was reoccupied during the Dark Ages, when King Vortigern attempted to build a castle here. The walls kept collapsing, and on consulting a wise man he was told that he must sacrifice a fatherless boy and sprinkle his blood on the ground. The boy, who turned out to be Merlin, the magician of Arthurian legend, told Vortigern that the reason the castle kept collapsing was that two dragons, one white and one red, were fighting in an underground pool. It was located, and the dragons exorcised; from their battle is said to have originated the red dragon as the symbol of Wales. Strangely enough, archaeological excavations have located an artificial pool on the hill, built in the 5th or 6th century AD to supply water to the fortress.

After Vortigern left Dinas Emrys, Merlin stayed on and built himself a fort, where his treasure is said to be still hidden. It is in a gold cauldron in a cave, the entrance blocked with earth and a huge stone, and it can only be located by the rightful owner who is a youth with yellow hair and blue eyes. When he approaches, a bell will ring and the stone will fall aside. *10 miles SE of Caernarfon; Dinas Emrys beside A498 1 mile NE of Beddgelert; inaccessible, but visible from road.*

Gelert's Grave. FAITHFUL HOUND. Gelert was the favourite dog of Prince Llewelyn, who in the 12th century lived close to Beddgelert. One day he and the princess went out hunting, leaving their baby son at home. Llewelyn noticed that Gelert was not with the dogs, and feeling uneasy he returned home where he found the cradle overturned, blood everywhere, and no baby to be seen. Gelert was there, covered with blood and wagging his tail, and in fury Llewelyn ran his sword through the dog. The dog's last cry was echoed by the cry of a baby, who was found beneath the cradle, safe and well. Under the bedclothes was a dead wolf, killed by the faithful Gelert. Full of remorse, Llewelyn had the dog buried in the meadow by the river and marked his grave with stones; the village that grew up nearby was called Beddgelert, Gelert's Grave.

It is a lovely story, but sad to say it is not true. It was concocted to promote the tourist trade in a previous century, taking as its starting point the village name, which in fact probably refers to the grave of a Celtic saint. However, the tradition of the faithful hound is recorded elsewhere in Europe, so the story itself was not fabricated - only its link with Beddgelert. *In village centre, signposted at footbridge over river (E of road bridge); follow path S by river in meadowland.*

BETWS-Y-COED

★ **Fairy Glen.** FAIRIES. People used to see the Tylwyth Teg (Little People) playing here, one of very many places in Gwynedd where they have been seen. *Fairy Glen is picturesque rocky valley of River Conwy 1 mile SE of town, easily accessible from bridge where A470 crosses river.*

BODEWRYD, ANGLESEY

Maen Pres (Brass Stone). TREASURE. A brass pan containing treasure was said to be buried here, its location being found by following the shadow cast by the stone at a certain time of day. It was also known as Carreg Lefn (Smooth Stone), and an alternative legend was that anyone reading the 'inscription' (really natural crevices looking like an inscription) would be rewarded by the stone moving to reveal the pot of gold. *3 miles SW of Amlwch; stone to N of lane from Bodewryd to Rhosgoch (SH 407902).*

CADER IDRIS

Cader Idris. GIANT. Cader Idris means Idris's Chair, Idris being the giant who was reputed to live on the mountain. His chair is a stone formation on top of the ridge, and anyone who sits in it overnight will become a poet, go mad or die. Three crags beside the Dolgellau-Machynlleth road were supposed to be pebbles thrown out of the giant's shoe. *3 miles SW of Dolgellau; walk to summit easy if strenuous: pony track starts ½ mile SW of Gwernan Lake Hotel at SH 698152.*

DYFFRYN ARDUDWY

Coetan Arthur (also known as **Carreg Arthur** and **Dyffryn Ardudwy Chambered Cairn**). TREASURE. Two prehistoric stone burial chambers which were once covered by a cairn of smooth pebbles still stand on a hillside above the sea. There is said to be treasure buried here somewhere, the location being revealed when the end of a rinbow touches the cairn. *5 miles NW of Barmouth; cairn at S end of village and E of A496, reached along path from road (SH 589229).*

LLANDWROG

Caer Arianrhod. DROWNED TOWN. According to tradition there are several lost areas of land, flooded by the sea, around the Welsh coast. Caer Arianrhod in Caernarfon Bay is three-quarters of a mile off the coastal hillfort Dinas Dinlle. It was formerly a castle inhabited by the evil lady Arianrhod, whose story is told in the old Welsh tales called the *Mabinogion*. Some women came ashore to fetch food or water, and when they looked back they saw that their town had been overwhelmed by the sea, perhaps because of the inhabitants' wickedness. It is said that sometimes, at low water, stones from the walls can be seen, and the high point of Dinas Dinlle is a good place to look out over the site of legendary Caer Arianrhod. *5 miles SW of Caernarfon; Dinas Dinlle ¾ mile W of Llandwrog and accessible from lane (SH 436563).*

NEWBOROUGH, ANGLESEY

Llanddwyn Island. HOLY WELL; DROWNED TOWN. A ruined church stands on this promontory which is one mile long and a quarter-mile wide. The church was dedicated to St Dwynwen, who is the Welsh St Valentine, the patroness of true lovers. According to legend, this came about following her refusal to marry Maelon Dafodrill, who then upset her by casting doubt on her good name, so that she prayed God to cure her of her love. An angel appeared in her sleep and gave her a philtre which cured her; given the same cure, Maelon turned into a lump of ice. Dwynwen was then granted three wishes: that Maelon should be unfrozen; that all true lovers who invoked her would either obtain their hearts' desire or be cured of their passion; and that she might never wish to be married. The wishes were granted, and she became a saint.

In later years the saint's well on the island was visited by people in love seeking some indication of their likely success, which was judged from the movement of small eels in the well.

There was also a tradition that the island was all that was left of a town, Cantref Waelod, which had been destroyed by the sea. *Newborough 10 miles SW of Menai Bridge; from village drive into Newborough Forest and park in car park near shore; walk W along beach to island, usually (except at very high tides) accessible by foot; saint's well on W coast by cove just N of church ruins.*

PENMAENMAWR

★ Druids' Circle (Y Meini Hirion). PAGAN RITUALS: MOVING STONE. Ten standing stones of the original 30 survive in this dramatically sited prehistoric stone circle. Archaeologists found buried inside the circle a cist containing a food vessel and the cremated remains of a child. Perhaps it was a sacrifice: folklore has embellished the theme by calling one of the stones the Stone of Sacrifice, the top of which looks as if it might have been shaped to hold a child. Traditionally, babies were placed in it for a few minutes during their first month to ensure good luck, and rainwater was taken from the cavity to sprinkle on the threshold of the house as a protection against witchcraft. The Deity Stone stands opposite it, and it was believed that if anyone used bad language near this stone it would lean over and strike the offender. A man who mocked the story and went up to the circle one night to shout words of blasphemy was found next morning dead, his body battered, at the foot of the Deity Stone. *Accessible by footpath from Penmaenmawr, starting at Graiglwyd Road on S of town; path signposted (SH 723747).*

RHYD-DDU

Llyn-y-Dywarchen. FAIRIES. The Land of the Fairies was said to extend from Cwm Hafod Ruffydd along the slope of Drws-y-Coed as far as Llyn-y-Dywarchen. On moonlit nights the local people would listen to the fairy music and watch them dancing. One young man fell in love with a fairy woman, seized her and locked her up in his house. She consented to be his servant if he could discover her name, and one day he overheard one of the fairies crying for his lost sister Penelop. After working for him for a while, Penelop agreed to marry him: they had two children and lived happily together for several years. One day while helping her husband catch a horse, Penelop was struck by an iron bit he threw towards her, and she vanished instantly, never to be seen again. Iron was known to repel fairies, and an open pair of scissors used to be hung above a child's cradle so that the combination of steel and the cross would preserve the child from abduction by the fairies.

Llyn-y-Dywarchen has a floating island, said to be blown about by the wind. In one version of the fairytale, the fairy wife who was touched by iron and spirited back to fairyland used to come and see her husband from time to time: she would stand on the floating island and he on the shore, while the two of them talked together across the water. *Rhyd-Ddu 3 miles N of Beddgelert; lake 1 mile NW, beside B4418 to Penegroes.*

Other Snowdonia Lakes. FAIRY COW; MONSTER; ARTHURIAN LEGEND. Equally rich in lore and legend, there are too many other lakes to describe fully here, but the following are worth visiting. At **Llyn Barfog**, near Aberdovey, a fairy cow and her offspring disappeared when a farmer was about to slaughter them. **Llyn Cynwch** is on the Nannau estate north of Dolgellau; Precipice Walk passes the lake. Here there was said to be a settlement with people living on the lake bottom, and a wyvern (monster) lived in the lake until it was beheaded by a shepherd with an axe on one of its forays into the hills. **Llyn Llydaw**, to the east of Snowdon, was one of the lakes where King Arthur's sword Excalibur was said to have been thrown by Bedivere. Other Arthurian legends are located in this area, such as his death on Snowdon and burial in Bwlch y Saethau (Pass of the Arrows).

ROEWEN

Maen-y-Bardd and Ffon-y-Cawr. GIANT. Evocative names are given to the many prehistoric sites surviving in North Wales, and these two are no exception. Maen-y-Bardd means Poet's Stone, and is a chambered tomb. It has had other names: Cwt-y-Bugail (Shepherd's Hut) and Cwt-y-Filiast (Greyhound Bitch's Kennel). Ffon-y-Cawr (the Giant's Staff) is a tall standing stone close by, also known as Picell Arthur (Arthur's Spear). A giant is said to have thrown his staff after his dog, who was sheltering in the 'shepherd's hut' instead of watching the sheep. *Roewen 3 miles SW of Conwy; sites along old green lane high above Conwy valley, beyond youth hostel; not accessible by car beyond hostel (Maen-y-Bardd: SH 741718; Ffon-y-Cawr: SH 738717).*

VALLEY, ANGLESEY

Llyn Cerrig Bach. TREASURE; GHOSTS. Sometimes real 'treasure' is found, as happened here in 1943 when the ground was being prepared for the construction of the air force station. Peat taken from the bog at Llyn Cerrig Bach was found to contain Iron Age metalwork: 141 items comprising weapons, chariot fittings (especially wheels), harness, iron currency bars, two bronze cauldrons, and gang-chains for holding captives by the neck. These items are thought to have been deliberately thrown into the lake, perhaps as votive offerings if it was a sacred lake. The druids had their last stronghold on Anglesey, until overcome by the Romans led by Paulinus in AD 60. The Latin historian Tacitus described the scene in his *Annals*:

The Fairy Glen at Betws-y-Coed, haunt of the Tylwyth Teg

The shore was lined by a motley battle array. Women were seen rushing through the ranks of soldiers in wild disorder, dressed in black, with their hair dishevelled and brandishing flaming torches. Their whole appearance resembled the frantic rage of the Furies. The druids were ranged in order, calling down terrible curses. The soldiers, paralysed by this strange spectacle, stood still and offered themselves as a target for wounds. But at last the promptings of the general - and their own rallying of each other - urged them not to be frightened of a mob of women and fanatics. They advanced the standards, cut down all who met them and swallowed them up in their own fires. After this a garrison was placed over the conquered islanders, and the groves sacred to savage rites were cut down.

None of the finds from Llyn Cerrig Bach dates from after AD 60. It is said that the ghosts of the Roman soldiers and druids now haunt the area of the lake. *Valley 3 miles SE of Holyhead; lake 3 miles SE of Valley, opposite airfield; road passes alongside (SH 306765).*

Maen-y-Bardd chambered tomb at Roewen

POWYS (NORTH)

CLATTER

Llynytarw. FAIRIES. The singing heard by the lake over many years was believed to emanate from the fairies who lived there. In 1936 it was reported in the press that a woman and her three children heard the 'sweetest singing imaginable' by the lakeside, but they looked in vain for the singer. *Llynytarw 2 miles NE of Clatter, itself 7 miles NW of Newtown; footpath from Bwlch y Garreg follows lake shore.*

HYSSINGTON

Church. SPIRIT LAID. The Roaring Bull of Bagbury was the spirit of a wicked squire who is said to have appeared after death as a savage bull that haunted the lanes and terrified the local people. A group of clergymen met at Hyssington church and enticed the bull there by the power of their prayers. He was so big that the church walls cracked, but the priests managed to diminish him in size and finally laid him in a snuffbox which, according to legend, was placed in the Red Sea for a thousand years. In another version, he was laid in a boot which was put below the church door-stone. If it were ever moved, the bull would be free again. *Hyssington $3\frac{1}{2}$ miles N of Bishop's Castle; church at N end of village.*

LLANWDDYN

Lake Vyrnwy. EVIL SPIRIT. In the days before the valley of Llanwddyn was dammed and flooded at the end of the last century to form a reservoir supplying water to Liverpool, it was believed to be plagued by a wicked spirit. Someone managed to trap the spirit beneath a large stone in the river, called Carreg yr Ysprvd or the Ghost Stone, and he was doomed to stay there until the water should work its way between the stone and the dry land – or until the river dried up, according to another version. There was great consternation locally when news came of the plans to flood the valley. The Ghost Stone, a boulder weighing 15–20 tons, would be in the way and would have to be removed, thus releasing the spirit to resume his evil ways. Eventually the stone was blasted, and all eyes were on the place where it had stood. In a pool of water sat a sleepy-looking frog, and the obvious question was asked: was this really a frog, or the evil spirit in frog's shape? Now it seems that all the fears were unjustified, as Lake Vyrnwy is today a placid stretch of water in a picturesque valley, haunted by plenty of wildlife but not by evil spirits. *10 miles SE of Bala; road follows lake shore; wildlife visitor centre at E end across dam.*

MONTGOMERY

Robber's Grave. GRASS WON'T GROW. Last century, a man sentenced to death for robbery swore his innocence, and from the scaffold declared that, as a sign of his innocence, no grass would grow on his grave. It was said that for many years the grave had a cross-shaped bare patch, but today it is hard to find. *6 miles S of Welshpool; grave in churchyard, on N side and with nameboard.*

PENNANT MELANGELL

★ **Church.** SAINT'S SHRINE. Melangell was the daughter of an Irish king who fled to Wales to avoid his plans for her marriage. She was living in this lonely valley in the Berwyn mountains in the 6th century when one day a local prince, Brochwel Ysgithrog, came hunting hares. One hare ran to Melangell and sheltered under her skirts, and the hounds dared not approach. The prince realized Melangell's saintliness and gave her land to build a chapel. From then on she became known as the patron saint of hares, and they were called in the area *wŷn bach Melangell* (Melangell's little lambs). Melangell lives on at the lonely church, for 15th-century carvings on the screen depict her encounter with the prince, and the reconstructed remains of her shrine are also on display. Her bed, Gwely Melangell, is in a cleft of rock about a quarter of a mile south of the church. *8 miles SE of Bala; church reached along lane from Llangynog.*

TRELYSTAN

Beacon Ring. FAIRIES. On the highest point of Long Mountain above the Severn valley, this Iron Age hillfort, now tree-covered, is full of atmosphere and was believed to be a fairy haunt. The long-distance Offa's Dyke Path passes through it. *2½ miles SE of Welshpool; pick up Offa's Dyke Path where it crosses lane from Trelystan to Leighton (SJ 265058).*

WELSHPOOL

Llyn Du. PROPHECY. It was believed that one day the lake would suddenly spread and engulf the town. *Between town and Powis Castle; footpath from town's main street towards castle passes above lake after ¼ mile.*

St Melangell's shrine in the church at Pennant Melangell

Powis Castle. GHOST. The castle was said to have been haunted by the ghost of a gentleman in gold-laced hat and waistcoat, who appeared one night to a spinning woman working there. Realizing he was a ghost, she spoke to him. He then led her to a closet and showed her a box under the floorboards, asking for it to be sent with its key to the Earl of Powis in London; if she could do that, he said, he would no longer haunt the house. She told the steward and his wife, and together they found the box and sent it to the Earl, who rewarded the spinning woman with comfortable accommodation for the rest of her life. *Powis Castle ¾ mile S of Welshpool; open to public (National Trust).*

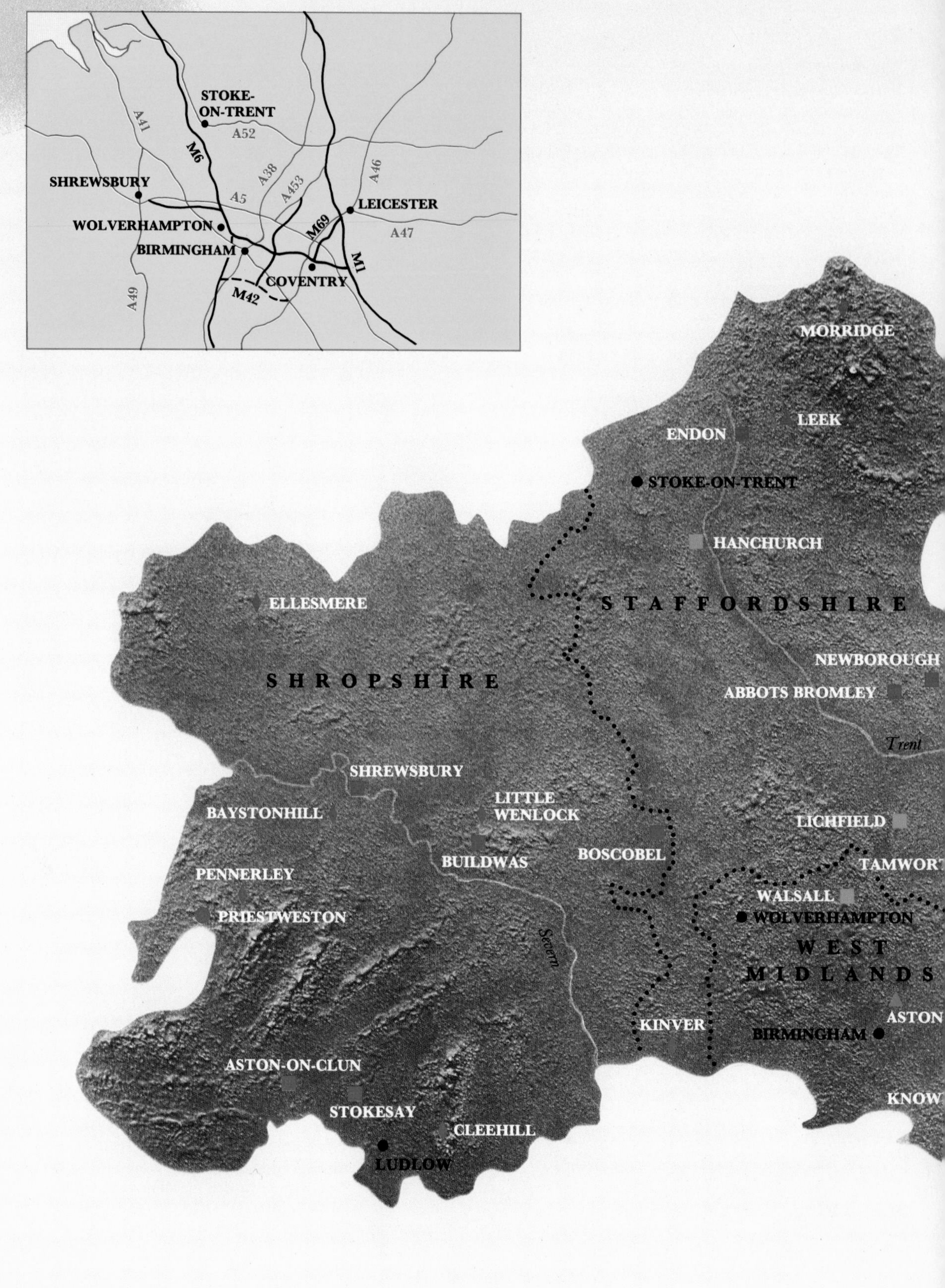
STOKE-ON-TRENT
A41
A52
M6
SHREWSBURY
A38
A453
A46
A5
LEICESTER
WOLVERHAMPTON
M69
A47
BIRMINGHAM
M1
COVENTRY
A49
M42
MORRIDGE
ENDON
LEEK
STOKE-ON-TRENT
HANCHURCH
ELLESMERE
STAFFORDSHIRE
NEWBOROUGH
SHROPSHIRE
ABBOTS BROMLEY
Trent
SHREWSBURY
LITTLE WENLOCK
BAYSTONHILL
LICHFIELD
BUILDWAS
BOSCOBEL
TAMWORT
PENNERLEY
WALSALL
PRIESTWESTON
WOLVERHAMPTON
Severn
WEST MIDLANDS
KINVER
ASTON
BIRMINGHAM
ASTON-ON-CLUN
KNOW
STOKESAY
CLEEHILL
LUDLOW

LEICESTERSHIRE SHROPSHIRE STAFFORDSHIRE AND WEST MIDLANDS

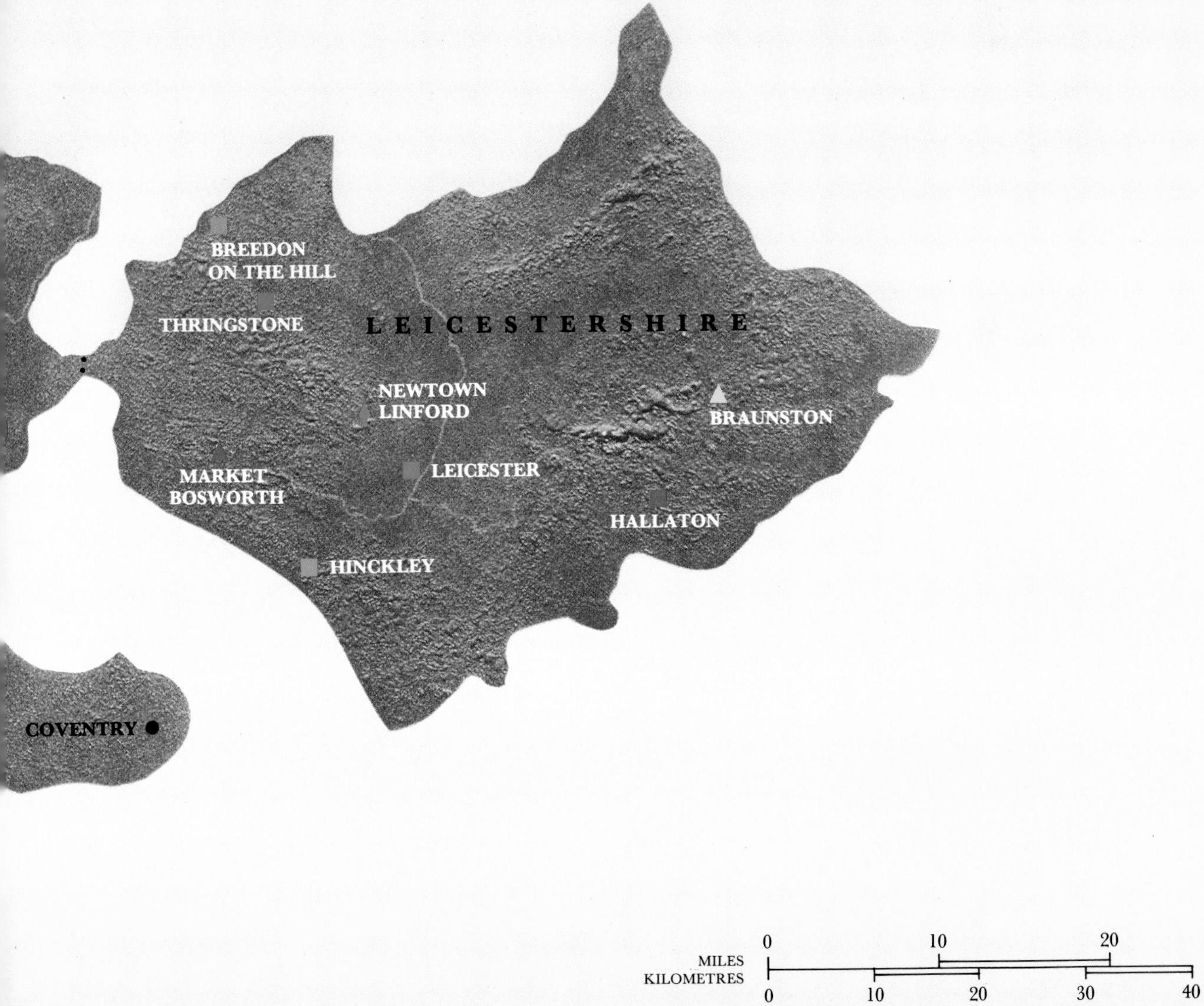

BREEDON
ON THE HILL
THRINGSTONE
LEICESTERSHIRE
NEWTOWN
LINFORD
BRAUNSTON
MARKET
BOSWORTH
LEICESTER
HALLATON
HINCKLEY
COVENTRY
MILES
KILOMETRES
0
10
20
0
10
20
30
40

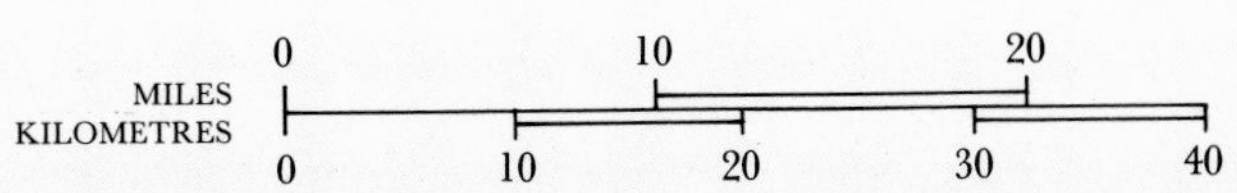

LEICESTERSHIRE

BRAUNSTON

Church. GODDESS CARVING. Outside the ancient church, which may date back to Norman times, can be seen a strange carved stone – a truncated body with two breasts topped by a hag-like head. Despite some people's suggestions that it is relatively modern, its appearance reinforces the feeling that it is very old, and may represent a goddess revered by pagan worshippers. For many years the stone was a doorstep, and the carving was only found when it was turned over. *2 miles SW of Oakham.*

Ancient carving, possibly of a pagan goddess, outside Braunston church

BREEDON ON THE HILL

★ **Church.** SITING LEGEND. Breedon church is very strangely and inconveniently situated, on a prominent hilltop high above the village. In the Iron Age there was a hillfort on the hill, later called the Bulwarks, but both it and the hill have been severely damaged by quarrying. Legend tells how the church was to be built in the village, but doves carried away the day's work every night, so the church was moved uphill to the new site that the birds had chosen. It is a church of Saxon origins, with some examples of fine Saxon sculpture, and there was a monastery here before the present building, founded in AD 675 by King Aethelbert. The church is dedicated to Hardulph, who is said to have been a hermit who lived on the hill before the church was built. This is clearly a very important ancient site, and it is sad that it has been so disfigured by the quarry. *8 miles SE of Derby; lane at W end of village leads to church.*

HINCKLEY

Church. BLEEDING TOMBSTONE; GHOST. Richard Smith, 20 years old, was murdered in 1727 by a recruiting sergeant who lost his temper and attacked him with his pike when Smith cracked jokes about the sergeant's attempts to do his job. Smith was buried in the churchyard, where his tombstone can be seen. It is said that it sweats blood every 12 April, the anniversary of his death. Ghostly footsteps pacing up and down the aisle inside the church have also been reported.

LEICESTER

Churches. GHOSTS. Several of the city's churches and religious buildings are said to be haunted. The former Holy Cross Priory on New Walk had the ghost of a former prior; and a house in the Newarke, built over the foundations of an old abbey church, was haunted by ghostly laughing voices and swishing skirts. The former 16th-century vicarage (demolished in the 1960s) to St Margaret's church was built on the site of a medieval bishop's palace, and many ghostly experiences were reported by the last residents. St Margaret's church itself was also haunted, by a ghostly man in dark clothes who was seen in the nave, sitting on the church steps, and by the vicarage gate. Two houses in St Martin's churchyard were said to be haunted; and a monk walked the passageway from the Guildhall to St Martin's. Ghostly footsteps were heard in Friar Lane, walking up to the main entrance of St Mary's church.

MARKET BOSWORTH

Bosworth Battlefield. KING'S WELL; GHOSTS. The Battle of Bosworth, which ended the Wars of the Roses on 22 August 1485, is where Richard III met his downfall. King Richard's (Dick's) Well, where he is said to have taken his last drink before going into battle, can be visited. We haven't heard that the battlefield is haunted, but there have been tales of a galloping headless soldier seen in lanes to the north; he may be connected with the battle, or he may be a Roman soldier, for witnesses have reported that he is bare-legged and wears a close-fitting helmet, and the Roman road called Watling Street (now the A5) is not far away. *2 miles S of Market Bosworth, reached from E–W lane between Shenton and Sutton Cheney; open to public.*

NEWTOWN LINFORD

Bradgate Park. GHOST; PHANTOM COACH; LEY. A large area of open country with woods, granite outcrops, a folly, bracken and deer has been preserved much as it was in Lady Jane Grey's day. This unfortunate girl, who was beheaded in 1554 while still in her teens, once lived in the now-ruined Bradgate House, which was the family home in the 16th century. Her ghost is said to appear on Christmas Eve, in a coach drawn by four headless black horses. They drive at speed along the road through the park and disappear into the ruins, among which she also appears as a White Lady.

Through Bradgate Park a ley passes, a 9½-mile alignment discovered by Paul Devereux and Ian Thomson. It links Oadby church, All Saints' church in Leicester, Woodgate crossroads, a standing stone in a field near Anstey, Anstey church, the haunted grounds of Bradgate House, and the notch on Old John Hill in Bradgate Park. *The Ley Hunter's Companion* contains further details. *Newtown Linford 5 miles NW of Leicester centre; one entrance into Bradgate Park here, another off B5330 W of Cropston, and third off lane on W side of park.*

THRINGSTONE

Grace Dieu Priory. UNDERGROUND PASSAGES; GHOST. The ruined nunnery in a roadside field seems untouched by the years, although modern traffic thunders past. There was a local belief that an underground passage linked the priory to Ashby-de-la-Zouch Castle 4¾ miles to the south-west, and another to Mount St Bernard's Abbey 2 miles to the south-east. These are unlikely, but more factual are the persistent reports of a ghostly woman in white seen along the A512 road, both close to the ruins and some distance away. When buses stopped for her, or if motorists looked back or stopped, there was apparently no woman to be seen. It is not clear if she was a phantom nun, or unconnected with the nunnery, though in local minds the two were naturally linked. She was seen one spring evening in 1961 by the village policeman, who was taking his dog for a walk in fields (now covered by a housing estate) half a mile south-west of the nunnery. He saw 'a white form in the shape of a long cloak and hood' which glided past him and disappeared in a hawthorn hedge. His dog growled and the hairs on its back rose; the air felt cold. *2 miles N of Coalville; priory ½ mile NE beside A512 to Loughborough.*

SHROPSHIRE

ASTON-ON-CLUN

Arbor Day. ANCIENT CUSTOM. Throughout the year the large black poplar tree in the centre of the village carries flags, which are renewed every 29 May when festivities are held. They commemorate a wedding in 1786, when the local squire's wife left money for the continuance of the custom. However, the date suggests also an Oak Apple Day ceremony (see *Boscobel*), and there is also a possibility that the custom may have originated a long time before, in the days of pagan tree worship. Today there are also a re-enactment by children of the squire's wedding, displays of morris dancing and a village fete. *9 miles NW of Ludlow.*

BAYSTONHILL

Bomere Pool. DROWNED VILLAGE; GIANT FISH. Where the pool now is there was once a village, whose inhabitants turned back to paganism from Christianity. To punish them, the story goes, the valley was flooded following heavy rains and the village was swept away. All efforts to drain the pool have been thwarted by some mysterious agency; and the bottom could not be located, however many waggon-ropes were tied together and let down into the water. There was also said to be a monster fish living in the pool, with a sword strapped to it. This sword belonged to Wild Edric, an 11th-century Shropshire hero, and would only be given up to Wild Edric's rightful heir. *2 miles S of Shrewsbury; Bomere Pool ½ mile SE of village, reached along track.*

BOSCOBEL

Boscobel House. ROYAL OAK. After King Charles II was defeated by Cromwell at the Battle of Worcester in September 1651, it is said that he fled north and took shelter at Boscobel House. The next day he left, fearing discovery, and found refuge for the day among the branches of an oak tree close by, where he avoided those searching for him. By night, he slipped away and journeyed to exile in Europe. At Boscobel House the room where he spent the night can be seen, as can the Royal Oak, said to have grown from an acorn from the tree in which he hid.

After 1660, when the monarchy was restored and King Charles II returned in triumph to London, the event was celebrated annually on 29 May, the date of his return, which became known as Oak Apple Day. Officially the name of the ceremony commemorated the oak tree in which he hid, but it probably also contained a strong element of pagan tree worship. Oak Apple Day used to be celebrated widely (for example, at Great Wishford in Wiltshire and *Castleton* in Derbyshire; see also *Aston-on-Clun*). *On Shropshire–Staffordshire border, 5 miles E of Shifnal; open to public.*

BUILDWAS

Buildwas Abbey. UNDERGROUND PASSAGE. An underground passage was said to connect the abbey with

The Needle's Eye, a cleft in the rock towards the summit of the Wrekin near Little Wenlock

Wenlock Priory 3 miles to the south-west - an unlikely distance for a tunnel to cover. However, in the 1860s archaeologists decided to check the story and did in fact locate an underground passage. They even followed it for 50 yards, until it became blocked by soil and debris. It was 10 feet high and 4 feet wide and well constructed, but there is no information as to whether it was heading in the right direction for Wenlock Priory. *2 miles NW of Ironbridge; abbey ruins on S side of River Severn, off B4378 to Much Wenlock; open to public*

CLEEHILL

Titterstone Clee Hill. GIANTS. The slopes of this prominent hill are littered with stones, said to be the missiles used by giants when they fought a battle here. *5 miles E of Ludlow; many footpaths cross hill.*

ELLESMERE

Cole Mere. LOST BELLS. A church here was destroyed by Cromwell's men and the bells thrown into the mere, so it is said. An attempt to raise them failed when, just as they were being drawn to the shore, one man said: 'In spite of God and the Devil we have done it.' The chains snapped and the bells sank to the bottom again. Sometimes they can be heard ringing on windy nights at the full moon, or on the church patron saint's anniversary. *2 miles SE of Ellesmere; footpath runs along SW shore.*

Great Mere. LEGEND OF LAKE'S ORIGIN. There are two versions of the origin of this 100-acre lake. In one, it was once fine meadowland, with a well of pure water which the villagers used. When a new tenant took over the farm he stopped this practice – and soon afterwards found his fields had flooded. But he had to continue paying rent on the drowned land. In the other version, the landowners charged a halfpenny for each bucketful of water fetched from the well, and the villagers prayed for an end to this oppression. They were rewarded when the well overflowed and flooded the field, so that there was plenty of free water for everyone. *E of Ellesmere and easily accessible.*

LITTLE WENLOCK

The Wrekin and Ercall Hill. GIANTS. Two giants are said to have dug earth out of the bed of the River Severn and formed the Wrekin so that they had a safe place to live. Bare patches on the hill were believed to be their footmarks. The Needle's Eye, a cleft in the rock on the summit, is the place where a giant's spade split the rock open when the two giants were quarrelling. A raven pecked the eyes of the giant with the spade, and a tear he shed formed the Raven's Bowl, a rock basin which is always full of water. That giant was subdued by the other and imprisoned inside Ercall Hill to the north, where at night he can sometimes be heard groaning.

In another version of the story, a cobbler met a giant carrying earth to bury Shrewsbury. He told him he had worn out all the boots he was carrying since leaving Shrewsbury, so the weary giant decided he would never get there; he dropped his load and the Wrekin was formed. The soil he scraped off his boots formed the Ercall. *Little Wenlock 3 miles S of Wellington; Wrekin to NW, prominent tree-covered hill and landmark for miles around; good (and steep) path to summit starts at NE where lane crosses between Wrekin and Ercall.*

PENNERLEY

★ **The Stiperstones.** DEVIL; GIANTESS. The highest rock on the rocky ridge is known as the Devil's Chair, being the place where he is supposed to have sat down to rest on a hot day while he was journeying from Ireland with an apronload of stones. His apron string broke when he got up, and the stones scattered all around; they are still lying there. In another tale the Devil sits on his Chair whenever he can, in the hope that his weight will push the rocks back into the earth and fulfil the prophecy that, when the Stiperstones sink into the earth, England will be ruined. A cairn of stones on the ridge was said to have been dropped by a giantess whose apron-strings were cut by the Devil, who found her trying to carry away his Chair. *Pennerley 9 miles SW of Welshpool; Stiperstones run for $1\frac{1}{2}$ miles to S and E of village; footpath beginning at car park (SO 369977) on lane between Ratlinghope and Pennerley runs along full length of ridge (good footwear needed).*

CALENDAR OF EVENTS

Easter Monday
HALLATON, Leicestershire. *Bottle-Kicking:* In a fierce competition between Hallaton and Medbourne, three small barrels are fought over for several hours; also a hare pie is blessed and then scattered about and scrambled for.

April/May/June (Ascension Day)
LICHFIELD, Staffordshire. *Beating the Bounds:* Led by the Dean and Chapter of Lichfield Cathedral, who stop in eight places for psalm-singing.

29 May
ASTON-ON-CLUN, Shropshire. *Arbor Day:* Tree decorated with flags (see entry for *Aston-on-Clun*).

May: Spring Bank Holiday weekend
ENDON, Staffordshire. *Well-Dressing:* One of the few well-dressing locations outside Derbyshire. Also at NEWBOROUGH in Staffordshire (May).

Early September
ABBOTS BROMLEY, Staffordshire. *Horn Dance:* Men wearing antlers perform a traditional dance (see entry for *Abbots Bromley*).

Arbor Day at Aston-on-Clun

PRIESTWESTON

Mitchell's Fold Stone Circle. GIANT; MAGIC COW; WITCH. Mitchell (or Medgel) was a giant who milked his cows at the site. Alternatively, Mitchell or Medgel was a witch who took advantage of a magical white cow that provided milk to all; she milked it into a sieve, whereupon it disappeared (and went to Warwickshire - see *Stretton-on-Dunsmore*). As a punishment, the witch was turned to stone (the tallest in the circle) and the others were set to guard her; or she was buried inside the circle. *Well sited on moorland with fine views into Wales; stone circle N of Corndon Hill and 1 mile NE of Priestweston (8 miles SE of Welshpool), reached by footpath from lane to S (SO 304983).*

Stokesay Castle, a 13th-century fortified house said to contain a hoard of gold

SHREWSBURY

Haughmond Abbey. UNDERGROUND PASSAGES. The abbey, now ruined, was said to be linked by underground passage to Holy Cross Abbey in the town centre. This 3-mile passage would have had to run beneath the River Severn. Likewise another passage, $3\frac{1}{2}$ miles long, to High Ercall, would have passed beneath the River Roden. If even a third of the underground passages allegedly existing in Britain had really been made, then there was at some time an army of extremely skilled tunnel builders - but there is no record of such a workforce. It has been suggested that 'underground passages' are really distorted memories of lines of natural earth energy, such as are also represented by leys (alignments of ancient sites). *Haughmond Abbey beside B5062 3 miles NE of Shrewsbury centre; open to public. Holy Cross Abbey in E town centre in Abbey Foregate; also open to public.*

STOKESAY

★ **Stokesay Castle.** GIANTS; TREASURE. One of the earliest fortified houses in England, dating from the 13th century, Stokesay Castle is said to be the hiding place of gold belonging to two giants. They kept their treasure in a chest, but one of them accidentally lost the key in the moat. Now the treasure is guarded by a raven which sits on the chest, waiting for someone to find the key. *7 miles NW of Ludlow; castle off A49 S of Craven Arms; open to public.*

STAFFORDSHIRE

ABBOTS BROMLEY

★ **Horn Dance.** ANCIENT CUSTOM. Its origins are shrouded in mystery, but all the evidence suggests that this is one of Britain's longest surviving customs, being at least a thousand years old. Throughout the day (the Monday after the Sunday following 4 September), the dancers perform at various points in and around the village. Six men carry reindeer antlers on their shoulders, accompanied by 'Maid Marian' (a man dressed as a woman), the Fool in jester's costume, a hobby horse, and a boy with a bow and arrow. Abbots Bromley is on the edge of Needwood Forest, and the dance can almost certainly be linked to deer hunting, but whether it merely confirms the villagers' hunting rights, or echoes a pagan act of ritual magic to ensure a good supply of deer, is unknown. *10 miles E of Stafford.*

HANCHURCH

Church. SITING LEGEND. The fairies were blamed for moving the stones from one site to another when building was taking place, and in the end the fairies' choice of site was accepted. *SW outskirts of Stoke-on-Trent.*

KINVER

Holy Austin Rock. GIANTS. On Kinver Edge, a sandstone ridge covered with woodland and heath, can be found Holy Austin Rock with its cave dwellings, some of them still inhabited into the 1950s. A giant was said to live here with his wife, and he took his water supply from a stone trough called the Giant's Water Trough. One day, after fetching water, he caught his wife being kissed by a giant who lived in Samson's Cave at nearby Enville. He threw a long javelin-shaped stone at him and it stuck in the ground, to become known as the Bolt Stone. Neither the stone nor the trough survives, but the caves can still be visited. *Kinver Edge National Trust land, SW of Kinver, itself 4 miles N of Kidderminster.*

The ancient Abbots Bromley Horn Dance, associated with deer hunting, is still performed every September

LEEK

Churchyard Cross. PROPHECY. The shaft of the 10-foot cross standing by the chancel door is said to be sinking lower into the ground every year, and the prophecy is that

When the Churchyard Cross shall disappear,
Leek town will not last another year.

MORRIDGE

Black Mere. MERMAID. It was said that animals would not drink the water of this pool, birds would not fly over it, and that a mermaid lurked there whose pleasure was luring unwary travellers to their deaths. When it was partially drained in the last century, it was said that the mermaid appeared to warn workmen that she would drown Leek if her pool dried up. A local public house commemorates the mermaid legend. *High moorland known as Morridge between Buxton and Leek; Black Mere S of A53 at ST 040613; Mermaid Inn ½ mile to SW.*

TAMWORTH

Tamworth Castle. GHOSTS. Offa, King of Mercia, had a palace at Tamworth in the 8th century. It was followed by a Saxon fortification in the 10th century, and then a Norman stone castle was built in the late 11th century. Parts of this early castle still survive, overlaid with later additions and alterations, and the castle's long history has resulted in some hauntings: a woman on the staircase to the Tower Room, and in that room; a woman on the terrace; as well as sundry sighs and groans. *Open to public.*

WEST MIDLANDS

ASTON, BIRMINGHAM

Aston Park. GHOST. A ghostly woman has been seen in the park; one person who saw her in 1974 sitting on the grass next to the tennis court said she wore an 'old-fashioned maroon dress' and had brown hair in a bun. She vanished when this witness and two companions were about 25 yards away. *Birmingham suburbs, off A38.*

KNOWLE

Church. SITING LEGEND. The church was going to be built on the hill above St Anne's Well, but every night the fairies removed the stones to the present site, until the builders gave in and relocated the building. Completed in 1402, it is a fine Perpendicular church. *2 miles SE of Solihull.*

WALSALL

St Matthew's Church. SITING LEGEND. The parish church was being built at Church Acre (now the Chuckery), but the fairies apparently decided that the hill where the church now stands would be a better location, so they removed the materials to the new site. The oldest part of the church is the crypt - 13th-century with some possible Norman remains - so there has been a church here for many centuries. There are some 15th-century misericords (carvings beneath choir-stall seats), the largest set in the West Midlands and Staffordshire, with a centaur and other beasts among the subjects depicted.

DERBYSHIRE LINCOLNSHIRE AND NOTTINGHAMSHIRE

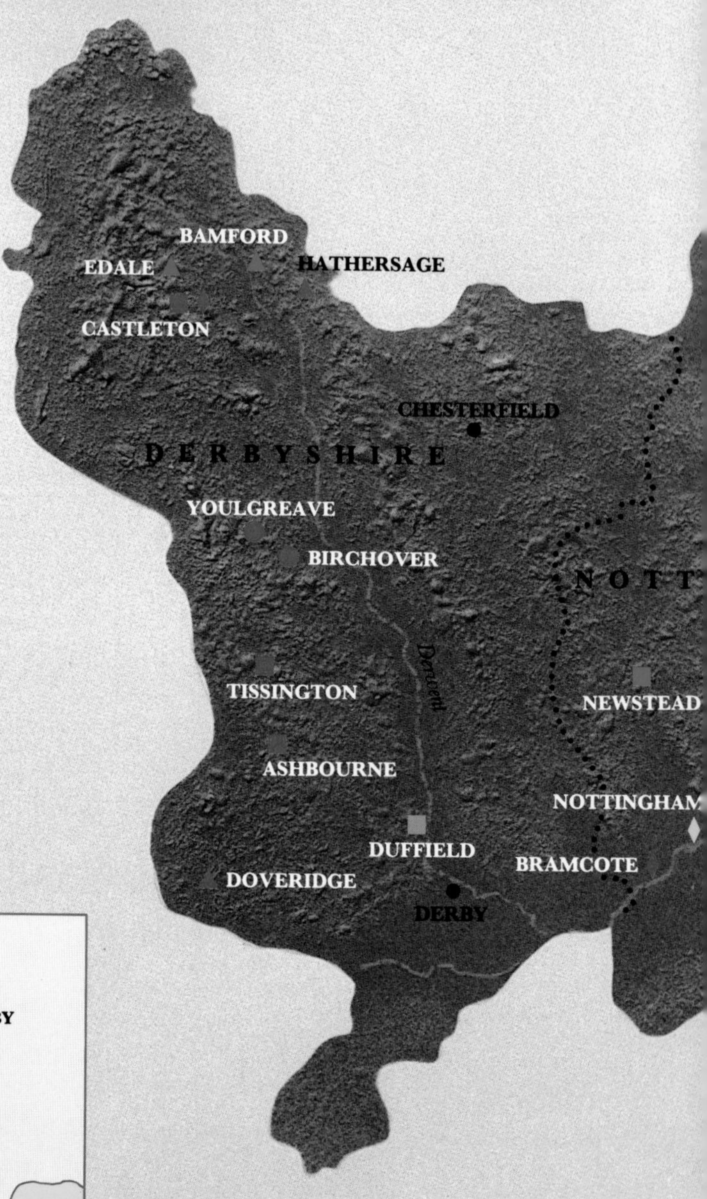

BAMFORD
EDALE
HATHERSAGE
CASTLETON
CHESTERFIELD
DERBYSHIRE
YOULGREAVE
BIRCHOVER
NOTT
Derwent
TISSINGTON
NEWSTEAD
ASHBOURNE
NOTTINGHAM
DUFFIELD
BRAMCOTE
DOVERIDGE
DERBY

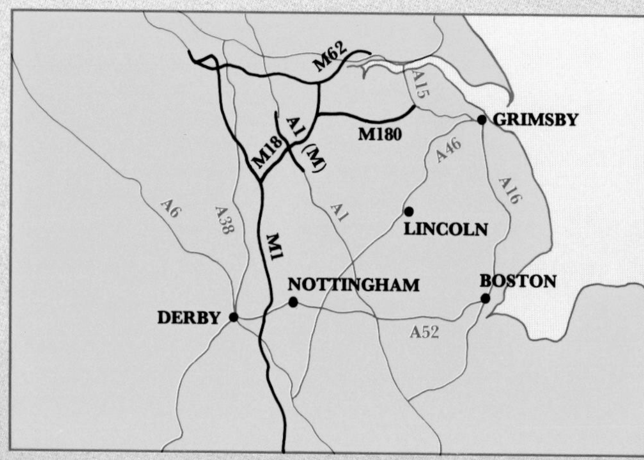

NORTH SEA
LAUGHTON
BLYBOROUGH
GLENTHAM
Trent
LINCOLN
BARDNEY
EDWINSTOWE
WELLOW
LINCOLNSHIRE
GHAMSHIRE
GUNBY
SKEGNESS
NEWARK
OXTON
DORRINGTON
CRANWELL
BOSTON
THE WASH
MILES
KILOMETRES
0
10
20
0
10
20
30
40

DERBYSHIRE

BAMFORD

Bridge near Shatton. GHOSTS; BOGGART (PHANTOM DOG). A ghostly old man – a farmer dressed in a knee-length smock and an old hat, and carrying a lantern with a tallow candle – was seen by several people in the hamlet of Shatton earlier this century. One lady walking home to Shatton from Bamford crossed the stone bridge over the River Noe and looked behind her, as she was afraid of walking alone in the dark. She saw the farmer, with 'white whiskers and rosy cheeks', which she noticed in the light of the lantern he carried. She hurried on, and saw him move on to the path to Offerton and Hathersage.

In the same area another lone walker saw a boggart, which he described as 'something terrifying and supernatural', not a dog or a ram – but as he mentioned those creatures it was presumably somewhat similar, and sounds like our old friend the phantom black dog. It blocked his way and wouldn't let him pass, so he found a gap in the hedge – but that too was blocked by the boggart. In the end he had to go by a longer route. *Bamford 10 miles NE of Buxton, and Shatton ½ mile SW.*

Well-dressing, a traditional custom still celebrated in a number of Derbyshire villages

BIRCHOVER

★ Nine Ladies Stone Circle, Stanton Moor and Rowtor Rocks. PETRIFACTION LEGEND; DRUIDS. Accompanied by a single standing stone, the King Stone, the stone circle has a name that suggests a tale of people turned to stone – perhaps for dancing on the Sabbath. There are numerous burial cairns on Stanton Moor, the area apparently having been used as a cemetery in the Early Bronze Age.

So-called 'druidic' relics can be seen at the other side of Birchover, behind the Druid Inn. Rowtor Rocks is a cliff with oddly shaped gritstone outcrops and vague druidic connections. It was of special interest to the Rev. Thomas Eyre, who in the late 17th century had three of the outcrops fashioned into seats, and also built Rowtor Chapel at the base of the cliff. There are also two 'rocking stones' on the cliff; and along the road to Winster are two pinnacles called Robin Hood's Stride. *Birchover 4 miles NW of Matlock; Stanton Moor to NE, reached along footpath off road to Stanton in Peak or off road to Stanton Lees (Nine Ladies: SK 249635); Rowtor Rocks W of village behind Druid inn.*

CASTLETON

Peak Cavern. THE OTHERWORLD; DEVIL. Four famous caves are located close to Castleton. Peak Cavern (also called the Devil's Arse) was said to be an entrance to the Otherworld. A 12th-century swineherd searching for a lost sow due to give birth went in to look for her; as he walked through the darkness he saw a light and came out on a wide plain where the harvest was being gathered. He found his sow with her litter, and returned safely home – to find it was still winter back in Derbyshire. Treak Cliff Cavern is said to be the Devil's home; and when, after heavy rain, water streams from the cave, it is said to be the Devil urinating. *8 miles NE of Buxton; Peak Cavern close to village.*

Oak Apple Day and Garland Ceremony. ANCIENT CUSTOM. Celebrations to commemorate the re-entry of King Charles II into London in 1660 at the Restoration of the Monarchy after the Civil War have got mixed up with rituals originating much further back in time. These are centred on the Garland, a hollow cone covered with flowers and over 3 feet high, which is worn by the Garland King as he rides round the village in the evening accompanied by his Lady or Queen and retinue of dancing girls. After the procession the Garland is removed from the King, and the posy of blooms topping the Garland is taken off. The Garland is then hauled to the top of the church tower and fastened to a pinnacle, the others having been decorated with oak boughs. As this strange custom takes place in May it is clearly one of the many ancient spring-time rites, and was probably originally celebrated on 1 May. There are clues to its ancient origins: the Garland King is the same as the traditional Jack in the Green or green man; and his Queen was until recently a man dressed as a woman, the 'she-male' being a symbol of fertility. The celebrations now take place on 29 May (or 30 May if the 29th is a Sunday).

DOVERIDGE

Churchyard. ROBIN HOOD. It was believed that Robin Hood and Maid Marian were betrothed under the old yew tree in this churchyard. *2 miles E of Uttoxeter.*

DUFFIELD

Church. SITING LEGEND. St Alkmund's church, dating back to 1300 or earlier, stands outside the village, close to the River Derwent. It was originally intended to be built nearer the village centre, on a hill close to Castle Hill where the former Norman castle (now demolished) stood. But when building was underway, in one night the Devil removed all the materials to the present site. The workmen recommenced on the first site, but again the materials were removed; finally the Devil got his way. *4 miles N of Derby.*

EDALE

Crossroads. PHANTOM HORSES; PHANTOM DOG. Some men walking home one night had reached the crossroads between the church and the railway station when they heard galloping horses. They made themselves ready to stop the animals, which could be heard getting steadily closer - but they could see nothing! The sounds passed the men, but despite the bright moonlight none of them saw anything; they agreed that the sounds had turned up the lane to Hope. Later they discovered that others had heard the same ghostly horses.

A mile to the west, at Upper Booth, a girl walking along one evening in 1930 saw a phantom black dog which passed through a wire fence. *5 miles NE of Chapel-en-le-Frith.*

HATHERSAGE

Churchyard. ROBIN HOOD. Little John, Robin Hood's right-hand man, was said to have been born in the village, and there were once several items of his to be seen. Now only his grave remains. The 10-foot grave is in the churchyard, and is clearly marked with a headstone. When it was opened in 1784, a 32-inch thighbone was found. But the people who kept it suffered misfortunes, so the bone was replaced in the grave. Little John's bow, 6 feet 7 inches long, together with arrows, some chain armour and a green cap, used to hang in the church, and the cottage where he is said to have died stood at the east end of the church until some time in the last century. There are places in the neighbourhood named after Robin Hood and Little John: Hood Brook, Little John's Well, Robin Hood's Cross and Robin Hood's Cave are a few examples. Robin Hood's Pricks were cairns in the Grindleford Bridge area. *10 miles NW of Chesterfield.*

YOULGREAVE

Nine Stones, Harthill Moor. MOVING STONES. There are only four stones, not nine - possibly the remains of a prehistoric burial chamber. Another name is the Grey Ladies, and it was believed that they danced at midnight. *1½ miles SE of Youlgreave, itself 2 miles S of Bakewell; stones E of lane from Alport to Elton (SK 227625).*

LINCOLNSHIRE

BARDNEY

Bardney Abbey and Tumulus. KINGS' BURIALS: SAINT'S SHRINE. Ethelred, King of Mercia, is said to have founded Bardney Abbey in the 7th century, and his burial place was traditionally the tumulus just east of the abbey site. His wife brought the bones of St Oswald, King of Northumbria, to Bardney after he was killed in battle, but it is said that the monks refused to open the door to allow the bones entry. During the night a pillar of light shot up to the sky, which the monks realized was a sign from Heaven, so they took in the bones and buried them. Afterwards many pilgrims came to the saint's shrine, where healing miracles were reported, until the abbey was destroyed by the Danes in 870. It was later rebuilt. Some relics from the 7th-century abbey can be seen in the parish church, and the high altar is said to be St Oswald's body-stone. *9 miles SE of Lincoln; abbey site and tumulus ¾ mile to N, W of B1202. Tumulus passed by two footpaths from B2102; abbey site reached along track from village (tumulus: TF 121708).*

BLYBOROUGH

Road to Grayingham. PHANTOM DOGS. A ghostly black dog haunted the lane near the fish pond. One woman who saw it when walking on this road nearly fainted: 'Quick as lightning, I upped wi' the umbrella I was a-carryin' an' lammed 'im one as 'ard as I could.' But the umbrella 'went clean thruff 'im' and the dog trotted on beside her. Lincolnshire is particularly well endowed with phantom black dogs, including others in lanes close to Blyborough, and the footpath south from Willoughton to Hemswell is reputed to have had a 'table-high' black dog. *7 miles NE of Gainsborough.*

CRANWELL

Byard's Leap. WITCH. When the local people decided to rid themselves of a tiresome witch, the story goes, a shepherd was chosen to stab her. He fetched all the horses to the pond, and the first one to raise its head from

Lane by Blyborough fishpond, said to be haunted by a phantom black dog

drinking when he threw a stone into the water was the one he had to mount. He did so and called the witch, who got up behind him on the animal, which was named Bayard. When the shepherd stabbed her in the breast, she clutched the horse's back with her long, sharp claws and he leaped with the pain. The jump carried him 60 feet, and the witch fell off his back into the pond and drowned. In another version, a knight was riding past when the witch jumped up behind him and Bayard made three leaps, marked by three stones 30 yards apart. Today the event is marked by two sets of four horseshoes 50 yards apart. *Cranwell 3 miles NW of Sleaford; Byard's Leap between B6403 and old road, near café and garage 2½ miles W of Cranwell.*

DORRINGTON

Church. SITING LEGEND. The present church stands on a hill outside the village, and it was said that its intended site had been inside the village, but the builders twice found their day's work undone at night. The third night they kept watch, but nothing happened. After they came back from breakfast they found the work undone again, with a very big stone taken uphill to the new site, so they decided to build up there after all. It is rumoured that there was a pagan temple on the hilltop site before the church. Christian churches were frequently built on former sacred sites - though whether to exorcise the pagan evil spirits or because paganism lingered within the Christian religion is not entirely clear. *4 miles NE of Sleaford.*

GLENTHAM

Church. DEVIL. If you ran round the church seven times, sticking a pin in the belfry door every time, and on the seventh time looked through the keyhole, you would see the Devil - or so it was said. *10 miles NE of Lincoln.*

GUNBY

Gunby Hall. GHOSTS. Sir William Massingberd built the Hall in 1700, after his daughter had eloped with a postilion rider whom Sir William shot dead. The ghosts of the lovers are said to haunt the Ghost Walk, a path near Gunby Hall. *7 miles W of Skegness; open to public (National Trust).*

LAUGHTON

Church. GHOST. In 1974, when workmen were repairing the church tower, they started hearing mysterious footsteps on the tower stairway. Eighteen-year-old Jeffrey Curtis heard them twice: 'It was as if somebody was coming up the tower but there was nobody there,' he said. 'I was a bit shaken at first, and did not want to be alone in the church for a few days after.' *8 miles SW of Scunthorpe.*

LINCOLN

Lincoln Cathedral. DEMON. Among the many fine carvings in the cathedral is one known as the Lincoln Imp, on a pillar in the Angel Choir. He was once alive, and proved troublesome when the cathedral was being built, so the priests exorcised him and turned him to stone.

The Major Oak, meeting place of Robin Hood and his men, near Edwinstowe in Sherwood Forest

SKEGNESS AREA

North Sea. SEA MONSTERS. There have been numerous sightings of sea monsters off the east coast this century. A boy holidaying at Trusthorpe one summer in the late 1930s was walking along the sea-wall when he saw a 'huge snake-like body' partially submerged 400 yards away. Off Chapel St Leonards in October 1966 a creature with a serpent-like head and 'six or seven pointed humps' was seen 100 yards offshore.

NOTTINGHAMSHIRE

BRAMCOTE

Hemlock Stone. DEVIL. The 30-foot block of red sandstone was said to have been a projectile thrown by the Devil at Lenton Priory from *Castleton* (where the Devil lives - see Derbyshire). In the 19th century, when the

CALENDAR OF EVENTS

February/March: Shrove Tuesday and Ash Wednesday
ASHBOURNE, Derbyshire. *Royal Shrovetide Football:* Street football with large scrums or 'hugs' often surrounding the ball.

April/May/June (Ascension Day)
TISSINGTON, Derbyshire. *Well-Dressing:* One of the first locations for this now-widespread custom of decorating wells with intricate flower pictures (see entry for *Tissington*). Well-dressing ceremonies can be found from May to August in many Derbyshire locations – WIRKSWORTH, ETWALL, YOULGREAVE, TIDESWELL, BAKEWELL, BUXTON, BARLOW and WORMHILL among others.

29 or 30 May
CASTLETON, Derbyshire. *Oak Apple Day and Garland Ceremony:* Procession carries garland of flowers to church tower (see entry for *Castleton*).

May: Spring Bank Holiday
WELLOW, Nottinghamshire. *Maypole Dancing.*

ancient druids were popularly believed in, the stone was believed to be a 'druidical altar'. It is probable that it had some significance in prehistoric times, though now its significance cannot be deduced. Close by there was a healing well called Sick Dyke, especially efficacious for rheumatism, and this sacred spring may have had a role to play when pagan rites were practised here. One and a half miles north, on Catstone Hill, is a similar but smaller stone called the Cat Stone. *1 mile E of Stapleford; Hemlock Stone on Stapleford Hill W of B6004.*

EDWINSTOWE

★ **Major Oak, Birklands Wood.** ROBIN HOOD. Here in the heart of Sherwood Forest can be found the Major Oak, a thousand-year-old oak tree still clinging to life, where Robin Hood and his men are said to have met, and hidden, because they were able to get inside the hollow trunk out of sight of the Sheriff of Nottingham. Other ancient trees in the wood have Robin Hood connections: Centre Tree marks the focal point of Robin's network of secret pathways, and Robin Hood's Larder is where he hung his game. Robin and Maid Marian were said to have been married in Edwinstowe church. *7 miles NE of Mansfield; Major Oak approached by footpath from B6034 N of Edwinstowe.*

Rufford Abbey. GHOST. The ruins are haunted by a monk with a skull for a face. *2 miles SE of Edwinstowe; open to public.*

NEWARK

St Catherine's Well. HOLY WELL. Sir Everard Bevercotes was slain here by his rival in love, Sir Guy Saucimer, and where the dead knight's head fell a spring began to flow. Sir Guy rode away, full of remorse, and later caught leprosy while abroad. He then had a vision of St Catherine, who told him the spring at Newark would cure his leprosy, so he returned and built a hermit's cell close to the spring. He had to move it when the site was flooded by a river, and built a chapel by the second St Catherine's Well. Today the site of the original well, in Devon Park close to the Civil War earthwork called Queen's Sconce, is marked, but the site of the second well is not known. *Close to River Devon (E bank) on W side of town.*

NEWSTEAD

★ **Newstead Abbey.** GHOSTS. Built in 1170 as a priory of the Black Canons, the abbey became the home of the Byron family after the Dissolution; it was haunted by a Black Friar, the sight of whom portended disaster. The poet Lord Byron saw him several times, including just before his unhappy marriage to Anne Milbanke. The ghost of 16th-century Sir John Byron is said to appear beneath his portrait, where he stands reading, and a White Lady has also been seen. In the grounds is an ornate monument of 1808 with a long epitaph to Byron's Newfoundland dog Boatswain. In his will, Lord Byron made a request to be buried with Boatswain in the vault beneath this monument, but his wish was not fulfilled. The monument is said to be where the church's high altar once stood. *Newstead 3 miles S of Kirkby-in-Ashfield; abbey (open to public) 1½ miles NE of Kirkby, reached from NE direction.*

NOTTINGHAM

Castle Rock. CAVES; UNDERGROUND PASSAGES. Castle Rock is riddled with tunnels and caves, the best known being Mortimer's Hole. This 107-yard-long passage was used in 1330 by Edward III and his followers to enter Nottingham Castle in secret and arrest Roger Mortimer, Earl of March, an adventurer who almost became king of England. Mortimer is said to haunt the passage. Other passages and caves lead from the cellars of the Olde Trip

Haunted Newstead Abbey, home of the poet Byron

to Jerusalem, the 'oldest pub in England', built into the sandstone rock below the castle. Before the city grew up, people lived in cave dwellings, and the name Nottingham derives from the Anglo-Saxon *snodenge* (caves) and *ham* (house). There are many other caves and passages under the city, some excavated, and a number of them can be visited (details can be obtained from the tourist information centre).

OXTON

Oxton Camp. ROBIN HOOD; LEY. Also known as Oldox, the camp is an Iron Age hillfort, small (2 acres) in area but in fine condition. It stands on Robin Hood's Hill, and close by on the north-west is a 20-foot-high mound 90 feet across; probably a round barrow, it is known as Robin Hood's Pot. A burial and a hoard of Roman coins have been found in the Pot. Paul Devereux and Ian Thomson identified a possible 14-mile ley passing through Oxton Camp. This alignment links Oxton church, Oxton Camp, Bilsthorpe church and moat, Boughton church, Walesby churchyard, and a ruined chapel by the River Maun. *The Ley Hunter's Companion* contains further details. *10 miles W of Newark; Oxton Camp 1 mile to N, reached along sunken lane from village.*

MAUGHOLD
ISLE OF MAN
PEEL
ST JOHN'S
CROSBY
DOUGLAS
BALLAKILPHERIC
PORT SODERICK
CREGNEISH
BALLASALLA
CASTLETOWN
LANGNESS
IRISH SEA
LANCASTER
LANCASHIRE
Ribble
BLACKPOOL
LONGRIDGE
CLITHEROE
PRESTON
RIBCHESTER
MELLOR
WALTON-LE-DALE
BURNLEY
BACUP
BOLTON
GREATER
MANCHESTER
MANCHESTER
Mersey
LIVERPOOL
MERSEYSIDE
BEBINGTON
APPLETON
ROSTHERNE
ANTROBUS
KNUTSFORD
CHESHIRE
MONK'S HEATH
CHESTER
OVER
CONGLETON
BEESTON
FARNDON
Weaver
0
10
20
MILES
KILOMETRES
0
10
20
30
40

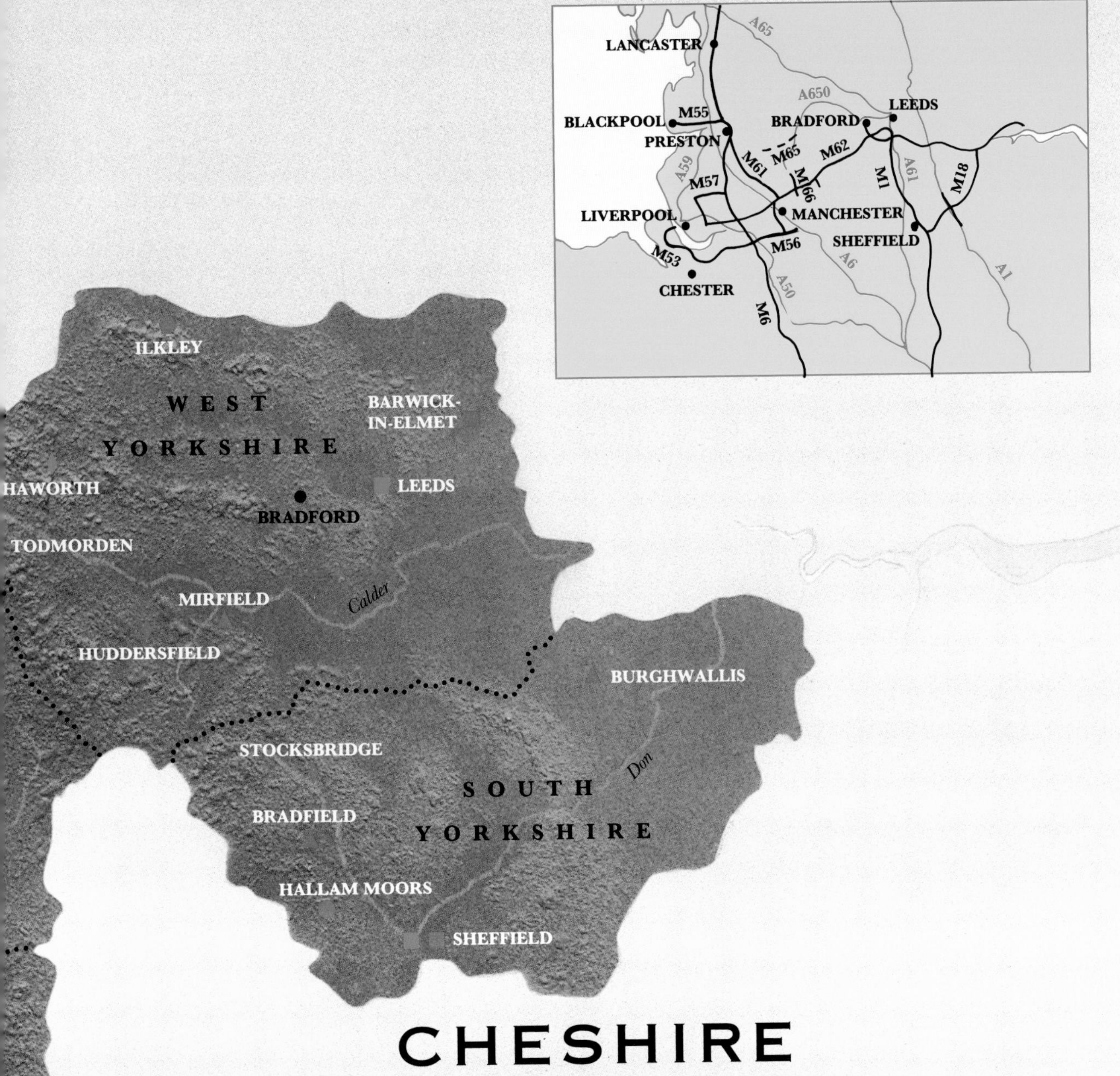

CHESHIRE GREATER MANCHESTER ISLE OF MAN LANCASHIRE MERSEYSIDE SOUTH YORKSHIRE AND WEST YORKSHIRE

CHESHIRE

ALDERLEY EDGE

★ **Alderley Edge.** ARTHURIAN LEGEND; MAGIC WELL. King Arthur is said to sleep in Alderley Edge, and one day a farmer leading a horse over the Edge met an old man who led him to a rock which he touched with a wand. An iron gate opened, and inside the farmer saw caverns where men and horses lay sleeping. The farmer's horse was needed to make up the numbers, so that they could all waken when George, son of George, became king. The farmer fled, leaving his horse behind. The wizard was Merlin, who is also remembered at a well in the woods. A natural spring under rocks, the Wizard's Well has an inscription reading: 'Drink of this and take thy fill, for the water falls by the wizard's will.' A face, older than the text, is also cut into the rock. *National Trust woods on Alderley Edge SE of village of same name, itself 1 mile S of Wilmslow; well reached from B5087 by following path signposted 'The Edge' and turning left where another path joins at right-angles.*

Carved head and inscription at the well on Alderley Edge

ANTROBUS

Souling Play. ANCIENT CUSTOM. At the beginning of November, on All Saints' and All Souls' Days, prayers were said for souls in purgatory and people sang a begging song for 'soul-cakes' which were given by the householders they visited. A soul-cakers' play, similar to a mumming play, was performed in some areas, and still survives in north-west Cheshire where it is performed in the pubs around Antrobus during the first two weeks of November. Among the characters are the Wild Horse (a horse's skull on a pole), King George, the Black Prince, the Quack Doctor, Mary (a 'she-male') and Beelzebub. *4 miles N of Northwich.*

APPLETON

Bawming the Thorn. ANCIENT CUSTOM. Bawming means adorning and decorating, and the thorn tree is hung with ribbons, garlands and flags annually in late June. The children dance around it singing a song, and then take part in sports and have tea. This genteel celebration is in contrast to the rowdy scenes which used to result when the Bawming was not solely a children's event and was followed by revelry and drunkenness, as a result of which the festival was banned during Victorian times. The ceremony is a possible survival of pre-Christian tree worship, or of midsummer fertility rites, and the original thorn was said to be an offshoot of the Glastonbury Holy Thorn. *3 miles S of Warrington.*

BEESTON

Beeston Castle. ROBIN HOOD; TREASURE. The castle stands on top of a prominent rock outcrop, and it was said that Robin Hood, who seems to have strayed from his usual haunts, shot an arrow at the crag from a barrow at Tilston Fearnall 2 miles away. It is worth climbing up to Beeston Castle for the views alone: they are superb - as far as the Welsh mountains to the west. Inside the 13th-century castle ruins can be seen a well, 366 feet deep, said to contain a treasure: 200,000 marks hidden by Richard II, or the Beeston family jewels - but nothing was found when the well was cleared out recently, nor were the demons seen which are said to guard it. *8 miles NW of Nantwich; open to public.*

CONGLETON

Bridestones Chambered Tomb. BRIDE'S BURIAL. Although this is a prehistoric burial chamber, it is in legend the burial place of the new bride of a general who followed her husband into battle and was killed near this place. *4 miles E of Congleton near Bridestones Farm, and reached off lane linking Ryecroft Gate with Congleton (SJ 906622).*

CALENDAR OF EVENTS

Good Friday
TODMORDEN, West Yorkshire. *Pace Egg Play:* Calder High School boys perform a traditional play at seven different locations including Mytholmroyd, Hebden Bridge, Midgley and Luddenden, ending at Todmorden.

Easter Saturday
BACUP, Lancashire. *Britannia Coconut Dancers:* Costumed dancers with blackened faces perform Nutters Dance around the streets, similar to morris dancing.

Easter Monday
PRESTON, Lancashire. *Egg-Rolling:* Children gather to roll decorated eggs down the hill slope at Avenham Park in Chapel Street; symbolic of new life in springtime.

May: first Saturday
KNUTSFORD, Cheshire. *Royal May Day:* May Queen, Jack in the Green, morris dancing, and especially 'sanding' - the ancient custom, performed nowhere else, of making pictures and designs with coloured sand in the streets.

May: Spring Bank Holiday
BARWICK-IN-ELMET, West Yorkshire. *Raising the Maypole:* Every three years (1987, 1990 etc.), the pole is refurbished, followed by celebrations (see entry for *Barwick-in-Elmet*).

June: third Saturday
APPLETON, Cheshire. *Bawming the Thorn:* Children dance around decorated bush (see entry for *Appleton*).

October/November: Hallowe'en and days following
ANTROBUS, Cheshire. *Souling Play:* Connected with the old custom of saying prayers for souls in purgatory (see entry for *Antrobus*).

26 December (Boxing Day)
HANDSWORTH, South Yorkshire. *Sword Dancing:* Traditional longsword dancing. Also at GRENOSIDE not far away (see entry for *Sheffield*, South Yorkshire).

Putting up the maypole, Barwick-in-Elmet

FARNDON

Farndon Bridge. GHOSTS. The ancient bridge across the River Dee links England to Wales. Built *c.*1345, it was said to be haunted by two children. They were the sons of Prince Madoc, left in the care of Roger Mortimer and the Earl of Warren when their father died. Sadly, the guardians had to get rid of the children for political reasons, and quietly dropped them off the bridge into the river. Now they haunt the area, their cries heard on stormy nights. *A534 crosses bridge, 5 miles NE of Wrexham.*

GAWSWORTH

Church and Maggotty's Wood. GHOSTS. Four monuments to members of the Fitton family feature

The Fitton monuments in Gawsforth church, often visited by the ghost of a lady-in-waiting to Elizabeth I

prominently in the chancel of the 15th–16th-century church, and the ghost who haunts the church is said to be Mary Fitton, a lady-in-waiting to Queen Elizabeth I. She comes out from behind the altar and looks at the family monuments. Maggotty's Wood, not far away, takes it name from a local eccentric of the 18th century, 'Maggotty' Johnson, who had himself buried there; his tomb can still be seen, as perhaps can his ghost. *3 miles SW of Macclesfield; Maggotty's Wood (National Trust) ½ mile NW of village (SJ 888702).*

MONK'S HEATH

Capesthorne Hall. GHOSTS. Apart from the lady in grey seen so often here, the owner has seen a line of figures going down the steps into the family vault in his private chapel, and his son once saw a ghostly arm in his bedroom, reaching towards the window. It disappeared as he approached it. *On A34 6 miles N of Congleton; open to public.*

OVER

Church. DEVIL. St Chad's church is now located outside the town, although originally, so it is said, it was in the centre. The Devil carried it off as soon as it was built, but the monks of Vale Royal rang their bells and this so alarmed him that he dropped it. Through the saint's power it landed unharmed, and remains today where the Devil dropped it. *Over is W part of Winsford; church at S end, on Church Hill.*

ROSTHERNE

Rostherne Mere. MERMAID; DROWNED BELL. Every Easter Sunday a mermaid was said to swim along an underground passage from the Mersey to the Mere, and people used to visit it on that day in the hope of seeing her, or hearing her sing. She would ring the sunken bell which lies on the lake floor, and sit on it singing. The bell had fallen into the water when being hung at Rostherne church, and was lost for ever when its fall was cursed by one of the workmen. *4 miles NW of Knutsford.*

GREATER MANCHESTER

BOLTON

Hall-i-th'-Wood. GHOSTS. Built in 1483, the half-timbered manor house is now a folk museum. Three ghosts have been seen here. One, a man 'dressed in green with a lace tunic, breeches and buckled shoes, carrying a sack over his shoulder', disappears through the wall where there was once a doorway. Upstairs a man in black has been seen, and a little old lady haunts the kitchen. *3 miles N of Bolton centre, on A58.*

MANCHESTER

Boggart Hole Clough, Blackley. BOGGART. The deep wooded valley, now surrounded by the city, is still a mysterious place. Its name comes from the boggart, a mischievous brownie who played tricks on everyone in the farmhouse here that he haunted (the farm no longer exists). *3 miles N of city centre, E of A664; footpaths cross valley.*

ROCHDALE

St Chad's Church. SITING LEGEND. The church was intended to be built down by the River Roch, but the materials were moved uphill by supernatural means, so it was built on its present hilltop site instead.

ISLE OF MAN

BALLAKILPHERIC

Giant's Quoiting Stone. GIANT. This standing stone is said to bear the marks of a giant's huge hands on top. There used to be five stones in a circle, all with the giant's marks, thrown by him from a mountain 2 miles to the north. *3 miles NW of Castletown, in field W of B44 just N of village (SC 221716).*

BALLASALLA

Fairy Bridge. FAIRIES. The A5 road between Douglas and Castletown crosses the Fairy Bridge, and at one time the islanders would doff their hats and greet the Little People here. The island used to be one of their strongholds, and a round barrow not far from the bridge was said to be one of their Fairy Hills. *Fairy Bridge 2 miles NE of Ballasalla, itself 2 miles NE of Castletown; Fairy Hill ½ mile SW of Fairy Bridge (SC 299714).*

CASTLETOWN

Castle Rushen. GIANT; UNDERGROUND PASSAGES; GHOST. A spellbound giant is said to be sleeping in underground apartments at the castle, discovered only after penetrating a warren of underground passages. A tunnel also linked the castle with Rushen Abbey at Ballasalla, 2 miles away. The building is haunted by a woman in grey, who has been seen by visitors and by the castle caretakers. *Open to public.*

CREGNEISH

Meayll Circle. GHOSTS. The stones form six T-shaped chambers which were originally covered by an earth bank, forming a chambered cairn where burials were placed in prehistoric times. A ghost army of men and horses was once seen nearby. *In SW tip of island; circle ¼ mile N of Cregneish, on Mull Hill E of lane N to Port Erin (SC 189677).*

CROSBY

St Trinian's Chapel. BUGGANE. The chapel is said to have never been finished, for every time they tried to put a roof on it, a buggane (a particularly nasty type of goblin) would rise from the ground and pull it down. *Beside A1 4 miles NW of Douglas.*

DOUGLAS

Saddle Road. FAIRIES. A strange-shaped stone sticks out of the wall in Saddle Road. It is said to be a fairy saddle turned to stone – the one they used when riding the vicar of Braddan's horses during the night.

LANGNESS

St Michael's Island. GHOSTS. People who drowned at sea were often buried in the graveyard of the little 12th-century church, now ruined, and the ghosts of these lost souls were sometimes seen sitting on the graves or walking up from the shore. The church is also haunted by the ghosts of pirate raiders, now imprisoned inside after murdering the priest, seizing his treasure, and drowning when they set sail. To hear their screams and curses, all you have to do is knock on the outside wall of the church. *Northernmost point of Langness, 2 miles E of Castletown.*

MAUGHOLD

Churchyard and St Maughold's Well. UNDERGROUND PASSAGE; FAIRIES; HOLY WELL. From the churchyard an underground passage was said to extend 9 miles in a north-westerly direction, to the earthwork Shan Cashtal south-west of Blue Point on the coast; it was used by the fairies. Maughold is famous as an early Christian centre, and the remains of early churches and carved cross-slabs can be seen in the churchyard. To the north-east, half a mile from the village, is St Maughold's Well, which flowed where the saint's horse landed. Its water was believed to cure many ailments, including sore eyes and infertility. Barren women would sit in the saint's chair nearby (no longer to be seen) and drink a glass of the well water. *3 miles SE of Ramsey.*

PEEL

Peel Castle. PHANTOM DOG; GIANT. The Moddey Dhoo, the Manx version of the giant phantom black dog of Norfolk, haunted Peel Castle, and was so familiar a sight to the soldiers in the guardroom that they took no notice when it came and sat by their fire. One night a drunken soldier said he would find out if it was dog or devil; he intended taking the castle keys alone to the Captain of the Guard, a journey which took him past the dog's lair. After a while the soldiers heard a loud noise and the foolhardy man returned, speechless; he died three days later. The dog was never seen again, and the passage where the soldier encountered it was closed off.

The legendary first ruler of the Isle of Man was Manannan Mac Lir (Manannan Son of the Sea), who was believed to be a giant and magician who could become invisible and travel wherever he wished. He lived in a castle on top of Barrule, and he had another vantage point now known as Manannan's Chair, an earthwork alongside a lane near Cronk-y-Voddy 3 miles north-east of Peel (SC 293857). He is said to be buried in a grassy mound 30 yards long which lies below the walls of Peel Castle, close to the sea. *Ruined castle on St Patrick's Isle.*

PORT SODERICK

Irish Sea. DROWNED ISLAND. In the sea off Port Soderick was said to be an island, submerged by the magician Finn McCool after he had been insulted by the people living there, whom he turned into blocks of granite. He allowed the island to surface for 30 minutes every seven years, and if during that time anyone could place a Bible on the island when it was at its original height above water, the spell would be broken. A girl called Nora, out walking with her sweetheart one autumn eveing, saw the island and rushed off to find a Bible, but she was too late, and pined away through disappointment. *3 miles SW of Douglas.*

ST JOHN'S

Tynwald, Giant's Grave and Slieu Whallian. RITUAL; GIANT; WITCHES. Tynwald Hill may originally have been a Bronze Age burial mound, but for centuries it has been a place of assembly, where at midsummer (5 July according to the old calendar) the parliament gathers and new laws are proclaimed in Manx and English. The hill is linked by a processional way to St John's church. Fifty yards to the north, a Bronze Age stone burial cist was discovered during road widening in the last century. This is called Giant's Grave and can still be seen. South of the village is the hill of Slieu Whallian where witches were punished by being rolled downhill in barrels full of spikes. It is haunted by the cries of a murdered witch, heard amid the howling wind.

LANCASHIRE

BURNLEY

Parish Church and Godley Lane. PHANTOM DOG; SITING LEGEND. One of the giant black dogs encountered in other parts of Britain was said to haunt the area of Burnley parish church and Godley Lane. He was called Skriker or Trash in Lancashire, the latter name from the splashing sound his feet made, 'like old shoes in a miry road'.

The church was intended to be built in Godley Lane, but every morning the workmen would arrive to find the stones and scaffolding moved to the present site. Traditionally they were moved by goblins in the form of pigs - pigs are sculpted on the south side of the steeple and on the old font. A black dog also haunted the Hurstwood area of Burnley, but the ghost was laid near Hoggarths Cross.

CLITHEROE

Peggy's Well. WATER SPIRIT. The stepping stones over the River Ribble at Brungerley Bridge had an evil reputation, for every seven years the river claimed a life here. Not far away in the grounds of Waddow Hall is Peggy's Well, and the spirit of the well was blamed for loss of life in the river. A mutilated stone figure which stood by the well was said to be Peggy of the Well, and to have been removed from the house where the servants blamed it for all problems and disasters. At one time, a bird, cat or dog would be drowned in the river on 'Peg's night' every seventh year, to appease the water spirit in the hope that it would not claim a human victim. *Brungerley Bridge ¼ mile NW of Clitheroe on B6478 to Waddington; Peggy's Well at SD 736426 in field near river; obtain permission to visit from Waddow Hall (Girl Guide Movement Training Centre).*

LONGRIDGE

Written Stone. EVIL SPIRIT. The stone, laid in place in 1655 by Ralph Radcliffe, is traditionally said to mark the site of a murder; alternatively a boggart plaguing a nearby farmhouse was imprisoned under it. A later owner of the farm saw the stone and decided to use it in the dairy. After it was laboriously moved there the family were plagued by trouble, so it was decided to take it back. The return journey proved much easier for the beasts carting it. Passing travellers sometimes experienced a strange atmosphere near the stone, and a doctor whose horse bolted when he rode past returned and challenged the spirit, whereupon 'something' materialized, lifted him off his horse and nearly choked him. *Longridge 7 miles NW of Blackburn; Written Stone in Written Stone Lane 2 miles NE at Dilworth, off B6243.*

MELLOR

Mellor Moor. FAIRIES. An underground city was believed to lie beneath the moor, swallowed up during an

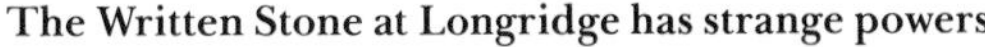

The Written Stone at Longridge has strange powers

earthquake, and on certain days its bells can be heard ringing as the inhabitants celebrate their festivals. Maybe they are the fairies, for it was also said that a fairy army is sometimes seen marching on the hillside, and during the last century a man near the earthwork on the top of the moor saw a 'dwarf-like man, attired in full hunting costume, with top-boots and spurs, a green jacket, red hairy cap, and a thick hunting whip in his hand. He ran briskly along the moor for a considerable distance, when, leaping over a low stone wall, he darted down a steep declivity, and was lost to sight.' This sighting may, surprisingly, be factual and not fictional, for there are many accounts even today of sightings of the Little People. *2 miles NW of Blackburn; Mellor Moor NE of village, crossed by footpaths.*

Dr John Dee and his assistant raising a corpse in St Leonard's churchyard at Walton-le-Dale

NEWCHURCH IN PENDLE

★ **Church and Pendle Hill.** WITCHCRAFT. The Pendle Hill area was notorious for its witches in the 17th century, and still today the reputation lingers. Groups of witches were tried in 1612 and 1633, and though the evidence against them was flimsy and unreliable, some were convicted and hanged. Today, a flat gravestone said to be the burial place of one of the victims, Alice Nutter, can be seen in the churchyard, though she was in fact buried in Lancaster. The stone bears a worn carving of a head and is south of the church. On the east side of the church tower is a witchcraft eye or Eye of God, put there to protect the church against witches in the 16th century. Some of the witches confessed to practising their magic in the Forest of Pendle south of Pendle Hill. *Newchurch in Pendle 4 miles N of Burnley; Pendle Hill 2 miles NW.*

RIBCHESTER

Hothersall Hall. BOGGART. When feeling in a good mood, the boggart will do chores for the family he lives with; but when irritated he will be a mischievous nuisance. Hothersall Hall had just such a boggart, whose nuisance value apparently exceeded his usefulness, for he was 'laid' under the roots of a large laurel tree in the grounds and cannot escape while the tree is still alive. To keep the spell and the tree alive, its roots must be periodically moistened with milk – which sounds like a libation or offering to the spirit of the tree. *Ribchester 5 miles NW of Blackburn, and Hothersall Hall 1 mile to W; footpath near church passes W by Hall on N bank of River Ribble.*

WALTON-LE-DALE

St Leonard's Churchyard. BLACK MAGIC. It was in this churchyard on 12 August 1560 that Dr John Dee, the occultist and scholar, together with an assistant, met to raise a body from the grave. The man had died without revealing where he had hidden his money, and they intended to ask him. At midnight in bright moonlight they opened the grave, removed the coffin lid and used incantations to animate the body. It rose out of the grave and stood before them. Not only did it give them the information they sought, but it also made some strange predictions concerning local people, which later came true. *2 miles SE of Preston.*

MERSEYSIDE

BEBINGTON

Poulton Road. GHOST. The area of Poulton Hall was said to be haunted by a nun who had been killed when on the way to a nunnery. In August 1970, a man driving along Poulton Road at night saw a girl in his headlights. Although he sounded his horn, she did not move and he had to stop his car. As he got out, she faded and disappeared. When this report appeared in the local press, another man reported a similar experience in the same road. He saw a girl with long hair and a long dark coat standing beside the road, so he stopped to see if she needed help. As he opened the passenger door, the girl 'slowly vanished into thin air'. *On Wirral, 3 miles S of Birkenhead; Poulton Hall S of B5137 and 1 mile W of Bromborough.*

LIVERPOOL

Speke Hall. GHOST. The half-timbered Tudor house has a haunted Tapestry Room. A woman has been seen near a window, and disappearing into the wall of a bedroom, in the place where a secret passage has been found. *8 miles SE of Liverpool centre, close to River Mersey; open to public (National Trust).*

SOUTH YORKSHIRE

BRADFIELD

Bailey Hill. TREASURE; UNDERGROUND PASSAGE; LEY; SITING LEGEND. The ancient mound stands not far from the church, its original purpose being unknown, but it was possibly a burial mound, possibly a Norman and/or Saxon fortification, possibly a local meeting place, and possibly all of these. Local people talk of treasure hidden in it, and an underground passage linking it with Castle Hill; this may be a folk memory of a ley alignment, for if the line of the underground passage is extended it cuts through Bar Dyke 2 miles to the north-west.

The fact that the church was sited close to Bailey Hill suggests that it was an ancient sacred site. This is confirmed by the legend that Bradfield church was to have been built at Low Bradfield, but every night the materials were moved to Bailey Hill, so in the end the pagan sacred site was adopted by the Christians. *6 miles NW of Sheffield centre.*

BURGHWALLIS

Robin Hood's Well. ROBIN HOOD. All around here was once Barnsdale Forest, where Robin Hood lived in early versions of his legend. His name still survives at Robin Hood's Well, at a lay-by west of Burghwallis close to the A1. The well has a cover designed by Vanbrugh. Loxley, on the western outskirts of Sheffield, was Robin Hood's birthplace according to one tradition, and there used to be Robin Hood place-names in the area. Robin Hood's Grave, so called, is at Kirklees Priory, *Mirfield* (see West Yorkshire). *Burghwallis 6 miles NW of Doncaster.*

HALLAM MOORS

Head Stone. MOVING STONE. Looking vaguely like a head, this tall pillar comprising several stones was also once called Stump John and Cockcrowing Stone. This last refers to the belief that it turns round on a certain morning when the cock crows. The stone has been found to align with other points, and may have been part of a system for making astronomical observations in prehistoric times. *6 miles W of Sheffield centre, ¼ mile S of A57 (at SK 255873), and prominent in landscape.*

SHEFFIELD

Beauchief Abbey. GHOSTS; LEYS; UNDERGROUND PASSAGE. Only the west tower now stands of the 12th-century abbey, the grounds of which (and of nearby Beauchief Hall) are haunted by a White Lady and a monk, among others. At least two leys pass through the abbey. One links the abbey with Norton church (echoed by an underground passage also said to join the two) 1½ miles away; the other begins at Bole Hill, Fulwood. (More details of these leys appear in *Strange Sheffield*, a booklet by David Clarke and Rob Wilson published in 1987.) *On S outskirts of Sheffield, E of A621 and accessible by footpath.*

The death of the Dragon of Wantley, whose lair was on Wharncliffe Crags at Stocksbridge

Handsworth. SITING LEGEND; GHOST; ANCIENT CUSTOM. The 12th-century church stands on a hilltop site, though originally it was intended to be built at Woodhouse. Each day's work was mysteriously undone and the stones moved to Handsworth, until the builders relocated it. Now the church is said to be haunted, a Grey Lady having been seen standing by the font, and strange presences felt.

Traditional sword dances are still performed at Handsworth. They symbolize death and resurrection, and are performed during midwinter. The symbolic death of a sacrificial animal or man is still incorporated in the dance performed by the Grenoside team (north-west Sheffield), whose leader wears a rabbit-skin hat and is symbolically decapitated by his colleagues. Grenoside and Handsworth are the two longest-established sword-dancing teams in the Sheffield area, but there are others in Yorkshire. *4 miles E of Sheffield centre.*

STOCKSBRIDGE

Wharncliffe Crags. DRAGON; UNDERGROUND PASSAGE. The Dragon of Wantley (a name derived perhaps from Wharncliffe, or a combination of that and Wortley, a local knight who destroyed villages to improve his hunting in the 16th century) was slain by 'More of More Hall', wearing a spiked suit of armour, who kicked the beast in an uncomfortable place in the nether regions. It is an unlikely tale, probably concocted to satirize local feuds, but possibly also incorporating much older local legends.

The dragon's lair was said to be on Wharncliffe Crags, where Dragon's Den is a cave below the rock face. There are also a Dragon's Well and Dragon's Cellar in the area.

Across the valley of the River Don on Townend Common is Allman Well, from which an underground passage is said to run to More Hall. Other dragon legends were linked to water sources, as is this to two wells and a river, and somewhere lurking among the accretions of centuries may be traces of pre-Christian rituals involving water. *Stocksbridge 5 miles NW of outskirts of Sheffield; Wharncliffe Crags to SE, at N end of Wharncliffe Wood (SK 298975). Paths and tracks run through woods to N and S. Allman Well Hill, across valley to W, also crossed by footpaths.*

WEST YORKSHIRE

BARWICK-IN-ELMET

Maypole Raising Ceremony. ANCIENT CUSTOM. Every three years, the maypole (86 feet high and said to be the tallest in Britain) is lowered on Easter Monday and then re-erected, newly painted, on Spring Bank Holiday Tuesday. This is celebrated by the crowning of the May Queen and maypole dancing. Although such festivities were revived in Victorian times, their origins go back much further to pre-Christian fertility customs. The first day of May was Beltane, a major date in the Celtic calendar, and throughout Britain various Maytime customs perpetuate its importance, albeit often in ways far removed from the original earthy practices. (See, for example, *Padstow* in Cornwall and *Castleton* in Derbyshire.) *7 miles NE of Leeds centre.*

HAWORTH

Haworth Moor. GHOST. The Brontë family lived in Haworth Parsonage, which is now the Brontë Museum, and Emily and Charlotte are buried at the parish church. Emily, who died in 1848 aged 30, was best known for her atmospheric novel *Wuthering Heights*, and she took her inspiration from the moors behind Haworth. Her ghost now haunts the moors around Top Withens and the narrow path to the Brontë Waterfall 2 miles from the parsonage, which was a favourite place of the sisters. *Haworth 3 miles SW of Keighley; moor to W; Pennine Way long-distance footpath crosses Haworth Moor, and lanes and paths lead up from Haworth.*

HUDDERSFIELD

Castle Hill, Almondbury. TREASURE; DEVIL; UNDERGROUND PASSAGES. In prehistoric times Castle Hill was the site of an Iron Age hillfort, and various legends have grown up around it over the centuries. A golden cradle is buried in the hill; the Devil jumped from Scar Top at Netherton to Castle Hilll; and underground passages link it to the village of Farnley Tyas to the south-east, as well as to other localities, such as Almondbury to the north, and across the River Colne. *2 miles S of Huddersfield centre, accessible by road (SE 153141).*

ILKLEY

★ Rombalds Moor. GIANTS. The moor south of Ilkley is littered with Bronze Age relics – cairns, rock carvings, hut circles, barrows, enclosures and stone circles. Some have intriguing names like the Twelve Apostles stone circle (SE 125450), Grubstones ring cairn (SE 136447), Pancake Stone (SE 134462) and Swastika Stone (SE 094470). The last two are among the class of carved prehistoric stones known collectively as cup-and-ring stones, though differing designs are also found, such as the swastika-like design on the stone of that name. Two cairns called the Skirtful of Stones (SE 138451) and the Little Skirtful of Stones (SE 140445) were believed to be piles of stones held in the apron of the giant Rombald's wife. She collected the stones to throw at her husband when they quarrelled, but her apron-strings broke. *Ilkley 9 miles NW of Bradford centre; moor to S, reached by footpaths from Ilkley.*

LEEDS

Kirkstall Abbey. GHOST; UNDERGROUND PASSAGE. The gatehouse, now housing a museum, is said to be haunted by an old abbot, and strange noises have been heard late at night. An underground passage is believed to link the 12th-century abbey, now ruined, to the City Varieties Theatre in Leeds. *3 miles W of Leeds centre, close to A65; open to public.*

Temple Newsam House. GHOSTS. The big Jacobean house, built in 1622, has several ghosts including an old woman in blue. Lord Halifax, whose ancesters built the house, saw her in 1908 as she crossed his bedroom; in the

Haworth Parsonage, home of the Brontë sisters; Emily's ghost is said to frequent the area round about

firelight he saw she had a shawl across her shoulders. A small boy has been seen stepping from a cupboard, and ghostly screams have been heard. *5 miles E of Leeds centre, signposted off A63; open to public.*

MIRFIELD

Robin Hood's Grave, Kirklees Priory. ROBIN HOOD. A mound in the park is said to be Robin Hood's grave, Robin having been taken to the priory when he became ill in old age. The prioress may have helped hasten his death by bleeding him for too long, either accidentally or at the suggestion of Sir Roger of Doncaster. Before dying, Robin summoned Little John; when he arrived Robin shot an arrow over the park, asking to be buried where it landed. *4 miles NE of Huddersfield centre, in private grounds of Kirklees Priory; for permission to visit, write to Estate Office, Kirklees Estate, Mirfield, West Yorkshire.*

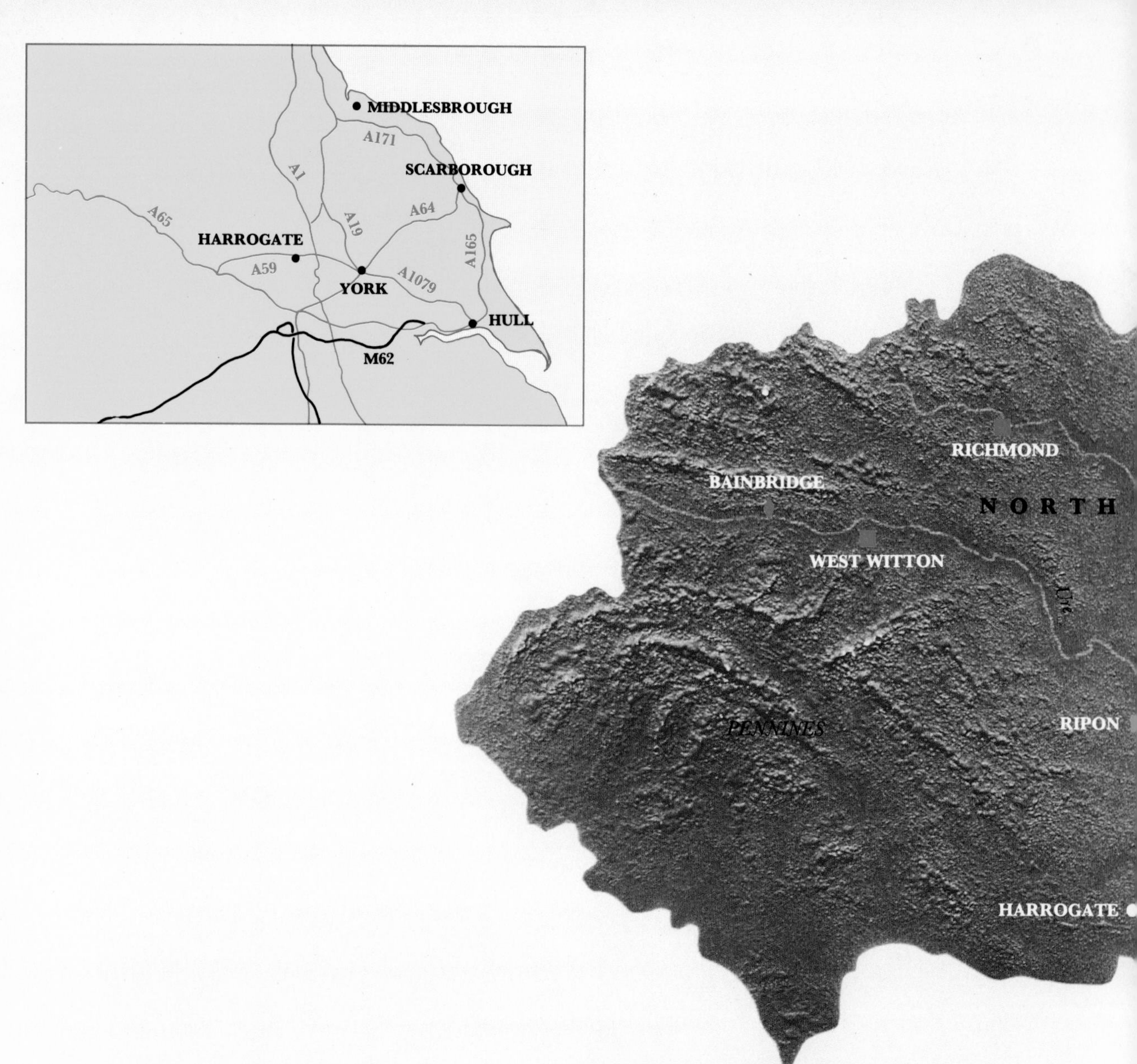

CLEVELAND HUMBERSIDE AND NORTH YORKSHIRE

0
10
20
MILES
KILOMETRES
0
10
20
30
40
MIDDLESBROUGH
CLEVELAND
GUISBOROUGH
MOORSHOLM
LYTHE
WHITBY
NORTH SEA
GOATHLAND
NORTH YORK MOORS
YORKSHIRE
SCARBOROUGH
THIRLBY
LOCKTON
Swale
NUNNINGTON
FILEY
WOLD
NEWTON
RUDSTON
BOROUGHBRIDGE
Derwent
Ouse
BURTON
AGNES
KNARESBOROUGH
YORK
LONG
MARSTON
HUMBERSIDE
LEVEN
BEVERLEY
HULL
WITHERNSEA
Humber
Bridge
Humber
BARNOLDBY
LE BECK
WILDSWORTH
HAXEY

CLEVELAND

GUISBOROUGH

Guisborough Priory. UNDERGROUND PASSAGE; TREASURE. From the ruined priory an underground passage was believed to extend to a field in Tocketts parish to the north. A chest of gold was hidden halfway along it, guarded by a raven, which changed to a devil when someone located the treasure.

MOORSHOLM

Gerrick Moor. ROBIN HOOD. Three tumuli in a line on the county boundary are known as Robin Hood's Butts - the place where he practised his archery. There are many tumuli scattered on the moors west towards Guisborough; one on Gisborough Moor was known as Hob on the Hill, Hob being the same as hobthrust, a mischievous spirit like a brownie, presumably believed to haunt the spot. *Gerrick Moor 2 miles SE of Moorsholm, itself 5 miles SE of Guisborough (Robin Hood's Butts: NZ 710116).*

HUMBERSIDE

BARNOLDBY LE BECK

Churchyard. PHANTOM BEAST. The 'shag-foal' said to haunt the churchyard seems to have been a cross between the familiar phantom black dog and a horse. Described as looking like a small horse, it would sit on its haunches like a dog and throw back its head before emitting unearthly cries. It was also seen in the lanes and fields round the village. *4 miles SW of Grimsby.*

BEVERLEY

Beverley Minster. UNDERGROUND PASSAGES. One of the finest Gothic churches in Europe, the Minster also has the largest collection of misericords (carvings beneath choir seats) in England. It is also, so legend has it, the starting point for two underground passages. One extends to the Abbey of Meaux 3 miles to the east, and was said to have been used to fetch food from Beverley when Meaux was being besieged. A woman who walked back and forth for three days carrying provisions died in the passage. Another passage is supposed to have led to Watton Abbey 7 miles to the north - rather too long a distance to be feasible.

BURTON AGNES

Burton Agnes Hall. GHOST; SKULL. In 1915 the then owner saw the ghost of a woman in fawn: while the family was taking tea in the house the ghost came from the garden, up the steps and in at the front door. Mrs Wickham Boynton conjectured that it was Anne Griffith, who was the daughter of the house's builder and died after being attacked by a robber. It is said that, before dying, she begged that her head be kept in the house she loved. After her burial in the churchyard, moaning noises were heard in the house until her head was dug up and brought home, where it stood on a table for many years. Later it was walled up in a niche prepared for it and there it remains, though hidden from view. The ghost is known as 'Owd Nance', and has been seen by visitors in recent years in an upstairs corridor. She also haunts the Queen's State Bedroom. *5 miles SW of Bridlington; open to public.*

HAXEY

Haxey Hood Game. ANCIENT CUSTOM. On 6 January, Christmas Day old-style, a ritual game of probable ancient origins takes place. The Hood, a 2-foot leather cylinder, is carried by the Fool, accompanied by 12 Boggans, the chief Boggan, and Lord of the Hood. By the churchyard the Fool mounts the Mowbray Stone and gives a speech of welcome before being 'smoked' by having a fire lit beneath his feet. Later the game begins, with the supporters of two pubs each trying to get the Hood back to their pub. A huge scrummage of men pushes to and fro for up to three hours until one of the pubs is reached. Traditionally the game originated in the 13th century when some local people retrieved Lady Mowbray's hood which had been blown off in the wind; but other possible origins include a type of street football, a fertility custom with the Hood having been the head of a sacrificial animal, or a Plough Monday custom (see *Goathland*, North Yorkshire). *6 miles NW of Gainsborough.*

LEVEN

White Cross. GHOST. The road at White Cross was said to be haunted by a headless woman who would leap up behind horsemen and slap their ears. Consequently the local people would travel miles out of their way to avoid passing the cross at night. *5 miles NE of Beverley; White Cross 1 mile S of Leven, on A165 to Long Riston.*

RUDSTON

★ **Rudston Monolith.** DEVIL; LEY. In the churchyard close to the church wall stands the tallest standing stone in England, at over 25 feet high. It was said to have been thrown here by the Devil, whose intention was to destroy the church, but having a bad aim, he missed.

A possible ley connects this stone to Willy Howe (see *Wold Newton*) as well as Willerby church, a tumulus on Staxton Brow, Gypsey Race and a cursus, and South Side Mount (see *The Ley Hunter's Companion* by Devereux and Thomson for more details). *5 miles W of Bridlington.*

The River Trent at haunted Jenny Hurn bend, Wildsworth

WILDSWORTH

River Trent. GHOST. A bend in the river north of Wildsworth is known as Jenny Hurn and had a reputation for being haunted. The ghost was small, man-like, with a seal's face and long hair, and he crossed the river in a boat like a large pie-dish, using oars the size of teaspoons. Another description was of a 'thing' that crawled out of the water and grazed in the fields. It had long hair, large eyes and walrus tusks. People would try to avoid passing close to the bend, for they felt uncomfortable there, and the boatmen said the same. *8 miles SW of Scunthorpe; Jenny Hurn bend on E side of river ½ mile NE of village, and lane to East Ferry passes right by it.*

WITHERNSEA AREA

North Sea. SEA MONSTERS. Strange sea creatures have been spotted off the Humberside coast, as off the coast of Lincolnshire further south (see *Skegness*, Lincolnshire). In the late 1930s, a woman living at Skiffing near Easington was lying on the beach and gazing out to sea when: 'Suddenly I saw a huge creature rise, it was of a green colour, with a flat head, protruding eyes, and a long flat mouth which opened and shut as it breathed; it was a great length and moved along with a humped glide.' When she called out to people nearby, the creature dived and did not reappear. In August 1945, a couple sitting on mud cliffs at Hilston saw 'a creature with a head and four or five rounded humps each of which was leaving a wake. It was moving rapidly but quite silently along shore northwards in face of a northerly wind.'

WOLD NEWTON

Willy Howe. FAIRIES; TREASURE; LEY. This fine round barrow was believed to be a fairy haunt, and a close encounter with them was described in detail by William of Newburgh in the 12th century. He told how a drunken man, returning home one night, heard the voices of people singing and decided to investigate. He was close by Willy Howe, and observed an open door leading into the mound. Looking inside, he saw a well-lit room filled with people at a banquet; one of the servants saw him and offered him a cup. He threw away the contents (knowing that to drink would put him in their power), but kept the goblet and ran off. The guests chased him, but he escaped and presented his prize to the king.

It was also said that treasure was hidden in the barrow. Some people dug and found a chest of gold, to which they fastened a team of horses, but as they pulled the chest sank deeper in, and it never has been recovered.

Willy Howe is on a ley alignment which also takes in *Rudston* monolith (see entry). *Wold Newton 6 miles SW of Filey, and Willy Howe 1 mile SE, just off lane to Burton Fleming and visible from track that passes its field (TA 061724).*

NORTH YORKSHIRE

BAINBRIDGE

Semer Water. DROWNED TOWN. A beggar (or maybe it was Christ) who asked for food at the town which once stood here was refused by all except a poor couple living in a cottage on the hill. He blessed their home, but cursed the town with the words:

> Semerwater rise, Semerwater sink,
> And swallow all the town,
> Save this little house on the hill
> Where they gave me meat and drink.

Next day the couple looked out and saw a lake covering the town in the valley. *Bainbridge 11 miles W of Leyburn; Semer Water 2 miles SW, visible from surrounding lanes.*

Wade's Causeway, a Roman road associated in legend with giants, near Goathland

BOROUGHBRIDGE

★ **Devil's Arrows.** DEVIL; ANCIENT CUSTOM; LEY. The three tall stones (there used to be four) were also known as the Devil's Bolts, and were said to have been thrown by the Devil from How Hill near Fountains Abbey; he was aiming them at the early Christian settlement at Aldborough. The stones are very impressive, being 18, 21 and 22½ feet tall, and clearly were of great importance to the people who erected them in prehistoric times, since the stone was brought from Knaresborough 6½ miles away.

In more recent centuries the St Barnabas Fair was held at the summer solstice in a field between the Devil's Arrows and Boroughbridge, and this is likely to have been the successor to pagan ceremonies held at the stones.

Two of the stones are on a ley discovered by Paul Devereux and Ian Thomson. Five miles long, the alignment links the stones with Cana Henge, a tumulus and another henge on Hutton Moor (more details are given in their *Ley Hunter's Companion*). *6 miles SE of Ripon; stones in fields W of village, on E side of A1 (SE 391665).*

FILEY

Filey Brigg. DEVIL; DRAGON; SEA MONSTER. There are two explanations for the long ridge of rocks known as Filey Brigg. In one version, they were built by the Devil. When he lost his hammer in the sea he plunged his hand in to find it, but brought out a fish. He exclaimed 'Ah! Dick!', and the fish, since then known as the haddock, carries the marks of the Devil's grasp on its shoulders.

The rocks were also seen as a dragon's bones – the dragon had terrorized Filey until it was drowned by local folk when it went down to the sea to wash parkin (sticky gingerbread) from between its teeth. (How it came to be eating parkin is too long a story to tell here!)

In 1934, a coastguard saw a real-life dragon at Filey Brigg: a 30-foot sea monster with eyes shining 'like torchlights'. *1 mile NE of Filey and reached by footpath.*

GOATHLAND

Plough Stots. ANCIENT CUSTOM. Plough Monday used to be celebrated widely in early January by a procession with 'plough stots' (youths acting as bullocks) dragging a plough around and stopping to collect money. Those who failed to pay would have their garden ploughed up. This was the time when the Christmas festivities were over and the farm work began again, usually with the spring ploughing, an important time in the farming calendar, and the original intention was to ensure a good growing season and harvest. A version of the plough stots custom, accompanied by sword dancing, is still enacted at Goathland. *7 miles SW of Whitby.*

Louven Howe and Lilla Howe. TREASURE. These are round barrows on Fylingdales Moor, where hidden treasure is said to be guarded by snakes, and any disturbance of the mounds will bring on violent thunderstorms. *3½ miles SE of village; footpaths pass by (Louven Howe: SE 887992; Lilla Howe: SE 889987).*

Wade's Causeway, Wheeldale Moor. GIANTS. The giant Wade's wife kept cattle on the moor, so he built her a road to enable her to reach them easily for milking. So legend has it; but in fact this road was built by the Romans, and once ran from Malton to Whitby. A 1¼-mile stretch on Wheeldale Moor has been excavated and

The ruins of Whitby Abbey, through which wanders the ghost of its 7th-century founder, St Hilda

preserved. Kerbstones and drainage culverts can be seen, and the large stones which now form the uneven road surface would originally have been covered with gravel, which has been washed away. *3 miles SW of Goathland; walk there from village, or go by car to S stretch at SE 803972.*

KNARESBOROUGH

★ Mother Shipton's Cave and Dropping Well. PROPHETESS; PETRIFYING WELL. 'Mother Shipton', born in 1488, was able to see into the future and became a famous prophetess. The cave where she was born, lived and made her prophecies is in woods at Knaresborough.

Close by is the Dropping Well, the water of which turns to stone any object placed in it; the process, which takes a year or so, is the result of the large amount of lime in the water. *3 miles NE of Harrogate; cave and well reached from A59; entrance on S side of River Nidd.*

LOCKTON

Hole of Horcum and Blakey Topping. GIANT. Another name for the Hole of Horcum, a deep valley like a natural amphitheatre beside the Whitby-Pickering road, is the Devil's Punchbowl, and it was said to have been formed when the giant Wade dug out a spadeful of earth. He threw it away to the east, and the hill called Blakey Topping was formed. *Lockton $4\frac{1}{2}$ miles NE of Pickering; Hole of Horcum $2\frac{1}{2}$ miles NE, W of A169; Blakey Topping $1\frac{1}{2}$ miles E of Hole of Horcum.*

The prehistoric Devil's Arrows at Boroughbridge, probable scene of pagan ceremonies

LONG MARSTON

Marston Moor Battlefield. GHOSTS. Oliver Cromwell defeated the Royalists on Marston Moor in 1644, and three hundred years later the ghosts of Cavaliers are still seen in the area. In 1932 two people driving across the battlefield on a misty November evening saw two men on the road. They were wearing large soft hats, dark plum-coloured cloaks and leggings. A bus passed and the car driver dipped his lights. When he put them up again, the men had gone. The driver and his companion stopped and searched, but there was no trace of them. In 1968 a group of tourists crossing the moor by car saw 'tramps' in the ditch, and on looking closer saw they were wearing 17th-century-style clothes. After passing them, the witnesses looked back, to find the 'tramps' had disappeared. They were seen again in 1973, and there have been other sightings. *Long Marston 7 miles W of York centre; battlefield to N, S of A59.*

LYTHE

Mulgrave Castle. GIANT. The old castle in Mulgrave Woods was said to be Wade's castle, built by the giant with the aid of his wife Bell. They also built Pickering Castle 18 miles to the south, and since they worked on one castle each but only had one hammer they used to shout out a warning as they threw it back and forth. Wade also built a road for his wife (see *Goathland*); and there are two sites said to mark his burial place not far away. One is Wade's Stone at East Barnby, where there were in fact two stones, and the other is to the north near Goldsborough, where again only one of two stones survives. *Lythe 3 miles NW of Whitby: Mulgrave Castle in woods 1 mile SW (NZ 840117); Wade's Stone S of A174 (NZ 831130); Goldsborough stone W of Barnby lane (NZ 830144).*

NUNNINGTON

Church. DRAGON. The effigy on the tomb of Walter de Teyes, a 14th-century knight, is said to be that of a dragon-slayer, Peter Loschy. On nearby Loschy Hill he fought the dragon for hours in what seemed a pointless battle, for every time the beast was wounded it rolled over and was instantly healed. Loschy therefore began to chop pieces off its body and his dog carried them away one by one, until there was nothing left of the dragon. But both hero and dog died from breathing the dragon's venom. *9 miles NW of Malton.*

RICHMOND

Richmond Castle. ARTHURIAN LEGEND; UNDERGROUND PASSAGE; GHOST. A man is said to have discovered a tunnel running into the hillside below Richmond Castle, and on venturing inside he saw King Arthur and his knights asleep at a round table. When he picked up the horn he saw on the table alongside a sword; they started to wake up, so he ran away. He heard a voice calling him:

> Potter Thompson, Potter Thompson!
> If thou hadst drawn the sword or blown the horn,
> Thou hadst been the luckiest man e'er born.

(Compare the legend of *Melrose*, Borders.)

The tunnel is also said to extend to Easby Abbey a mile away. A drummer boy was sent to explore it, and his drumbeats were heard until he reached the halfway mark. The boy never returned, but ghostly drumming is sometimes heard. *Castle S of town; Castle Walk along hillside below walls is in area where tunnel was said to begin.*

THIRLBY

Gormire Lake. DROWNED TOWN. An earthquake is said to have swallowed up a town, with all its buildings and inhabitants, the site being immediately covered by a lake. It is said to be bottomless; but sometimes chimneys and roofs can be seen by people taking a boat out on to the water - or so it is said. *4 miles NE of Thirsk; lake 1 mile SE of village; footpath follows E shore from A170.*

WEST WITTON

Burning Bartle. ANCIENT CUSTOM. After dark in late August a little-known custom is followed here, when Bartle (an effigy like the November guy) is paraded through the village and finally burnt. This custom, taking place on the feast of St Bartholomew, to whom the church is dedicated, is probably a survival of the custom of taking the saint's statue through the parish on his feast day, mixed up with a legend about the death of a giant who lived on Pen Hill. *3 miles SW of Leyburn.*

WHITBY

★ **Whitby Abbey.** GHOSTS. The abbey was founded by St Hilda in AD 657, and now her ghost is said to haunt the ruins. A coach-and-four pulled by headless horses has been seen tearing along the road to the abbey; and treasure-seekers looking for the riches rumoured to be buried in the grounds felt someone tapping them on the shoulder and turned to see a tall white figure with no head. At dawn on old Christmas Day, faint echoes of a choir may be heard in the ruins.

YORK

Treasurer's House and Holy Trinity Church. GHOSTS. With its wealth of old buildings York is inevitably rich in ghosts. One of the most famous sightings is that of Harry Martindale, who was a young plumber in 1953 when he saw part of a Roman army walk through the cellar of the Treasurer's House where he was working. He saw up to 20 soldiers, some on horseback. Other people have also seen them. Holy Trinity church was said to be haunted by a phantom nun, who used to appear on Trinity Sunday. One worshipper in 1876 saw her pass and repass outside the east window. She may be the last abbess of the convent formerly attached to the church. *Treasurer's House in Chapter House Street; open to public (National Trust); Holy Trinity church in Micklegate.*

CALENDAR OF EVENTS

6 January
HAXEY, Humberside. *Hood Game:* Traditional 'football' game (see entry for *Haxey*).

January: Saturday after 6th
GOATHLAND, North Yorkshire. *Plough Stots:* Longsword dancing (see entry for *Goathland*).

February/March: Shrove Tuesday
SCARBOROUGH, North Yorkshire. *Shrovetide Skipping:* The Pancake Bell is rung at noon as a signal to start cooking pancakes. In the afternoon hundreds of people congregate on the promenade to spend the afternoon in communal skipping.

August: first Saturday
RIPON, North Yorkshire. *Feast of St Wilfred:* Pageant celebrates saint's arrival in Ripon. A man dressed as the saint rides on a white horse to the cathedral, which is dedicated to St Wilfred.

August: Saturday nearest to 24th
WEST WITTON, North Yorkshire. *Burning Bartle:* Effigy burned after parade (see entry for *West Witton*).

The Haxey Hood Game

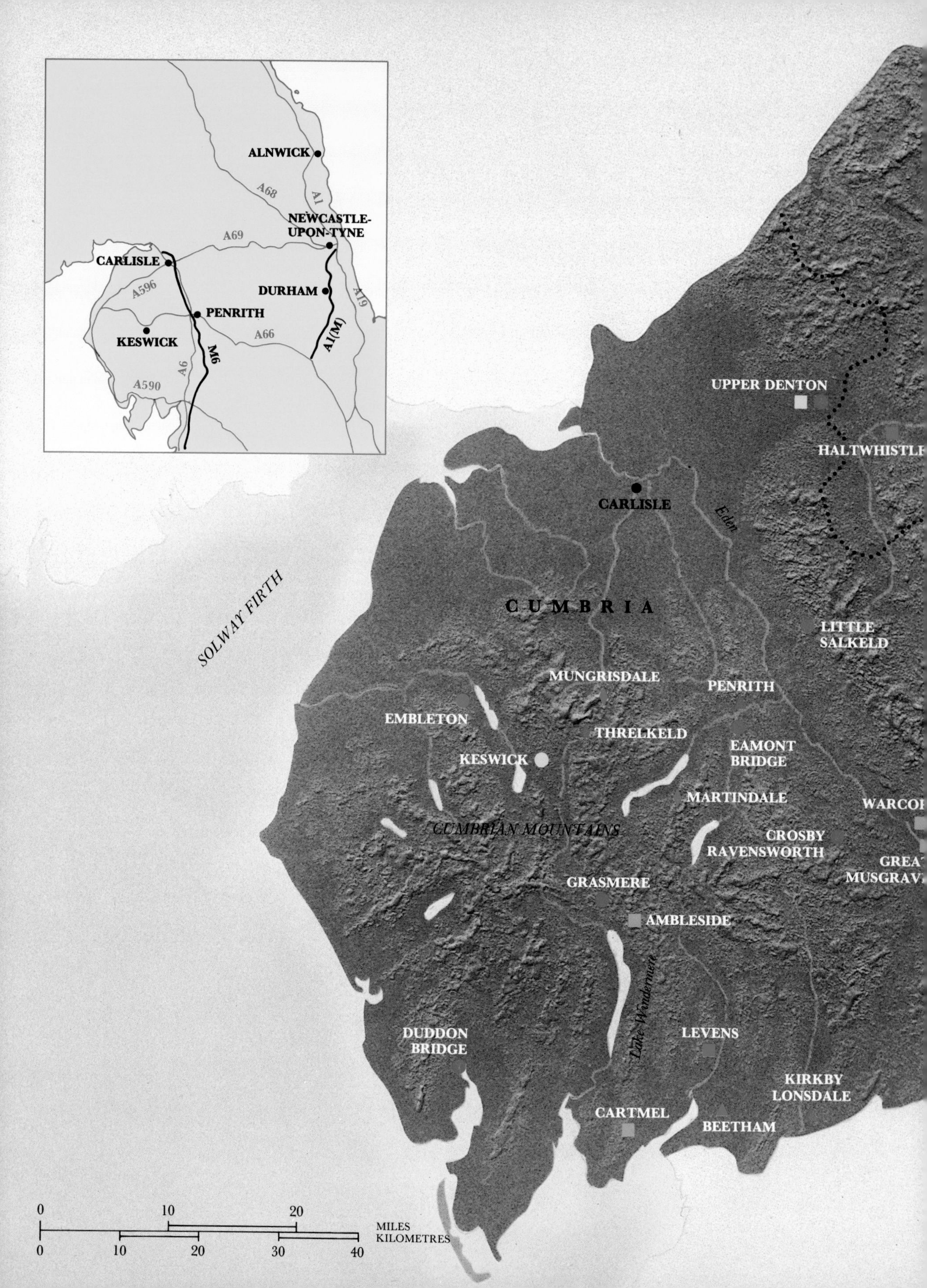
ALNWICK
A68
A1
NEWCASTLE-
UPON-TYNE
A69
CARLISLE
DURHAM
A596
A19
PENRITH
KESWICK
A66
M6
A1(M)
A6
A590
UPPER DENTON
HALTWHISTLE
CARLISLE
Eden
SOLWAY FIRTH
CUMBRIA
LITTLE
SALKELD
MUNGRISDALE
PENRITH
EMBLETON
THRELKELD
EAMONT
BRIDGE
KESWICK
MARTINDALE
WARCOP
CUMBRIAN MOUNTAINS
CROSBY
RAVENSWORTH
GREAT
MUSGRAVE
GRASMERE
AMBLESIDE
Lake Windermere
DUDDON
BRIDGE
LEVENS
KIRKBY
LONSDALE
CARTMEL
BEETHAM
0
10
20
MILES
KILOMETRES
0
10
20
30
40

CUMBRIA DURHAM NORTHUMBERLAND AND TYNE AND WEAR

CUMBRIA

BEETHAM

Fairy Steps. RITUAL; FAIRIES. The steps are cut into limestone, and if you can climb them without touching the walls on either side you can make a wish which will come true. The name of the steps indicates the local belief in the presence of the Little People. *8 miles S of Kendal; steps signposted to W of church.*

CARTMEL

Church. SITING LEGEND. A group of monks who arrived in this part of Lancashire (as it was before the boundary changes in 1974) decided to build a monastery and found a hill with a fine view. As they began their preparations, a voice spoke to them seemingly from nowhere, saying: 'Not there, but in a valley, between two rivers, where the one runs north, and the other south.' They travelled through the north of England in search of this strange valley where rivers ran in opposite directions - and found it close to where they had originally started work. They built their church midway between the two streams on a firm island, and they also built a chapel on the hill of their first choice, but this no longer survives. Today the fine medieval church at Cartmel, dating back to the 12th century, is all that survives of their priory. *1½ miles NW of Grange-over-Sands; original site was Mount Bernard 1 mile W, accessible by footpath.*

CROSBY RAVENSWORTH

Robin Hood's Grave. ROBIN HOOD. A cairn on Crosby Ravensworth Fell was at some time in the past identified as Robin Hood's grave - though why he should be buried out here, far away from his usual haunts, is not clear (see *Mirfield*, West Yorkshire, for a more likely burial site). *5 miles SW of Appleby; cairn 2½ miles S of village, reached by footpath from there or from Orton to S (NY 617107).*

DUDDON BRIDGE

Swinside Stone Circle. BURIED CHURCH; UNCOUNTABLE STONES. The stone circle is also known as Sunken Kirk, from the belief that a church was buried here. Did this come from some vague memory of pagan religious rituals once performed on this spot? The stones were also thought to be uncountable. *Duddon Bridge 5 miles NE of Millom; circle reached from paths up to Swinside Fell (SD 172882).*

EAMONT BRIDGE

King Arthur's Round Table. ARTHURIAN LEGEND. There are two prehistoric henge monuments (ceremonial earthworks) not far apart, the most southerly being known as King Arthur's Round Table or Arthur's Castle. Apart from the names, the connection with King Arthur is tenuous, though in the 18th century games and sports were held there, which could possibly have been a faint echo of the jousting and tournaments held by the knights at their Round Table. *1 mile SE of Penrith, beside A6 and S of junction with B5320 (NY 523284).*

EMBLETON

Elva Hill and Castle Howe. FAIRIES. Names similar to 'elf-howe' indicate that the hill or burial mound was thought to be a place where the Little People lived. Other such places in Cumbria were Elf Hill near Millom, Elfa Hills in Hutton-in-the-Forest and Elf Howe in Kentmere. A man returning home to Bewcastle one night was nearly dragged into a fairy hill, but he carried a page from the Bible in his pocket as a charm and so was safe from kidnap. Other protective charms were rosaries, crosses, iron and steel. Elva Hill at Embleton has a stone circle on its south-east slope. Not far away is Castle Howe, in woods on the shore of Bassenthwaite Lake; this was another fairy fort where little men in green were seen. *Elva Hill 3 miles NE of Cockermouth; lane passes W–E along S slopes of hill (NY 179318); Castle Howe at NW end of Bassenthwaite Lake, off A66 (NY 202308).*

GRASMERE

Dunmail Raise. KING'S BURIAL; TREASURE. The cairn is said to mark the burial place of Dunmail, last king of Strathclyde and Cumbria, who was defeated here in AD 945 by Malcolm, King of Scotland, and Edmund, King of the Saxons. The king's golden crown was traditionally thrown into Grisedale Tarn. *Cairn visible from A591 (on bank between double carriageways) 2½ miles NW of Grasmere; Grisedale Tarn 2½ miles NE of Grasmere, accessible by footpath from Grasmere.*

KESWICK

★ Castlerigg Stone Circle. PREHISTORIC RITUALS; MYSTERIOUS LIGHTS. One of the most spectacularly sited stone circles in the British Isles, Castlerigg (also known as the Keswick Carles) clearly was an important site when first constructed - but what was its purpose? John Glover, one researcher who has been trying to find out, observed the phenomenon of shadow paths. At sunset on the summer solstice the tallest stone casts a long shadow. This shadow was possibly used by the ancients for astronomical calculations, because at Candlemas (2 February) it points to the sunrise.

Earlier this century, two men walking home to Keswick at night passed close to the stones and saw white lights moving around. One came straight towards them, but it went out as it drew near. Mysterious lights of this kind may be of supernatural origin, or they may be formed as a result of earth movements (similar to earthquake lights), or they may be a phenomenon called ball lightning. At present, although similar lights are quite often seen worldwide, their true nature and origin are unknown. *1½ miles E of Keswick, beside lane (NY 292237).*

KIRKBY LONSDALE

Devil's Bridge. DEVIL. According to legend, an old woman's cow had strayed across the River Lune and she could not get it back because the river had risen in the meantime. As she stood gazing across, wondering what to do, the Devil happened to come by and said he would build her a bridge by morning if she agreed that he could have the first living thing to cross the new bridge. She agreed, and so the Devil set to work. By dawn he had finished, and when the old woman appeared he demanded payment. So she threw a bun across the bridge and her dog ran after it. Letting out a howl of rage, the Devil flew off. Children used to be shown the Devil's fingermarks on a coping stone on the bridge, and the Devil's Neck-Collar which he left on the bank, now between the old and new bridges.

In his hurry to complete the work, the Devil is supposed to have dropped several loads of stones around the area: the Devil's Apron Strings on Casterton Fell, for instance, and the Apronful of Stones near Settle. He also dug out a hole known as the Devil's Punch Bowl in a field beyond Ruskin's View at Kirkby Lonsdale. He buried a church in it, and if you listen with your ear to the ground the bells can be heard - or so children were once told. *10 miles SE of Kendal; bridge to SE, crossing River Lune.*

KIRKBY STEPHEN

Pendragon Castle. ARTHURIAN LEGEND. Built in the 12th century, the small castle is now ruined. In the days before it was built it is said that King Arthur's father,

Castlerigg stone circle at Keswick, an impressive prehistoric site whose purpose is still unknown

CALENDAR OF EVENTS

February/March: Shrove Tuesday
ALNWICK, Northumberland. *Shrovetide Football:* Unconventional football match with 40 players and goalposts decorated with laurel leaves.

February/March: Shrove Tuesday
SEDGEFIELD, Durham. *Shrovetide Football:* Played with a hard ball the size of a cricket ball, everyone trying to touch it for good luck as it is kicked around the village.

4 July (Old Midsummer Eve)
WHALTON, Northumberland. *Baal Fire:* Midsummer bonfire (see entry for *Whalton*).

August: Saturday nearest to 5th
GRASMERE, Cumbria. *Rushbearing Ceremony:* Religious custom dating back to the time when church floors were covered with rushes. Also performed at WARCOP (29 June), AMBLESIDE and GREAT MUSGRAVE (both first Saturday in July).

31 December (New Year's Eve)
ALLENDALE, Northumberland. *Tar Barrel Procession:* Burning the old year out (see entry for *Allendale*).

Tar Barrel Procession at Allendale

Uther Pendragon (head dragon or chief), tried to divert the River Eden to make a moat round the mound, so that it would be well protected against enemies. But he did not succeed, and a local rhyme ran:

> Let Uther Pendragon do what he can,
> Eden will run where Eden ran.

There is no evidence that Uther Pendragon ever built a fortification on the hill. *Castle 4 miles S of Kirkby Stephen, W of B6259.*

LEVENS

Levens Hall. GHOSTS. The Elizabethan house incorporates a 14th-century pele-tower, and there is a famous topiary garden in the grounds. Several ghosts have been seen in recent years: a black dog which rushes downstairs, a Pink Lady seen in the house and garden, and a Grey Lady who haunts nearby Levens Bridge. A gipsy who died of starvation in the 18th century after being turned away from the house cursed the Lady of Levens, saying that no male heir would be born until the

Despite its name, King Arthur's Round Table at Eamont Bridge is prehistoric

River Kent dried up and a white stag was born in the park. These conditions were fulfilled in the 1890s, when the river froze and a pale stag was born – subsequently a boy was born to the family. *4 miles SW of Kendal; Hall beside A6 ½ mile SE of village: open to public.*

LITTLE SALKELD

★ Long Meg and Her Daughters. WITCHES; PETRIFACTION LEGEND; UNCOUNTABLE STONES; RETRIBUTION; RITUALS. The stone circle is said to be a witches' coven turned to stone by the wizard Michael Scot when he found them holding a sabbat. Meg may have been Meg of Meldon, a local 17th-century witch. The stones (around 66 of them, forming one of Britain's largest stone circles) were said to be uncountable, and if anyone arrived at the same number twice the spell would be broken – no one seems to have succeeded yet. Anyone trying to move any of the stones would bring on fearsome storms; and if a piece should be broken off Long Meg (the tallest stone) she would bleed. Prehistoric carvings can be seen on Long

Meg – a cup-and-ring mark, a spiral and an incomplete circle. These, along with the apparent positioning of two of the largest stones east and west in the directions of the spring and summer equinoxes, point to prehistoric rituals perhaps intended to mark the movements of the heavenly bodies. Not far away is another group of stones, Little Meg, where spiral carvings can be seen. Perhaps these two sites were somehow linked in the performance of ancient rituals. *5 miles NE of Penrith; Long Meg ½ mile NE of Little Salkeld, along track from lane to Glassonby (NY 571372); Little Meg ¼ mile further NE, off same lane (NY 577375).*

Giant's Grave in the churchyard at Penrith

MARTINDALE

Sandwick Rigg. FAIRIES. The Lake District is rich in fairy lore, one particularly interesting tale – said to be true – coming from Ullswater. In 1857 Jack Wilson of Martindale saw a group of fairies dancing on Sandwick Rigg one moonlit night. When they saw him, they climbed up a ladder into a cloud; he tried to follow, but they drew up the ladder and disappeared.

This tale is intriguing because it overlaps with present-day reports of UFOs. When the occupants of these craft are seen, they are often described as small in size. Could it be that some of the 'fairies' of earlier centuries were perhaps the same as the UFO entities reported today? *On S side of Ullswater, 8 miles SW of Penrith.*

MUNGRISDALE

Souther Fell. GHOSTS. On Midsummer Eve 1735, a phantom army was seen on the mountain; and again two years later on the same evening; and again in 1745. There was never any trace of the passage of real soldiers and horses, and the terrain was not suitable for such an event. The sightings may have been optical illusions (though there were plenty of witnesses), or may have been prophetic visions of coming military events. *Mungrisdale 7 miles NE of Keswick; Souther Fell 1 mile SW.*

PENRITH

Giant's Grave. KING'S BURIAL. In St Andrew's churchyard two stone pillars, formerly crosses, stand 15 feet apart, with four 'hog-back' tombstones between them. Together they are said to mark the grave of a giant, the 6th-century King Owein (Yvain of French Arthurian legends) or Ewan Caesarius, who was a boar-hunter. The legend also tells how the grave was opened in the 16th century to reveal the bones of a huge man.

THRELKELD

Blencathra. ARTHURIAN LEGEND. This mountain is one of the places were King Arthur is said to be sleeping, awaiting the call to awaken and lead the fight against his (and our) enemies. The tradition may have arisen from the mountain's earlier name, the Rackes of Blenkarthure. *Threlkeld 3 miles NE of Keswick; Blencathra 1 mile to N.*

UPPER DENTON

Camboglanna Roman Fort. ARTHURIAN LEGEND. The similarity of the name to Camlann has led to the suggestion that this was the site of King Arthur's last battle. But there is no archaeological evidence. Some Roman remains survive on the site, which was a fort on Hadrian's Wall, and excavations are currently revealing more structures. *6 miles NE of Brampton; approached from N along lane to Birdoswald.*

Church. ANCIENT STONES; WITCH. The Saxons built this church using stones from Hadrian's Wall, and a Roman arch, probably from Camboglanna, was re-erected in the chancel.

An 18th-century witch, Margaret Teasdale, is buried in the churchyard. She died in 1777 aged 98, and the epitaph on her tombstone reads:

What I was once, some may relate,
What I am now is each man's fate;
What I may be, none can explain,
Till He that called me, calls again.

She was probably the basis for the character Tib Mumps in Sir Walter Scott's *Guy Mannering*. It was said that gruesome relics found in her house after her death proved her involvement in black magic. *Upper (or Over) Denton 6 miles NE of Brampton.*

DURHAM

BISHOPTON

Castle Hill. FAIRIES. A 60-foot mound marks the site of a Norman castle. Locally it was called Fairy Hill, and its occupants did not take kindly to disturbance. When attempts were made to cart the hill away, voices were heard asking, 'Is all well?'

'Yes,' was the workmen's reply.

The voice responded, 'Then keep well when you are well, and leave the Fairy Hill alone.'

But work continued, and soon the workmen found a large oak chest which needed several men to shift it. They hoped it was full of treasure, but were disappointed to find only nails. *6 miles NE of Darlington; hill at SE end of village.*

DURHAM

★ **Durham Cathedral.** SITING LEGEND. The cathedral was founded as a shrine for the body of St Cuthbert. Anticipating a Viking raid, in AD 875 the monks were carrying his incorrupt body in a coffin from Lindisfarne; they also had other precious relics with them, like the head of St Oswald and St Aidan's bones. Miracles were said to occur wherever they rested. As they approached Durham in 995, after many years of wandering, a monk had a vision in which the saint asked that his body be laid to rest at Dunholme. They found this place, a hill by the River Wear, and here the shrine was built. Today the site of the original shrine and the burial place are marked by a statue of St Cuthbert holding the head of St Oswald.

HURWORTH

Road to Neasham. BROWNIE. The one-mile stretch of road was said to be haunted by a brownie called Hob Headless. After being exorcised he was laid to rest beneath a large stone by the roadside; anyone who sat on the stone was believed to be unable to get up again. The brownie was laid for 99 years and a day, and the time is nearly up, so trouble could break out again on the road before long. *3 miles SE of Darlington centre.*

LAMBTON

Lambton Castle. DRAGON. According to legend, the young Lambton heir caught a strange worm in the River Wear and threw it into a nearby well. It grew and grew,

Castle Hill at Bishopton, site of a Norman castle and associated in local legend with fairies

and when too large for the well it returned to the river. By night it coiled itself round Worm Hill near Fatfield, and was a terrible sight to see. Its appetite was gargantuan, and at Lambton Castle it was given a trough of milk daily - it would tear up trees unless given the milk of nine cows. Knights tried to kill it, but the pieces they chopped off immediately reunited.

It was finally defeated when the Lambton heir returned from the Crusades. He asked a wise woman's advice on killing it, and she told him to cover his armour with spear-heads. But before encountering the beast, he had to vow to kill the first living thing to meet him afterwards. If he failed to do this, no Lord of Lambton would die in his bed for nine generations. Dressed in his armour with its sharp spear-heads, he took his sword and stood on a rock in the river. When the worm appeared, he struck out at it; the creature coiled itself round him, but was badly injured by the spear-heads and the knight was able to cut it in two. One part was carried away in the river, so the dragon could not re-form itself. As the hero returned, blowing his bugle to announce his triumph, his aged father, forgetting the vow, rushed forward to congratulate him. Feeling unable to kill his father, the knight instead slew his dog which had also come rushing forward. But it was no use - the curse took effect for nine generations. *2 miles NE of Chester-le-Street; castle grounds now Lambton Pleasure Park, 200 acres with drive-through safari section including lions and elephants - but no dragon!*

NORTHUMBERLAND

ALLENDALE

Tar Barrel Procession. ANCIENT CUSTOM. On New Year's Eve a traditional ceremony of burning the old year out is still performed. Just before midnight, 40 or 50 men with blazing tar barrels on their heads meet in the town centre and parade through the streets. At the turn of the year they light a bonfire in the marketplace, and then the 'guisers' (men in fancy dress) go first-footing. *8 miles SW of Hexham.*

BAMBURGH

★ Bamburgh Castle, the Spindlestone and Bamburgh Church. ARTHURIAN LEGEND; DRAGON; SAINT'S DEATH. An earlier castle than the Norman and 18th-century one seen today may have been Joyous Gard, the castle of Sir Lancelot in Arthurian legend.

In another age, the people of Bamburgh were terrorized by the 'Laidley Worm', a dragon which was supposed to be the king of Northumbria's daughter who had had a spell cast on her by her wicked stepmother. The milk of seven cows was fed daily to the worm in a stone trough. The king's son, not knowing the worm's true identity, volunteered to despatch the monster. The place where he went to fight the worm is called the Spindlestone, a whinstone pillar 2 miles south-west of Bamburgh. But the worm refused to fight and revealed who it was, whereupon the spell was broken and the princess regained her human shape. The stepmother was turned into a toad, and now lives in St Elmund's Well at the castle.

Saints Oswald and Cuthbert were both associated with Bamburgh. King Oswald (before he became a saint) had his palace on the present castle site in the 7th century AD, and after his death his arm was kept as a holy relic in the church at Bamburgh until stolen by a monk. St Aidan died in AD 651 in a shelter at the church preceding the existing building, and a shrine in the present church now marks the place. A crypt was rediscovered below the church in the last century, where the saint's relics were probably displayed. Carvings of Saints Oswald, Aidan and Cuthbert (see *Durham* and *Holy Island*) can be seen in the church. *16 miles SE of Berwick upon Tweed; castle open to public.*

BELLINGHAM

St Cuthbert's Well. HOLY WELL. Also known as Cuddy's Well (Cuddie or Cuddy is a local name for the saint), this spring is said to have been found by St Cuthbert, who was a dowser. *14 miles NW of Hexham; well in grassy lane outside churchyard wall.*

CALLALY

Callaly Castle. SITING LEGEND. A 15th-century pele-tower is incorporated into the mansion, which was originally planned for Castle Hill half a mile to the south-east. But when work started, the stones were moved nightly to the present site. One version of the story tells that it was the Lord of Callaly's wife who wanted the site moved from Castle Hill, so she got her steward to undo the day's building every night. When her husband sat up to watch for the culprit, she dressed the steward as a wild boar and told him to dance among the stones and pull them down, singing that only a castle built where the Lady wished it would ever stand. Believing supernatural powers to be at work, the Lord gave in. *8 miles SW of Alnwick; castle open to public at weekends and on bank holidays.*

HALTWHISTLE

Featherstone Castle. GHOSTS. The castle, now partly used as a young people's holiday centre, comprises a 14th-century pele-tower and an adjoining Jacobean mansion. Legend tells of a tragedy which befell the Featherstonhalgh family after a daughter was married. The wedding party went out on horseback but had not returned by evening. Early next morning they returned - but in silence, and when they drew close the baron saw that blood streamed down the faces of everyone in the

Holy Island, for many centuries a place of Christian pilgrimage

party. When he recovered his senses they had gone, and so he sent out a search party which found them lying dead in a lonely dell, all murdered. A rejected suitor may have been responsible. On the anniversary of the slaughter, the ghostly party is said to ride again to the old castle. *Haltwhistle 15 miles W of Hexham; castle $2\frac{1}{2}$ miles SW, close to lane.*

HARBOTTLE

Drake Stone. HEALING STONE. Children were taken up to the Drake Stone when ill, for it was once believed that if they were passed over the top of this huge natural sandstone rock, they would be cured. *8 miles NW of Rothbury; Drake Stone in Harbottle Hills $\frac{3}{4}$ mile W of village, reached by foothpath from road to Alwhinton (NT 921044).*

HAZELRIGG

St Cuthbert's Cave. SAINT; GHOST. Cuddie's Cave was said to be one of the places where St Cuthbert's body was rested when being taken from Lindisfarne to Durham. The cave was haunted by the Hazelrigg Dunny, the ghost of a reiver who had buried some treasure nearby and then forgotten where. He sometimes took the form of a dun-coloured horse, which explains the name Dunny. *$7\frac{1}{2}$ miles W of Bamburgh; cave on Greensheen Hill, reached by footpath from Holborn Grange N of Hazelrigg (NU 059352).*

HOLY ISLAND

Lindisfarne Abbey. SAINTS; GHOSTS; PHANTOM DOG; RITUAL. The island has been a place of pilgrimage for centuries; its religious importance began in AD 635 when St Aidan came here as a Christian missionary and was appointed the first bishop. After his death, St Cuthbert came in 664 as prior of the abbey; but after 12 years he retired to the largest of the Farne Islands and lived as a hermit, with only a small stone cell and oratory. Nine years later he was called back to Lindisfarne to become bishop. He died in his cell at the hermitage, having been taken back there when he realized he was dying in 687. His body was kept in a coffin beside the altar in Lindisfarne abbey church, and when opened 11 years later the body was found to be incorrupt. Opened again in 1104, it was still incorrupt. He now lies in *Durham* cathedral (see entry). But a part of him still remains on Holy Island, for traditionally his ghost is said to haunt the abbey and the island. On stormy nights he can be heard hammering on an anvil on the shore, as told in a poem by Sir Walter Scott:

> On a rock by Lindisfarne,
> St Cuthbert sits, and toils to frame
> The sea-born beads that bear his name;
> Such tales had Whitby's fishers told,
> And said they might his shape behold,
> And hear his anvil sound;
> A deafening clang - a huge, dim form,
> Seen but, and heard, when gathering storm
> And night were closing round.

(The 'beads' are fossils called crinoids, which could be found on the shore after a storm.)

A ghostly white dog has also been seen in the abbey ruins. A stone in the churchyard called the Petting Stone (perhaps the base of St Cuthbert's Cross) was visited by new brides who jumped over it to ensure a successful marriage. *Off NE coast 10 miles SE of Berwick; Holy Island can be reached on foot across sands, or by car across causeway, at low tide; priory ruins still stand by S shore; St Cuthbert's hermitage in Farne Islands can be visited by boat from Seahouses.*

HOLYSTONE

Lady's Well and Five Kings. HOLY WELL; STANDING STONES. Traditionally associated with St Ninian, Lady's Well feeds a pool where a Celtic cross now stands. It is said that Paulinus baptised three thousand people here at Easter in AD 627, but documentary evidence seems to be lacking. The place-name 'Holy Stone' suggests that this was a sacred place even before Christianity took it over, with an ancient stone as well as an ancient well.

A Roman road once passed by the well, and to the south are five barrows (prehistoric tombs) and five standing stones known as Five Kings, traditionally put up as memorials to five brothers who were kings. These stones range from 5 to 8 feet in height, but one is fallen. *7 miles NW of Rothbury; Lady's Well (National Trust) ¼ mile N of village, reached along footpath; barrows and standing stones on Holystone Common ½ mile S of village and reached by footpath (barrows: NT 953020; Five Kings: NT 955015).*

HOUSESTEADS

Broomlee Lough. ARTHURIAN LEGEND; TREASURE. This is one of several lakes in Britain where it is claimed King Arthur's sword Excalibur was thrown when he lay dying. It is also said to conceal a box of treasure, hidden here by the owner of a castle on Sewingshields Crag, and seemingly now unrecoverable. *On moors below Hadrian's Wall and Housesteads Roman fort, 10 miles NW of Hexham.*

King's Crag and Queen's Crag. ARTHURIAN LEGEND. King Arthur and his Queen, Guinevere, are here seen as giants; the King had his chair on King's Crag, while Guinevere sat on Queen's Crag. They had a quarrel, and Arthur threw at Guinevere a rock which hit her comb and fell between the two rocky outcrops, the toothmarks made by the comb still being visible. King Arthur is said to lie sleeping in a cave below Sewingshields Castle, just to the south. A farmer who found the cave failed to follow the correct procedure of drawing the sword, then cutting the garter and blowing the horn - all these items lay on a table. He cut the garter but did not blow the horn, so although Arthur awoke he fell asleep again. (See *Melrose*, Borders, and *Richmond*, North Yorkshire, for similar legends.) *½ mile NE of Broomlee Lough.*

ILDERTON

Threestone Burn Stone Circle. TREASURE. Now only 11 stones, this circle is said to have once had 12, and anyone finding the missing stone will also find treasure. But a farmer who located 13 stones got no treasure. *Ilderton 4 miles SE of Wooler; circle 3 miles SW, out on moors and reached by footpath from Ilderton or Langlee (NT 971205).*

SEATON DELAVAL

Seaton Delaval Hall. GHOST. Designed by Vanbrugh and said to be his masterpiece, the house was completed in 1728. An unidentified ghost, of a woman in a grey dress, has been seen at a window in the west wing. *3 miles NW of Whitley Bay; open to public.*

WHALTON

Baal Fire. ANCIENT CUSTOM. On Old Midsummer Eve (4 July), a midsummer bonfire is lit in the village. It is possibly the last genuine survivor of a widesread rural custom intended to bring fertility to crops and cattle (see our book *Earth Rites* for details of many similar customs which have now died out). Children would dance round the fire and scramble for sweets and pennies, while young couples would jump through the dying flames 'for luck' (i.e. to promote fertility). *5 miles SW of Morpeth.*

YEAVERING

Battle Stone. GIANT; ROYAL SITE. Also known as the Druid's Lapful, this stone was said to have been dropped from a druidess's apron when the string broke. It stands at the foot of the hill which is crowned by Northumberland's largest hillfort, Yeavering Bell.

To the west, now marked only by a stone monument, was the site of Ad Gefrin, an Anglo-Saxon royal township where King Edwin had his palace and the Christian missionary Paulinus came in AD 627 (see *Holystone*). The site was abandoned around AD 670. *3 miles NW of Wooler; standing stone ½ mile W of Yeavering (NT 930303), S of B6351; Ad Gefrin ½ mile further W (NT 926305).*

TYNE AND WEAR

JARROW

Church. BEDE'S CHAIR; MAGIC. The Venerable Bede, the famous Dark Age scholar, spent most of his life in the monastery at Jarrow until his death in AD 735. The remains of the monastery can still be seen beside St Paul's church. Inside the church, which has Saxon origins, is an old chair known as Bede's Chair, though the truth of this belief is debatable. It was said to have magical powers, and single women would take chips of wood from it to put under their pillows in the hope of placing a spell on the man they dreamed of. New brides would sit in the chair to ensure they would have children, and pregnant women hoping for a pain-free birth would drink water in which pieces of wood from the chair had been soaked. *2 miles W of South Shields; church on S side of River Tyne, N of A185.*

SUNDERLAND

Hylton Castle. BROWNIE. The 'Cauld Lad of Hylton' was a mischievous spirit which haunted the 15th-century tower house. He untidied neat work, and tidied up any untidiness. The servants banished him by leaving out for him a green cloak and hood, which he seized with glee, being so delighted with the gift that he left the house and never returned. *In NW Sunderland at Castletown.*

TYNEMOUTH

Black Middens. DEVIL. The Devil was said to have carried apronsful of stones to block up the entrance to the River Tyne, because the inhabitants of Newcastle looked as if they were becoming religious and he wanted to spoil their town. However, one morning he met a woman as he brought a load of stones, and was so startled that he dropped his load and fled, never to return. The stones with which he had partially blocked the river are now known as the Black Middens. *On N side of river mouth, SW of North Pier.*

WASHINGTON

Washington Old Hall. GHOST. Originating in the 12th century, the Old Hall was home to the ancestors of George Washington, the USA's first president. A ghostly lady in a long grey dress has been seen in the upstairs corridor. *5 miles W of Sunderland; open to public (National Trust).*

St Paul's church at Jarrow and, beside it, the ruins of the monastery associated with St Bede

SCHIEHALLION
BEN LAWERS
Loch Tay
GLEN ALMOND
OBAN
COMRIE
IONA
CENTRAL
Earn
LOCH AWE
Teith
ABERFOYLE
Forth
KILMICHAEL GLASSARY
STIRLING
JURA
LINLITHGOW
DUMBARTON
GOUROCK
GLASGOW
KILCHOMAN
Clyde
ISLAY
STRATHCLYDE
ARRAN
LANARK
FIRTH OF CLYDE
KINTYRE
MACHRIE
AYR
KILMORY
Nith
LENDALFOOT
DUMFRIES AND GALLOWAY
STRANRAER
GLENLUCE
KIRKMABRECK
WIGTOWN
WHITHORN
0 10 20 MILES
0 10 20 30 40 KILOMETRES

CENTRAL
AND
SOUTHERN SCOTLAND

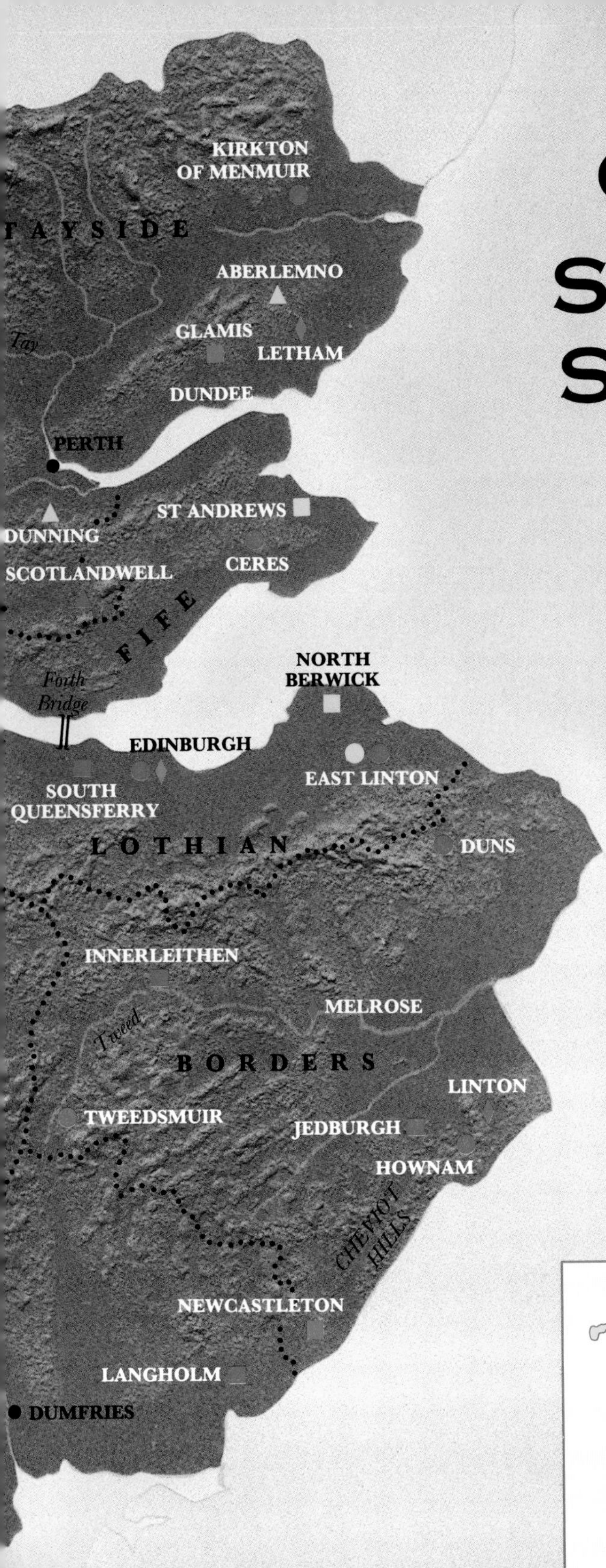

KIRKTON OF MENMUIR
TAYSIDE
ABERLEMNO
GLAMIS
LETHAM
Tay
DUNDEE
PERTH
ST ANDREWS
DUNNING
SCOTLANDWELL
CERES
FIFE
Forth Bridge
NORTH BERWICK
EDINBURGH
EAST LINTON
SOUTH QUEENSFERRY
LOTHIAN
DUNS
INNERLEITHEN
MELROSE
Tweed
BORDERS
LINTON
TWEEDSMUIR
JEDBURGH
HOWNAM
CHEVIOT HILLS
NEWCASTLETON
LANGHOLM
DUMFRIES

OBAN
A85
PERTH
DUNDEE
A82
A83
A9
M90
M9
A80
GLASGOW
M74
M8
EDINBURGH
A7
A68
A1
A71
AYR
A74
A77
A76
JEDBURGH
DUMFRIES
A75
STRANRAER

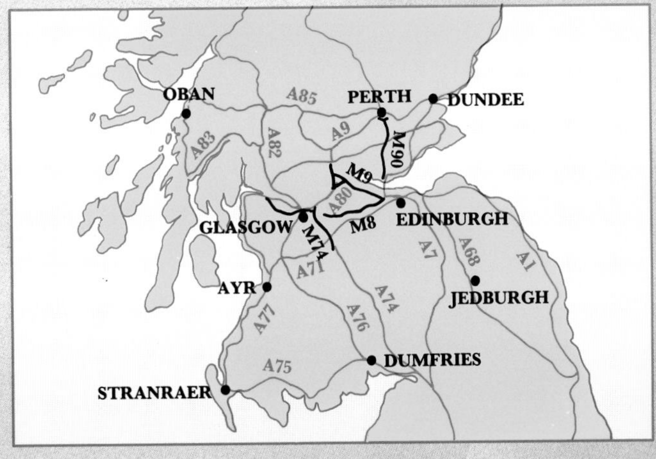

BORDERS

DUNS

Edin's Hall Fort and Broch. GIANT. Red Etin, who lived in the fort, was a three-headed giant, killed by a boy who gave the correct answer to the giant's riddles. In another tale, the giant died by drowning when crossing a river. A one-ton boulder at the site was said to be a pebble he shook from his shoe. *4 miles N of Duns and signposted on A6112 (NT 772603).*

HOWNAM

Hownam Shearers. PETRIFACTION LEGEND. A hundred yards south of Hownam Rings hillfort is a line of 28 stones said to be people turned to stone for reaping on the Sabbath. *Hownam 7 miles E of Jedburgh; stones ¾ mile E of village, reached by footpath (NT 791192).*

LINTON

Linton Hill and Church. DRAGON. A monstrous 'worm' (serpent or dragon) living on Linton Hill is said to have terrorized the surrounding area with its ravenous appetite, so a local hero, John Somerville, killed it by fixing a wheel of burning peats to his lance and thrusting this down the worm's throat. Thereafter the event was commemorated in the crest of the Somervilles, a worn carving of which can still be seen over Linton church door. From the churchyard Linton Hill can be clearly seen, with the marks said to have been left by the worm where he coiled himself round the hill. *6 miles SE of Kelso; church off B6436.*

MELROSE

★ **Eildon Hills and Melrose Abbey.** MAGIC; FAIRIES; ARTHURIAN LEGEND; TREASURE. In legend the hills got their shape when an evil spirit, at the command of the

Hermitage Castle at Newcastleton, a place of dark and evil legends

CALENDAR OF EVENTS

February/March: Shrove Tuesday (usually)
JEDBURGH, Borders. *Jethart Ba':* Traditional ball games played through town streets, using about 15 balls; the games start at Mercat Cross.

1 March
LANARK, Strathclyde. *Whuppity Stourie or Scoorie:* Children run round the church carrying paper balls on end of long strings, then scramble for coins thrown to them. It may be an ancient magic ritual to drive winter away.

July: second or third week
INNERLEITHEN, Borders. *Burning of the Deil:* Devil's image burnt on a bonfire, followed by torchlight processions, to celebrate St Ronan overcoming the Devil.

July: last Friday
LANGHOLM, Dumfries and Galloway. *Common Riding:* Horsemen follow their standard-bearer along a traditional route, with elaborate ceremonies like sod-cutting and proclamations.

Early August
SOUTH QUEENSFERRY, Lothian. *Burryman's Parade:* A man covered head to foot with burrs and carrying flower-decked staffs walks the town throughout the day before the Ferry Fair, collecting money. This very ancient custom brings luck to the town, and may be pre-Christian in origin.

31 December (New Year's Eve)
COMRIE, Tayside. *Flambeaux Procession:* Traditional midnight torchlit procession originating in pagan fire rituals to keep away evil.

The South Queensferry Burryman

magician Michael Scot, split one large hill into three. In the Iron Age a great hillfort was built on top of the northernmost hill, the still visible ramparts forming the largest hillfort in Scotland.

A Roman fort was also built in this area, at Newstead, east of Melrose, and it was somewhere near here that Thomas the Rhymer (Thomas of Erceldoune) met the Fairy Queen. She took him into her kingdom under Eildon and he lived in fairyland for three years, though it seemed like three days to him.

In another tale Canonbie Dick, a horse trader who was riding over the hills at night, saw an old man who bought the horses Dick had been unable to sell. Dick made several sales to the old man on subsequent occasions, and one night was taken by him into the hill called Lucken Hare. Inside Dick saw a large cavern where lay horses and knights all sleeping - and the old man revealed himself to be Thomas of Erceldoune. He gave Dick the choice of drawing a sword or blowing a horn, saying that he would die if he chose wrongly. Dick chose the horn and blew a blast on it, whereupon all the knights and horses awoke. He grabbed the sword, and heard a voice crying:

> Woe to the coward that ever he was born;
> Who did not draw the sword before he blew the horn.

Then he found himself whisked out of the hill in a whirlwind and was found lying on the bank by some shepherds, to whom he told his strange tale before he died.

Melrose Abbey, reputed to be the burial place of the wizard Michael Scot

Though steep in places, the 4-mile Eildon Walk beginning off the B6359 in Melrose will take you through the hills and past the place where Dick entered them; the hills can also be clearly seen from the surrounding roads. *Eildon Hills just S of Melrose, 3 miles E of Galashiels; Melrose*

In one version the knights were King Arthur's men; and there are many other hills in Britain where they are believed to lie sleeping, awaiting the call to come to the country's aid. It is also said that there is so much gold in the Eildon Hills that sheep grazing there develop yellow teeth.

In Melrose Abbey the wizard Michael Scot is said to lie buried. He was a real person who lived in the 13th century, but there is no proof that he practised magic. He was a leading scholar, and in his writings condemned magic, but he expressed an interest in science and astrology, and somehow an assortment of tales of magical feats, mostly located around Cumbria, Northumberland and southern Scotland, have become attached to his name.

Abbey open to public, and grave alleged to be Scot's next to double piscine in south transept chapel nearest to presbytery, set into floor and with cross on it.

NEWCASTLETON

Hermitage Castle. GHOSTS. The castle looks partly sunk into the ground, 'unable to support the load of iniquity which had been long accumulating within its walls', according to John Leyden in Sir Walter Scott's *Border Minstrelsy*). An early owner responsible for the castle's reputation was Lord Soulis, around whom bloodthirsty legends grew up: that he had a familar called Redcap, a spirit who continued to haunt the castle; that he practised black magic and committed murder; and that he was finally taken to Nine Stane Rig stone circle in the hills nearby, rolled up in a sheet of lead, tipped into a red-hot cauldron and melted. Lord Soulis still haunts the castle, as do some of the people who met their deaths here.

A woman in white seen in the castle may be Mary Queen of Scots, who nearly died of fever while at Hermitage. *5 miles NE of Newcastleton; castle W of B6399 running S from Hawick; open to public.*

TWEEDSMUIR

Giant's Stone. GIANT. The three standing stones at this site are said to be the place where Jack the Giantkiller killed his final victim – final because the mortally wounded giant managed to kill Jack before dying himself. Jack hid behind one of the stones to shoot the giant, and now they mark his burial place. *Tweedsmuir 12 miles N of Moffat; stones lie beside lane running S from village, ½ mile S (NT 095239).*

CENTRAL

ABERFOYLE

Fairy Hill and Churchyard. FAIRIES. The Rev. Robert Kirk lived at Aberfoyle in the 17th century, and it was there that he wrote his famous *Secret Commonwealth of Elves, Fauns and Fairies.* He was a seventh son, a position said to confer second sight, and this may have influenced his later interests. Among his other literary and parish work, he collected information on fairies from his parishioners at Balquhidder and Aberfoyle.

He is said to have been taking an evening walk on the Fairy Hill near his manse when he collapsed and died, on 14 May 1692, aged 48. According to the tradition which grew up afterwards, he appeared to a relative and gave him a message, saying he was not dead but a captive in fairyland. He said he would appear at the christening of his posthumous child, and his cousin was to throw a knife over the apparition; this would break the spell, because iron has physical power against fairies, and Kirk would then be able to return to the world. He appeared at the christening as promised, but in his amazement the cousin forgot to throw the knife and Kirk disappeared, never to be seen again. He had been buried in the churchyard, but it was believed that the coffin was full of stones. His grave is covered by a horizontal slab of red sandstone with an inscription in Latin. Also of interest are the cast-iron mort-safes to stop body-snatchers taking the corpses away. *8 miles SW of Callander; grave and mort-safes in old burial ground S of village.*

STIRLING

Stirling Castle. ARTHURIAN LEGEND; GHOSTS. In 1478 William of Worcester said that 'King Arthur kept the Round Table at Stirling Castle'. This 'Round Table' may have been a raised earth platform where medieval entertainments were held, now part of the formal garden called the King's Knot, though the mound to be seen today is unlikely to have been the original Round Table, and almost certainly had no connection with King Arthur.

The ancient castle itself has seen many historic events, including the crowning of Mary Queen of Scots, in 1543, and it is probable that the ghosts reportedly seen there are echoes of these events. A woman in a long pink dress has been seen walking from the castle to the church, while a Green Lady haunts various parts of the castle. Her appearances seem to precede disasters like serious fires. Ghostly footsteps have also been heard in the Governor's Block, and in the 1820s a sentry found dead with a look of horror on his face may have encountered whatever it was that made the footsteps.

Neolithic Cairnholy II chambered cairn

DUMFRIES AND GALLOWAY

GLENLUCE

Glenluce Abbey. MAGIC. The wizard Michael Scot (see *Melrose*, Borders) is said to have lured the plague to the abbey during an outbreak in the 13th century, and locked it into the vault. *8 miles SE of Stranraer; abbey 1 mile NW of Glenluce.*

KIRKMABRECK

★ Cairnholy Cairns. GRAVES; TREASURE. Two Neolithic chambered tombs in close proximity, labelled by the archaeologists Cairnholy I and Cairnholy II, were traditionally known as the burial places of Galdus, a mythical Scots king, and of a bishop of Whithorn who was killed in a 14th-century battle. The name Cairnholy may derive from *Carn Ulaidh*, treasure cairn. Interesting structures well sited above the sea, the cairns are worth a visit. *5 miles SW of Gatehouse of Fleet, reached along lane off A75 at bend (NX 518531).*

WHITHORN

Whithorn Priory. ANCIENT RELIGIOUS CENTRE. This is one of the oldest Christian centres in Britain, St Ninian having established here the first church in Scotland in the early 5th century. In this locality are numerous visible remains of the early religious activities: St Ninian's Cave near Glasserton, St Ninian's Chapel at Isle of Whithorn, many carved stones in Whithorn Museum and at Kirkmadrine church, in addition to the remains at Whithorn itself, which are currently being excavated. The ruined priory and cathedral are medieval, but the excavations in the field to the south have revealed the remains of structures dating back to the 5th century. The finds include graves with coffins made from split logs, coins, pilgrims' badges and fragments of sculpted crosses. White quartz pebbles and cattle teeth found in the graves may have been lucky charms. *10 miles S of Wigtown.*

Whithorn Priory, a focus of Christian worship for 1500 years

WIGTOWN

Torhouse Stone Circle. GRAVE; MYSTERIOUS LIGHT. This is another place where the mythical King Galdus was said to be buried (see *Kirkmabreck).* Not far away was a cairn whose cist-slab was removed in the 19th century to be used to cover a water conduit; several people claimed to have seen a light at night, moving from the cairn along the route that the slab was carried, and then rest on top of the slab for a while. *3 miles W of Wigtown beside B733 (NX 382565).*

FIFE

CERES

Norrie's Law. TREASURE. This Bronze Age cairn gets its name from Tammie Norrie, a cowherd who was buried here after blowing his horn and then dying in fulfilment of an old prophecy which involved the gold believed to be buried in the hill to the south called Largo Law - so much of it that the fleeces of the sheep lying on the hill turned yellow. The cairn was also said to have been formed by the Devil, or by the wizard Michael Scot, or to contain a warrior in silver armour, buried upright on his horse.

In fact, excavations in 1819 (which were probably responsible for the cairn's present mutilated state) revealed a cache of 7th-century Pictish silverware, in addition to bones and a food vessel. The silver was clearly placed in the cairn many years after its original construction, and its discovery proves that some legends of hidden treasure may be more factual than fictional (though in all likelihood the buried warrior tale postdated the find of hidden silver). *2½ miles S of Ceres, itself 2½ miles SE of Cupar, close to track to Bonnyton off Blackmuir of New Gilston road (NO 409073).*

ST ANDREWS

St Andrews Cathedral. WITCHCRAFT; GHOST. Many witches were burnt at St Andrews during the 16th and 17th centuries, on a hill to the west that was known as Witch Hill and also on Methven's Tower, but no trace remains today of this terrible period in the city's history. The large and fine cathedral only survives in ruinous form, the area of the round tower being haunted by a woman in a long white or grey dress. She has been seen more than once in the last 20 years. A couple who saw her in 1975 thought she was a real woman, and watched her as she moved towards them; they were curious because she was wearing a veil, uncommon today. As they looked at her, she vanished.

LOTHIAN

EAST LINTON

Traprain Law and Loth's Stone. ANCIENT SETTLEMENT; BURIAL TRADITION. Although it is difficult to imagine it now, the hill of Traprain Law was the site of a 40-acre settlement which was once the capital of the

Votadini tribe, and items discovered during excavation indicate that the hill was occupied for a thousand years, possibly continuously, from the 7th or 8th century BC into post-Roman times.

Close by is a standing stone known as Loth's Stone, traditionally marking the burial place of 'King Loth', who gave his name to Lothian. A stone burial cist was discovered near here in 1861, but there was no clue as to who was really buried there. *Traprain Law beside minor road just S of East Linton; Loth's Stone just S of hill near track (NT 578741).*

EDINBURGH

Arthur's Seat. ARTHURIAN LEGEND. There are traces of an early settlement on the hills of Holyrood Park, and this hillfort may once have been a major centre comparing in importance to Traprain Law (see *East Linton*). There are also slight hints in certain Arthurian legends that King Arthur fought a battle here, and although this is for various reasons unlikely, the name of Arthur's Seat shows that in tradition at least the hill was linked to Arthur. It used to be the custom to wash in the dew on Arthur's Seat on May Day morning, and then to wish at St Anthony's Well. *Well near ruined St Anthony's Chapel above St Margaret's Loch, on N side of Holyrood Park; Arthur's Seat to S.*

Calton Hill. FAIRIES. In the 1660s a ten-year-old boy from Leith was said to have been given the gift of second sight by the fairies. Every Thursday night he went to Calton Hill and entered fairyland through huge gates only visible to those with the gift of fairy vision. He played the drums for fairy dances, and watched the festivities to which he was so mysteriously drawn, so much so that no efforts could restrain him from his weekly visits. *In central Edinburgh, E of cathedral.*

LINLITHGOW

St Michael's Church and Linlithgow Palace. GHOSTS. It is said that the ghost of an old man dressed in a long blue gown appeared to King James IV of Scotland inside this church and warned him that he would be killed in battle at Flodden. The Scottish poet David Lindsay was with the King and saw the ghost. His prophecy came true, for the King did not heed the warning and died in battle in 1513.

In the adjacent royal palace where both King James V and his daughter, Mary Queen of Scots, were born, James IV's queen is said still to await her husband's return, in the room known as Queen Margaret's Bower. The ghost of a woman (also Queen Margaret?) has been seen near the main palace entrance. Dressed in a bluish gown, she walks towards the church before disappearing. She is usually seen around nine o'clock on April mornings, and sometimes also in September. *7 miles SE of Falkirk; palace open to public.*

NORTH BERWICK

Old Kirk Porch. WITCHES; DEVIL. A famous coven of witches was active here in the late 16th century, their best-known exploit being their attempt to wreck the ship carrying King James VI and his new bride, Princess Anne of Denmark. The witches used spells and incantations and threw a dead cat into the sea, in order to blow up a storm which almost succeeded in capsizing the ship. The King took a special interest in the subsequent treason trial, and the group claimed to be working under the instructions of the Earl of Bothwell. Some of the witches were executed, and Bothwell was banished.

Little remains in North Berwick of the places where the witches met, although the porch of the Old Kirk, where the Devil allegedly met with the witches, still stands. *North Berwick on coast; porch of Old Kirk on mound by harbour.*

STRATHCLYDE

LOCH AWE

Loch Awe. SACRED WELL; MONSTER; GHOST. Before Loch Awe existed, there was a sacred spring on the summit of Ben Cruachan, which had to be covered by a stone every evening. One night a woman called Bera, whose task it was to look after the spring, was too tired and fell asleep. Three mornings later she awoke to find that the valley was submerged under water from the spring, and Loch Awe had been formed. A great monster was believed to live in the lake, and in hard winters when the people heard the ice on the lake cracking they would say it was being done by the monster.

The old chapel of Killineuer at the foot of the loch bears the marks of a ghost's hand on its lintel. It happened when a tailor who didn't believe in ghosts spent the night in the chapel. He passed the time knitting stockings and refused to look at the ghost; but when he finally looked up he rushed from the chapel with the ghost in pursuit, and the ghost hit the lintel as he grabbed for the tailor. *B840 runs along loch-side and passes close to chapel 1 mile E of Ford.*

DUMBARTON

Dumbarton Rock. SITING LEGEND. The prominent rock, an isolated volcanic plug, was thrown here by witches, according to legend, when they were chasing St Patrick out of the country on the Devil's instructions. St Patrick sailed off in a boat and the witches could not follow him across running water, so they tore a lump from a nearby hill and threw it after him. In fact from early times the rock was a fortress, and was the capital of the kingdom of Strathclyde from the 5th to the early 11th century. The name Dumbarton comes from the Gaelic *Dun Breatann*, fort of the Britons. *Dumbarton on N bank of Clyde estuary; rock projects into estuary on E side of mouth of River Leven; remains of Dumbarton Castle on rock (18th and 19th centuries) can be visited.*

St Columba's Cell on the Isle of Iona, with the abbey church in the background

GOUROCK

Granny Kempock Stone. WITCHES; DEVIL; RITUALS. In 1662 Mary Lamont confessed that she and her companions in witchcraft had danced round the stone with the Devil, and had planned to throw the stone into the sea in order to harm the fortunes of the fishermen. The stone had for a long time been regularly visited by fishermen who brought gifts and a basket of sand which they would sprinkle at the foot of the stone as they circled it, asking for good weather, calm seas and a large catch. This ritual may be a relic of much older prehistoric rites practised at this 7-foot standing stone, as also may be the practice of newly-weds to walk hand in hand around it, in hopes of a happy marriage. *Now protected by ugly iron railings, on Kempock Point in Gourock (W of Greenock).*

ISLE OF IONA

★ **Isle of Iona.** HOLY ISLAND; GHOSTS. St Columba founded a Celtic monastery here in AD 563, and since that time numerous religious structures have been built, Christianity having managed to survive here despite pagan invasions. Nothing remains of Columba's first monastery, though the remains of St Columba's Cell are on top of Tor Abb about 30 yards west of the abbey church. In addition to the restored abbey church, there are three early Christian stone crosses. Iona, the island in the west thought to be nearest to Heaven, was a favoured burial place, and 48 Scottish kings are said to lie here as well as others from Ireland, Norway and France. The first was Kenneth MacAlpin, who may have built the 9th-century Chapel of St Oran which still stands in the ancient burial ground.

The island is full of atmosphere, and it feels like going back in time fourteen hundred years to stand in the small bay in the south of the island where St Columba landed, for little has changed. Past events also cast their shadow over the island in phantom shapes: ghostly monks have been seen, wearing brown robes and apparently unaware of human witnesses; a fleet of ghostly Viking longboats, re-enacting a long-past raid, was observed; and ghostly music and bells have been heard. *Cars not allowed on island, off SW coast of Mull.*

KILCHOMAN, ISLE OF ISLAY

Church. ANCIENT RITUALS. In the churchyard is a carved Celtic cross with a cup-marked stone below it, one cup containing a marble ball. The ritual followed by visitors was to turn the ball three times sunwise in its cup, and leave a coin as an offering. By this action a wish would be granted. At Kilchiaran, 2 miles to the south-west, is a ruined chapel where another cup-marked stone can be found, again used in a wishing ritual. *7 miles W of Bridgend.*

KILMICHAEL GLASSARY

Dunadd. INAUGURATION SITE. Dunadd is a Dark Age hillfort, but the most interesting feature to visitors is the strange rock carvings on the summit. There is a boar, some ogham writing (ogham was a strange script formed of groups of straight lines above and below a central horizontal line), a basin and a footprint. The boar is Pictish in design, and may date from the late 7th or early 8th century, at which times the Picts besieged Dunadd fort. The Picts also learned ogham writing from the Scots of Dalriada, who themselves brought it from Ireland when they settled in Argyll in the 5th century. The basin and footprint at Dunadd were probably used in inauguration ceremonies; the fort is traditionally the capital of the kingdom of Dalriada, and the place where the kings of Dalriada were inaugurated. The new king would place his foot in the footprint to show that he would follow in the footsteps of his predecessors. Other carved footprints have been found, and a pair can be seen at Clickhimin broch in the Shetland Isles. The Dunadd footprint was also known as the Fairy's Footprint. *Kilmichael village 3 miles N of Lochgilphead; Dunadd 1 mile W, off A816 to Kilmartin.*

KILMORY, ISLAND OF ARRAN

Torrylin Cairn. RETRIBUTION LEGENDS. As with so many prehistoric burial chambers, this long cairn has been dug into for whatever treasure might be found inside. Very often, local people would avoid interfering with a sacred site for fear of the consequences: storms might blow up, or evil strike at a transgressor. In this case, it was said that the thief who took away a large skull from the cairn was followed home by the powers he had unleashed, and the walls of his house shook as if struck by a strong wind. He rushed back to the cairn to rebury the skull, but was still haunted day and night until finally he was thrown from his horse and killed. *At S of island, along track off A841 at Kilmory (NR 955211).*

LENDALFOOT

Carleton Castle. GHOSTS. The striking ruined castle, perched on a rocky ridge, is said to be haunted by ghostly screams, perhaps echoing down the centuries from the time when the baron who lived there is said to have pushed seven wives over the cliff (the eighth pushed *him* over). *Lendalfoot on coast 6 miles SW of Girvan; castle ½ mile inland.*

MACHRIE, ISLAND OF ARRAN

Machrie Moor. GIANT; PREHISTORIC ASTRONOMY. There is a group of stone circles and standing stones on this lonely Arran moorland, one of the circles being a double circle, with a ring of eight granite boulders inside another ring of granite stones. This structure, known as Fingal's Cauldron Seat, is reputed to have been made by the giant Finn McCool and to have been the place where he cooked his meals in a cauldron. He tied his dog Bran to a holed stone in the outer circle.

Other structures lie buried beneath the peat, and it is possible that in the early Bronze Age this place may have been an astronomical observatory. *On W of island, S of river named Machrie Water and reached from A841 at NR 895330.*

TAYSIDE

ABERLEMNO

★ **Churchyard and Roadside.** PICTISH SYMBOL STONES. Three fine stones can be seen in outdoor settings here, the best being in the churchyard. This sandstone cross-slab has a battle scene on one side and an intricately carved cross on the other. It is a regular-shaped stone with Christian symbolism, and therefore dates from some time after AD 700. The battle scene reveals a wealth of detail in the weapons and armour, and above the soldiers are

Symbol stone at Aberlemno, with carved battle scenes and Pictish symbols

carved some of the more enigmatic Pictish symbols, including a 'Z-rod' at left and a possible double-handled mirror at right.

More stones can be seen by the road in the village. One is another cross-slab, and there is also a stone without Christian symbolism, and with the symbols carved on an unshaped rock - therefore from an earlier period. They include a serpent, mirror and comb, Z-rod and double disc - all common Pictish symbols, though their meaning remains in dispute.

There are many more fine Pictish symbol stones dotted around central and eastern Scotland, with good collections in museums at Meigle and St Vigeans north of Arbroath. *5 miles NE of Forfar; church down side lane, and two stones beside B9134.*

BEN LAWERS

Ben Lawers. FAIRY CATTLE. Herds of fairy cattle were believed to graze in a few areas of the Highlands and Islands, one of the places being Ben Lawers. They were dun-coloured and had no horns, and like other fairy cows their real home was the sea. When the Ben Lawers cows were ready to mate, they would go down to Loch Tay and call for the water bull. *A827 Aberfeldy–Killin road runs between Ben Lawers and Loch Tay.*

DUNNING

Witch Memorial. WITCH. The persecution of so-called witches was rife in Scotland during the second half of the 17th and the early 18th centuries. It is doubtful whether many of the old women picked upon were guilty of anything more than eccentricity, but the ignorance and hatred of the mob resulted in many of their victims being burned to death. One such execution is recorded with a memorial of stones just outside Dunning, where in 1657 Maggie Wall was burned as a witch. *8 miles SW of Perth; memorial close to B8062 to Auchterarder.*

GLAMIS

Glamis Castle. GHOSTS. Tradition assigns to this fine castle a secret room, where a monstrous child who eventually became the earl lived hidden from the world until his death in the 1920s. It was also said that one of Glamis' ghosts was Macbeth, who allegedly murdered Duncan here. Others in a long list of ghostly visitors include 'Earl Beardie', who played cards with the Devil and lost, a tongueless woman, a negro servant boy and a gibbering madman up on the roof. In recent times the ghost seen most often appears to be the White or Grey Lady who haunts the chapel. She has been seen kneeling in a pew by Lord Strathmore and Lady Granville, on separate occasions, and by numerous other witnesses. *10 miles N of Dundee; open to public.*

GLEN ALMOND

Clach Ossian (Ossian's Stone). BURIAL SITE. Only since the 18th century has this been known as the burial place of Ossian, a legendary 3rd-century Gaelic warrior and poet. When the road was made in 1730 the stone was moved and bones or ashes found; they were reburied nearby to avert ill-fortune. *Beside A822 in Glen Almond, 6 miles NE of Crieff (NN 895306).*

KIRKTON OF MENMUIR

White Caterthun Hillfort. WITCH. The remains of massive stone walls can be seen on the hilltop, traditionally built by a witch in one morning. She brought the stones in her apron, and work stopped when her apron strings broke, dropping the largest stone outside the wall. *Accessible by footpath from lane 5 miles NW of Brechin; across lane is Brown Caterthun hillfort (NO 548660).*

Glamis Castle numbers Macbeth among its many ghosts

LETHAM

Battlefield. GHOSTS. In AD 685 the Battle of Nechtanesmere was fought at Letham; in 1950 a ghostly re-enactment of its aftermath was witnessed by Miss E.F. Smith, who was driving home to Letham late one winter's night. Her car skidded into a ditch, so she decided to walk the rest of the way. As she neared Letham she saw people carrying flaming torches, and her tired dog which she was carrying began to growl. During 12 minutes she saw people examining corpses as if looking for their dead comrades. The clothes she described later to historians matched well with those worn by Pictish warriors carved on some symbol stones. *Letham 4 miles SE of Forfar; battlefield beside lane to W, from Dunnichen to Milldens.*

SCHIEHALLION

Schiehallion. FAIRIES; GHOSTS; STRANGE CREATURES. 'The Fairy Hill of the Caledonians', at the eastern end of Rannoch Moor, is an especially haunted part of this barren moorland, where all kinds of strange beings were believed to roam. Water horses lived in the lochs, and evil spirits haunted the hills. People passing by Schiehallion would sometimes see the shadowy form of a ghost dog. The Fairy Well on its slopes is marked by stones: the fairies who dwelt there could grant wishes and cure diseases. On May Day girls dressed in white brought offerings of flowers. *10 miles NW of Aberfeldy; ascent of Schiehallion only possible by very experienced mountain walkers, but minor road E from Kinloch Rannoch passes close to hill.*

SCOTLANDWELL

Holy Well. HEALING WELL. Robert Bruce, King of Scotland 1306-29, suffered from leprosy, and this is one of three wells in Scotland said to have been responsible for his cure. King Charles II also came to the well, as did Mary Queen of Scots. The present structure only dates from 1858, but the well itself is very much older. *On A911 4 miles E of Kinross.*

CAPE WRATH
DURNESS
BEN LOYAL
OUTER HEBRIDES
CALLANISH
LEWIS
LOCH SHIN
LOCH
BORRALAN
LAIRG
ULLAPOOL
DORNOCH
WESTERN ISLES
NIGG
LOCH GARVE
TRUMPAN
TROTTERNISH
LOCH ACHILTY
MUNLOCHY
HIGHLAND
INVERNESS
DUNVEGAN
CULLODEN
LOCH
MULLARDOCH
BRACADALE
KYLE OF
LOCHALSH
LOCH ALSH
SKYE
LOCH NESS
GLEN
SHIEL
LOCH
DUICH
KINCRAIG
INVERGARRY
MALLAIG
INNER HEBRIDES
MUCK
FORT WILLIAM
MULL
IONA
MILES
KILOMETRES
0
10
20
0
10
20
30
40

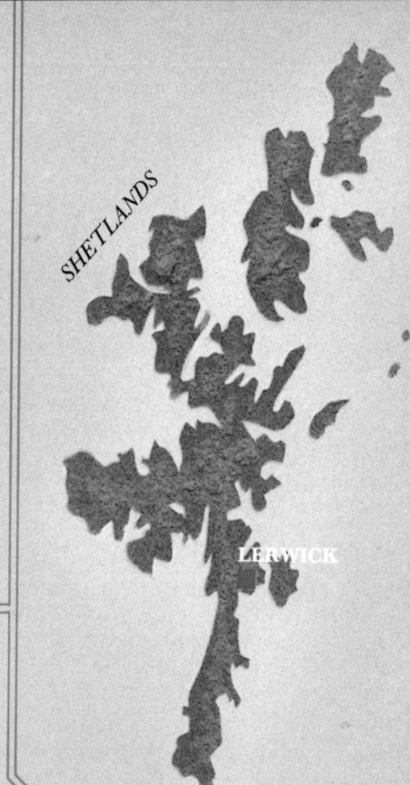

FRASERBURGH
BURGHHEAD
URQUHART
ULDEARN
RIVER SPEY
GRAMPIAN
CHAPEL OF GARIOCH
PITYOULISH
MIDMAR
LUMPHANAN
ABERDEEN
BEN MACDHUI
MUCHALLS
BRAEMAR
STONEHAVEN

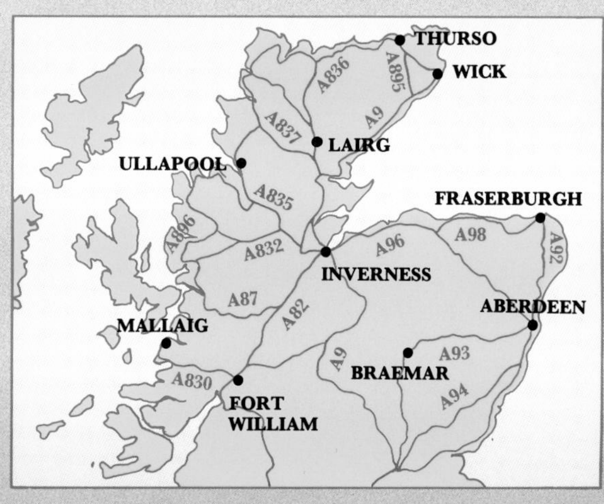

NORTHERN SCOTLAND

GRAMPIAN REGION

BEN MACDHUI

Ben Macdhui. GHOSTLY GIANT. This Cairngorm peak may be home to an unusual occupant – the Big Grey Man. Climbers have been followed by ghostly footsteps, as was Professor Norman Collie who in 1891 heard an 'eerie crunch, crunch' behind him as he walked down the mountain through mist. Seized with terror, he ran 4 or 5 miles downhill. On another occasion, someone camping alone overnight on the summit saw 'a great brown creature ... swaggering down the hill'. It was tall (at least 20 feet), covered with short brown hair and had a large head. Climber Tom Crowley saw 'a huge grey figure' in the 1920s when descending Braeriach not far away. It seemed to have pointed ears, long legs and feet with talons, and Crowley too fled down the mountain. We have not heard of any recent sightings of the Big Grey Man, but climbers should beware! *10 miles NW of Braemar; only accessible to experienced mountain walkers.*

CHAPEL OF GARIOCH

Maiden Stone. PETRIFACTION LEGEND; PICTISH SYMBOL STONE. Janet of Drumdurno is said to have fled from the embraces of a warlock, praying for help, and she turned to stone as he seized her. This 10-foot red granite pillar is in fact a Pictish symbol stone, carved with strange beasts and symbols which obviously had a significance fifteen hundred years ago but which are now difficult to decipher. There are many such Pictish symbol stones in this part of north-east Scotland. *Chapel of Garioch 4 miles NW of Inverurie; Maiden Stone 1 mile further NW, beside lane (NJ 703248).*

LUMPHANAN

Macbeth's Cairn. BURIAL TRADITION. Macbeth is said to be buried in this cairn. *NW of village, itself 9 miles NW of Banchory, and reached along path from A980 (NJ 578053).*

MIDMAR

Midmar Stone Circle. PAGAN AND CHRISTIAN OVERLAP. Keen observation will often reveal that a Christian church has been built on a previously pagan site: the churchyard may be circular, there may be a standing stone in the churchyard, or an earthwork at the site. Here at Midmar pagan and Christian structures stand side by side, the well-preserved stone circle taking pride of place in the churchyard. It is a 'recumbent stone circle', with one large stone lying on its side, a type peculiar to this area of Britain. *6 miles N of Banchory, alongside B9119 (NJ 702059).*

MUCHALLS

Muchalls Castle. GHOST. The castle is traditionally haunted by a young woman dressed in green, of whom there have been several sightings this century. A visitor in the 1970s saw her in an upstairs dining room, facing a wall, 'as if looking into a mirror and patting her hair into place. Her dress was terribly old-fashioned and was an unusual lime colour.' She could not have been a real person, for she vanished as the witness entered the room. *4 miles NE of Stonehaven; castle W of village.*

RIVER SPEY

River Spey. MONSTER. The river was believed to demand one life a year. Drownings were blamed on the White Horse of Spey, a beautiful creature that was really a kelpie (water horse) in disguise. He would offer a ride to weary travellers, and then when they were on his back he would gallop off and plunge into the river.

URQUHART

Deil's Stanes. DEVIL. It is best to avoid being at this stone circle at midnight, because if you walk round it three times the Devil will appear. *Urquhart 4 miles E of Elgin; stones close to crossroads ¾ mile to N (NJ 290640).*

HIGHLAND

LOCH ACHILTY

Loch Achilty. DEVIL. The Devil used to bathe in this loch, it was said, and after he had spent a night in its cool waters they would be steaming hot. His soap, made of tallow, sulphur, ashes and ground-up toad bones, covered the loch with dirty suds, but these gradually changed into white water lilies which thrived in the warm water. *1 mile W of Contin, itself 2 miles SW of Strathpeffer; road off A832 runs along N side of loch.*

AULDEARN

Churchyard, Inshoch Castle and Standing Stones. WITCHES; DEVIL. In the 17th century there was a coven of witches at Auldearn, and in a witch trial held there in 1662 Isobel Gowdie confessed to many weird activities, though it is not clear how great a part her vivid imagination played in her confession. She claimed to have been 'baptised' into witchcraft by the Devil in the churchyard at Auldearn, and to have first met the Devil at Inshoch Castle. Some standing stones at Auldearn are possibly the remains of a stone circle, and here the witches practised their craft - again as mentioned in Isobel Gowdie's confession. *2 miles SE of Nairn; standing stones in woodland S of A96 (NH 925553); ruins of Inshoch Castle 1 mile to NE.*

BEN LOYAL

Ben Loyal. DWARVES. The mountain is said to be magnetic and to distort compass readings. A large smelting furnace at its heart, using the iron ore in the mountain, is operated by dwarves, according to legend. At a standing stone called the Stone of the Little Men you could leave a silver coin and a model or drawing of any metal object you desired, which would be made by the dwarves and left by the stone. *5 miles S of Tongue.*

LOCH BORRALAN

Loch Borralan. WATER HORSE. Fishermen were said to be at risk from the beautiful water horse living in this loch. Two who saw it were so taken by its beauty that they stopped to admire it - and were never seen again. Nothing was found but their rods, the fish they had caught and a large horse's hoofprints. *Just SE of Ledmore, itself 13 miles NE of Ullapool; A837 runs close to loch-side.*

BRACADALE, ISLAND OF SKYE

Dun Gharsainn or Garsin. FAIRIES. As with so many of these prehistoric forts, the fairies were believed to have once lived here, and would regularly go out to dance in the moonlight. After a farmer took some stones from the dun to build a cattle shelter, the fairies left for good. *8 miles SW of Portree close to road around head of Loch Beag (NG 361387).*

CAMSTER

★ **Grey Cairns of Camster.** ANCIENT RITUALS. Both legend and history are silent when one searches for answers to the many questions provoked by a visit to some of Britain's finest prehistoric sites. Out on the moors of north-east Scotland can be seen two very interesting Neolithic burial chambers, one a round chambered cairn, the other a long cairn. The 20-foot-long passage in the round cairn is only 2½-3½ feet high, so although it can be entered it is not recommended to anyone suffering from claustrophobia! Broken pots, charcoal, ashes and human skeletons have been found, but they only show that burial rites of some kind were performed here. What these people of around six thousand years ago believed about death is not known, but it is clear from the surviving structures that they were skilful craftsmen: their chambered tombs are the oldest large stone structures in Britain. Will any construction being erected in the late 20th century still be around in AD 8000? *Cairns close together beside N-S minor road which leaves A9 E of Lybster, 10 miles SW of Wick (ND 260442).*

CAPE WRATH

Cape Wrath. GHOST; MERMAID. Remote and sparsely populated, there is little more than a lighthouse at Cape Wrath and it is an eerie place. A ghost - a tall man dressed like a sailor - has been seen more than once in the last few years, and the remains of Sandwood Cottage seem to be a focus for the haunting. At Sandwood Bay, a local man saw a mermaid in 1900. His dog saw her first, lying on a ledge looking at them. She was human-sized and beautiful, and apparently waiting for the tide to take her back out to sea.

The prehistoric round chambered cairn at Camster

CULLODEN

St Mary's Well. GHOSTS; HOLY WELL. This area is best known for the battle fought in 1746 when in a brief, 40-minute skirmish twelve hundred Highlanders under Prince Charles Edward Stuart were slain. This event has left its echoes in the form of ghosts in the area of the commemorative cairn.

But there is also a famous holy well here, which until the early years of this century was visited by coachloads of pilgrims on the first Sunday in May. St Mary's Well is a rag well where offerings of rags are hung in the tree branches, and the water was believed to have health-giving properties. It was also believed that on 1 May the water turned to wine for a short time. *Well in Culloden Wood, 3 miles E of Inverness, reached by footpath from Blackpark (NH 723453).*

Eilean Donan Castle on Loch Duich, said to be haunted by a Spanish soldier

DORNOCH

Witches Stone. WITCH; GHOST. In 1772 Janet Horne had the doubtful honour to be the last person executed for witchcraft in Scotland. The place where she was burned to death is marked by a slab of rough blueish stone, and it is said that her ghost haunts the spot on autumn nights when the moon is waning. *In garden near golf course.*

LOCH DUICH AND LOCH ALSH

Loch Duich and Loch Alsh. MONSTERS; GHOST. The seal-people come to Loch Duich in the evening, and sometimes mermen too. It was believed that seals were really human beings who were forced to take the form of seals, being allowed to return to their human appearance every once in a while.

Since Loch Duich is a sea loch, other strange creatures sometimes put in an appearance here: there have been several sightings of sea monsters in both Loch Duich and Loch Alsh to the west. Dr Farquhar Matheson had a close sighting in September 1893 when he was with his wife in a small boat on Loch Alsh. He saw 'a long, straight, neck-like thing as tall as my mast' moving towards them, and continued.

> Then it began to draw its neck down, and I saw clearly that it was a large sea-monster – of the saurian type, I should think. It was brown in colour, shining, and with a sort of ruffle at the junction of the head and neck. I can think of nothing to which to compare it so well as the head and neck of the giraffe, only the neck was much longer, and the head was not set upon the neck like that of a giraffe; that is, it was not so much at right angles to it as a continuation of it in the same line. It moved its head from side to side, and I saw the reflection of the light from its wet skin .... I saw no body – only a ripple of water where the line of the body should be. I should judge, however, that there must have been a large base of body to support such a neck.

The famous Eilean Donan Castle stands at the northern end of Loch Duich and is said to be haunted by the ghost of an 18th-century Spanish soldier. *A87 runs along N shores of both lochs, from Kyle of Lochalsh to Shiel Bridge.*

DUNNET

Dwarwick Head. MERMAID; TREASURE. A mermaid who fell in love with a fisherman and gave him gold and jewels became jealous of his attentions to human girls, so she took him to a cave under Dwarwick Head and showed him piles of treasure from ships sunk in the Pentland Firth. As he gazed at it, the mermaid sang to him and he

CALENDAR OF EVENTS

11 January
BURGHHEAD, Grampian. *Burning the Clavie:* Midwinter fire festival, when burning tar barrel is carried through the town at night.

January: last Tuesday
LERWICK, Shetland. *Up-Helly-A:* Fire festival celebrating the end of the Yule festivities: a 30-foot model Viking ship is taken through the town in a torchlit procession, and at the sea the torches are thrown into the ship, setting it alight.

25 December and 1 January
KIRKWALL, Orkney. *Boys' and Men's Ba' Games:* Street football can last up to 6 hours as large teams try to take 3lb ba' to opposite ends of the town.

31 December (New Year's Eve)
STONEHAVEN, Grampian. *Swinging the Fireballs:* New Year welcomed in by men swinging burning balls of rags and tar through the town, with pipe band accompaniment.

A model Viking longship is burnt in the Up-Helly-A festivities at Lerwick

fell asleep, waking to find himself bound with gold chains. He remains there still, guarded by the jealous mermaid. *N side of Dunnet Bay.*

DUNVEGAN, ISLAND OF SKYE

Dunvegan Castle. FAIRIES. The Macleod clan, at Dunvegan Castle since the 13th century, are said to be protected by a fairy flag given them by the fairy wife of a 14th-century Macleod chief. She was recalled to fairyland, and left her husband at Fairy Bridge after giving him the flag. It was said to save the clan if unfurled when they were in dire peril, but only three times, and it has already been used twice in battles in the 15th and 16th centuries. During the Second World War young members of the clan carried photographs of the flag with them. Today the original (a silken banner thought in reality to date from the 7th century and to have come from Syria or Rhodes) is on show in the drawing room at the Castle. *Castle 1 mile NW of Dunvegan; Fairy Bridge 2 miles to NE, close to junction of A850 and B886.*

DURNESS

Smoo Cave. DEVIL. In the 17th century Lord Reay was said to have been a student of the Devil. One day while exploring Smoo Cave his dog came rushing out 'howling and hairless', and Lord Reay realized that the Devil was inside. Before the two could meet again the cock crew, and the three witches who were with the Devil knew that dawn was approaching; the four of them blew holes in the cave roof and took off, thus avoiding a confrontation. *E of Durness, close to A838.*

Dunnet Bay, where a mermaid is said to have fallen in love with a fisherman

LOCH GARVE

Loch Garve. WATER HORSE. The water horse living in this loch carried off a girl to live in his fine house below the surface, but she felt cold and so he fetched a local mason to the loch by trickery: masquerading as a real horse, he let the man catch his bridle and mount him, and then he galloped off to the loch. He persuaded the mason to build him a proper fireplace and chimney. Afterwards, the mason only had to go to the loch-side and say 'Fish', and next day a basketful would be waiting for him. Now, a large patch of water at the eastern end never freezes when the rest of the loch does, and this is said to be where the water horse's chimney is located. *A832 4 miles W of Strathpeffer passes loch.*

GLEN SHIEL

Glen Shiel. GHOSTS. Phantom warriors have been seen fighting a ghostly battle - perhaps a re-enactment of the Battle of Glen Shiel of 1719, when Spaniards fought with the Jacobites against the Hanoverians.

INVERGARRY

★ **Well of the Heads.** HEAD CULT. In the 1660s seven men were beheaded in revenge for a murder and the heads were washed in a spring. Following this event the spring became known as Tobar nan Ceann (Well of the Heads), and in 1812 a monument was erected which is topped by a dramatic depiction of the severed heads.

Although this particular 'head well' has a neat explanation for its name, it is interesting that there are plenty of other wells having a connection with severed heads, and it is likely that all these tales are a relic of the Celtic head cult. The Celts venerated the head as the source of all the attributes they most admired - like fertility, healing, prophecy and wisdom - and they displayed the severed heads of important enemies. Heads and faces appear widely in Celtic artefacts, and the Celtic tradition of carving stone heads has survived in some remote areas even to the present day. *Monument beside A82 and Loch Oich, 1 mile S of Invergarry.*

INVERNESS

Tomnahurich Hill. FAIRIES; SLEEPING PROPHET. Here, inside this 'hill of the yews', the fairy queen was said to hold her court. A fiddler who fell asleep on the hill awoke to find himself being invited to play at a party. After accepting, he was taken to an underground palace where he played until he was exhausted. He shouted out a holy name and found himself lying on the river bank. But a hundred years had passed in the world outside during his one night in fairyland. According to another version of the story there were two fiddlers, who were gone two hundred years 'overnight' and crumbled into dust when they got back to the real world.

The 13th-century prophet Thomas the Rhymer is said to be buried in the hill; alternatively he is only sleeping, accompanied by his men and white horses, and will come to Scotland's aid when she needs him. *Today hill is cemetery 1 mile out of town centre, beside A82 to Loch Ness.*

KINCRAIG

Church of Insh. MAGIC BELL. This site has been used for worship since the 7th century, and inside the present church is an ancient square bell of cast bronze, said to have magical powers. It would fly through the air to those who needed it for healing purposes, singing as it flew. No one could prevent its return to Insh: it would always fly back home. *On hillock jutting out into Loch Insh just S of Kincraig, itself 6 miles NE of Kingussie; bell chained to windowsill.*

ISLAND OF MUCK

Island of Muck. FAIRIES. In the early years of this century the Rev. Alexander Fraser, who was minister of the island, was told by a local inhabitant about two boys aged ten and seven who had met some fairies only a few days before. They had found a tin on the beach and were trying to break it open when two tiny boys with green vests appeared. They could speak Gaelic, and asked the boys about their home and family. The human boys also saw a tiny boat with a tiny woman dressed in green, and a dog the size of a rat. She invited them aboard for a meal, but they refused, so she gave them walnut-sized loaves of fairy bread, which they ate. Then the fairies left in their boat, saying that they would not return, but others of their race would.

The two boys were found by their sister sitting gazing out to sea. When she spoke to them they came out of their apparent trance and were frightened by the memory of their experience, although they had not been scared at the time. This strange tale, which is reportedly true, is uncannily similar in many respects to present-day reports of encounters with UFOs and UFO entities.

LOCH MULLARDOCH

Loch Mullardoch. PHANTOM COTTAGE. Two experienced mountain walkers were descending Beinn Fhionnlaidh in May 1987 when they saw a two-storey cottage on the loch shore below them. They were surprised, as they didn't know of a cottage at that point, so they headed towards it. They lost sight of it behind a hillock, and when they reached the loch shore there was no cottage to be seen. They later found that there had been a lodge at the loch, but it was under water since flooding in the 1950s. *Loch Mullardoch 7 miles W of Cannich, but W end where cottage was seen only accessible on foot; only experienced mountain walkers should attempt to visit area.*

MUNLOCHY

Cloutie Well. HOLY WELL. Also known as St Boniface's Well, this is a rag well, one where sick people visiting for a cure will leave behind a small piece of cloth attached to a tree or bush. The rag may originally have been an offering to the spirit of the well, or the pilgrims may have believed that, if the rag was first rubbed on the afflicted part before being left on the bush, as it rotted so the disease would be cured. It was certainly believed that anyone destroying the rags would take on the donor's illness, which may explain why there are so many rags at the Cloutie Well (a rough estimate by a recent visitor put the number at fifty thousand). *Beside A832 ½ mile NW of Munlochy (NH 641537).*

LOCH NESS

Loch Ness. MAGIC WELL; LAKE MONSTER. The loch now fills a valley 24 miles long, but it is said that the glen was once a fertile landscape until a mother distracted by her crying child left the cover off a magic well. While she was away, the well overflowed and drowned the valley. The fleeing people cried out, 'Tha loch nis ann!' (There is a lake there now!), from which the loch got its name.

The loch has long had an eerie reputation, with rumours of strange creatures: there was in legend a water horse there, and even as early as the 6th century St Columba is said to have had a confrontation with a 'fearsome beastie' which fled at the sound of the saint's commanding voice after it got within a few feet of the saint's companion, who had jumped into the water after a boat. It had already killed a local man.

Whether that was the same sort of creaure as the famous Loch Ness Monster of the 20th century is impossible to tell. No one is even sure if there ever have been monsters in the loch, and even with all the modern technology of the late 1980s there is still no solution to the mystery. Those who have seen the monster are convinced of its existence; while the sceptics claim that people are misidentifying familiar animals and birds, like ducks, deer and otters, or wave patterns caused by boats or wind, or pieces of wood and mats of rotting vegetation. Until someone can produce the monster itself, dead or alive, there can be no answer - even photographs are unreliable because hoaxes cannot be ruled out.

Loch Ness is not the only inland lake in Scotland where monsters have been reported. 'Nessie' is certainly the most famous monster, but there is also 'Morag' in Loch Morar, and strange creatures have also been seen in Lochs Lochy and Shiel, among others. A number of monster sightings have also been reported from sea lochs (see *Loch Duich and Loch Alsh*), but whether these are the same types of creatures as seen in the inland lochs is not known. They might be: the inland lochs are all connected to the sea by rivers along which the creatures could travel. *Good views of loch from main road on W shore and from Urquhart Castle.*

NIGG

Nigg Bay. BURIED LAND. The Sands of Nigg are said to cover a low-lying fertile valley with fields, a village and a church. During a storm, the sea came in past Cromarty and covered the land with sand and water. Local fishermen believed that, when it was dangerous to set sail, they would hear the bells of the submerged church ringing

The Loch Ness Monster, photographed from Urquhart Castle in 1977

to warn them. There may be more than a grain of truth in this legend, because in many places around the British coast sizeable areas of land have been submerged over the centuries. *N of Cromarty Firth, between Cromarty and Tain.*

PITYOULISH

Loch Pityoulish. WATER HORSE. A black horse was said to live in the loch, and anyone bathing was warned to be very careful and never to put his head under the water. One cautionary tale told how some boys playing by the shore saw a fine black horse with a silver saddle, bridle and reins grazing close by. They grabbed the reins, whereupon the horse galloped into the loch pulling the boys with it. Only one survived: he had used a knife to cut off his fingers holding the reins. *2 miles NE of Aviemore; loch lies just off B970.*

LOCH SHIN

Loch Shin. WATER HORSE; DEVIL. A golden horse is said to live in the loch. In the early days of Christianity he agreed to help a local priest build a church, fetching stones from a dun where the fairies lived and carrying them across the loch on his back. The fairies were displeased that their fortress was being plundered, and thereafter the water horse was out of favour with them. Water horse legends are told of many of Scotland's lakes, and some people believe that these beasts were the forerunners of the present-day lake monsters reportedly seen in numerous lochs (see *Loch Ness*).

There is also a Devil story from Loch Shin. A young couple saw a man fishing from a stone at the loch-side, and asked him if he could spare a couple of trout for their supper. At the sound of a human voice, the angler turned into a ball of flame that set fire to the heather and sent the young couple running for home. *NW of Lairg.*

TROTTERNISH, ISLAND OF SKYE

Old Man of Storr. PETRIFACTION LEGEND. An old couple supposedly met giants with magical powers while out looking for a lost cow, and were turned to stone as they looked back when running away. The stone pillar which formed the wife has fallen, but the Old Man still stands. *7 miles N of Portree, W of A895.*

TRUMPAN, ISLAND OF SKYE

Heaven Stone. PROPHECY. In the churchyard of the old church at Trumpan stands a stone with a hole in it. With eyes closed, you have to try and put your finger in the hole. If you are successful at the first attempt, you will go to Heaven; if not, your route leads the other way. *In N of Vaternish, about 8 miles N of Dunvegan.*

Rags hung up by the sick hoping for a cure at the Cloutie Well, Munlochy

ORKNEY ISLANDS

BURWICK, SOUTH RONALDSAY

Ladykirk Stone. SAINT; OATH-SWEARING SITE. Two footprints on this stone in St Mary's church are said to be those of St Magnus, who crossed the Pentland Firth standing on it when no boat was available. More likely it was a 'swearing stone' on which kings stood to make their royal oaths. *At S end of island.*

HOY

Dwarfie Stane. GIANT; DWARF. On the bare hillside, a sandstone block 28 feet long was turned into a tomb in prehistoric times; it is unique in Britain. A passage and two cells were hollowed out, and the blocking stone lies beside the entrance. One legend improbably describes the tomb as the home of a giant and his wife; more logical is the belief that a dwarf or troll lived there. *In N of island; stone lies short distance off road to Rackwick (HY 243005).*

STENNESS, MAINLAND

★ **Maes Howe.** ANCIENT RITUAL; TREASURE. One of Britain's finest prehistoric burial chambers, it was built around 2500 BC by skilled craftsmen. The passageway was positioned so that the midwinter sun shone down it and lit up the inner chamber. This also happened at a few other tombs, notably Newgrange in Ireland, and just as the midwinter sun marked the return of vitality to living things, so its entry into these tombs could have symbolized the continuance of life for those who had died, in the form of their living descendants.

Viking visitors to the tomb over 3500 years after its construction left runic engravings about a 'great treasure',

The standing stones at Callanish on the Isle of Lewis

and saying that they had taken treasure away. But this may refer to a tradition that treasure was hidden there, similar to the belief at other burial mounds. *5 miles NE of Stromness, just off A965.*

Stones of Stenness and Ring of Brodgar. ANCIENT RITUALS. Both sites are prehistoric henges (circular Neolithic ceremonial earthworks) with standing stones. The Ring of Brodgar has 27 stones in a circle, the Stones of Stenness four; both originally had more, and they may have been linked by a line of stones, of which the 18½-foot Watch Stone remains. At the New Year, couples wishing to marry would go to the Temple of the Moon (Stones of Stenness) and then to the Temple of the Sun (Ring of Brodgar), performing a set ritual at each, before finally clasping hands through a hole in the Stone of Odin (no longer there). Sick people would also walk three times round the Stones of Stenness in hopes of a cure. *Not far from Maes Howe; both sites beside B9055 between Loch of Stenness and Loch of Harray.*

WESTERN ISLES

★ CALLANISH, UIG, ISLE OF LEWIS

Callanish Stones. PETRIFACTION LEGEND; ANCIENT RITUALS. The Gaelic name *Fir Bhreig* (false men) was used for these stones, as they looked like human figures from a distance. There was also a legend that they were giants turned to stone by St Kieran for failing to embrace Christianity when he came and preached to them. But modern research suggests that this elaborate layout of standing stones, comprising an avenue and a cross formation, originally had some astronomical purpose: it may have been a prehistoric observatory. In particular, the lunar cycle seems to have been of importance, with especially dramatic events taking place every 18½ years when the moon passes low over the horizon and appears to be among the stones. This last happened in 1987 and will not occur again until 2008.

Sunrise on Midsummer Day was another important time, according to legend, for then the 'Shining One' would walk along the avenue. Men and women would exchange betrothal vows among the stones, and even consummate their marriages there to ensure a happy future. Although all real knowledge of the stones' original purpose is lost, and today we only have vague legends and traditions to guide us, aided by painstaking long-term observations by dedicated researchers, it is very clear that this has always been a special place. The local people would visit the stones at midsummer and on May Day, despite the disapproval of the church elders, for they instinctively felt drawn to the stones and knew they must not neglect them. On these occasions the respect for the Old Religion proved greater than that for the New. *13 miles W of Stornoway.*

FURTHER READING

BORD, JANET and COLIN, *Mysterious Britain* (1974), Paladin/Grafton Books

—— *The Secret Country* (1978), Paladin/Grafton Books

—— *A Guide to Ancient Sites in Britain* (1979), Paladin/Grafton Books

—— *Earth Rites: Fertility Practices in Pre-Industrial Britain* (1983), Paladin/Grafton Books

—— *Sacred Waters: Holy Wells and Water Lore in Britain and Ireland* (1986), Paladin/Grafton Books

—— *Ancient Mysteries of Britain* (1987), Paladin/Grafton Books

—— *Modern Mysteries of Britain: 100 Years of Strange Events* (1987), Grafton Books

DEVEREUX, PAUL, and IAN THOMSON, *The Ley Hunter's Companion* (1979), Thames and Hudson (out of print). Part of this book reissued as *The Ley Guide: The Mystery of Ancient Alignments* (1987), Empress, PO Box 5, Brecon, Powys, LD3 7AA

DEVEREUX, PAUL, and NIGEL PENNICK, *Lines on the Landscape: Leylines and Other Linear Enigmas* (1989), Robert Hale

GREEN, ANDREW, *Ghosts of Today* (1980), Kaye and Ward

KIGHTLY, CHARLES, *The Customs and Ceremonies of Britain* (1986), Thames and Hudson

MICHELL, JOHN, *The New View Over Atlantis* (1983), Thames and Hudson (a classic work on Britain's sacred places)

—— *The Traveller's Key to Sacred England: A Guide to the Legends, Lore, and Landscape of England's Sacred Places* (1989), Harrap Columbus

MILLER, HAMISH, and PAUL BROADHURST, *The Sun and the Serpent* (1989), Pendragon Press, PO Box 888, Launceston, Cornwall, PL15 7YH (investigation of the St Michael Line)

SHUEL, BRIAN, *The National Trust Guide to Traditional Customs of Britain* (1985), Webb and Bower with Michael Joseph

WALKER, CHARLES, *The Atlas of Occult Britain* (1987), Hamlyn

WESTWOOD, JENNIFER, *Albion: A Guide to Legendary Britain* (1985), Grafton Books

INDEX

DATE DUE			